I Think Our Son Is Gay

1

OKURA

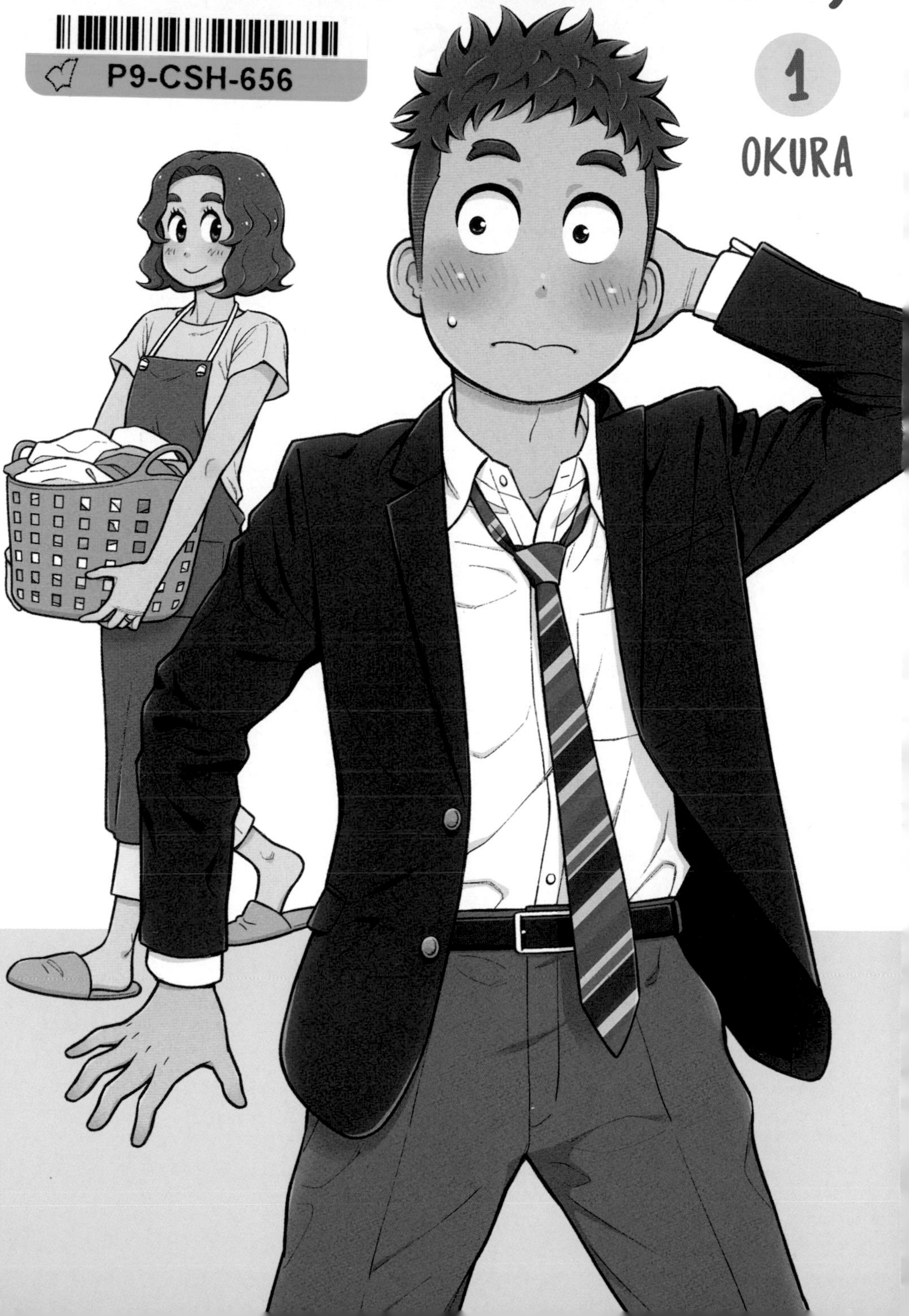

I Think Our Son Is Gay

CONTENTS

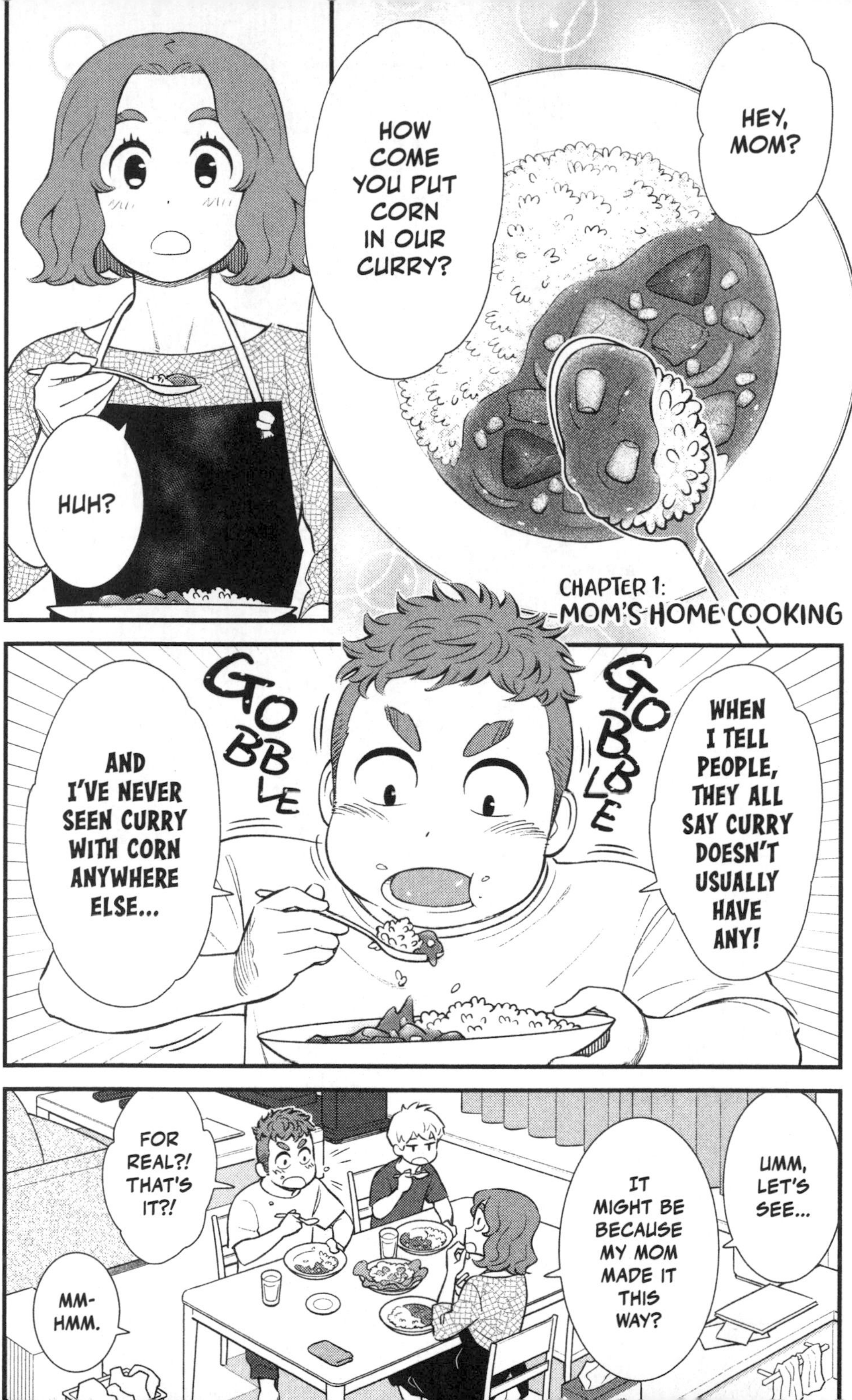
HEY, MOM?
HOW COME YOU PUT CORN IN OUR CURRY?
HUH?
CHAPTER 1: MOM'S HOME COOKING
WHEN I TELL PEOPLE, THEY ALL SAY CURRY DOESN'T USUALLY HAVE ANY!
GOBBLE
GOBBLE
AND I'VE NEVER SEEN CURRY WITH CORN ANYWHERE ELSE...
UMM, LET'S SEE...
IT MIGHT BE BECAUSE MY MOM MADE IT THIS WAY?
FOR REAL?! THAT'S IT?!
MM-HMM.

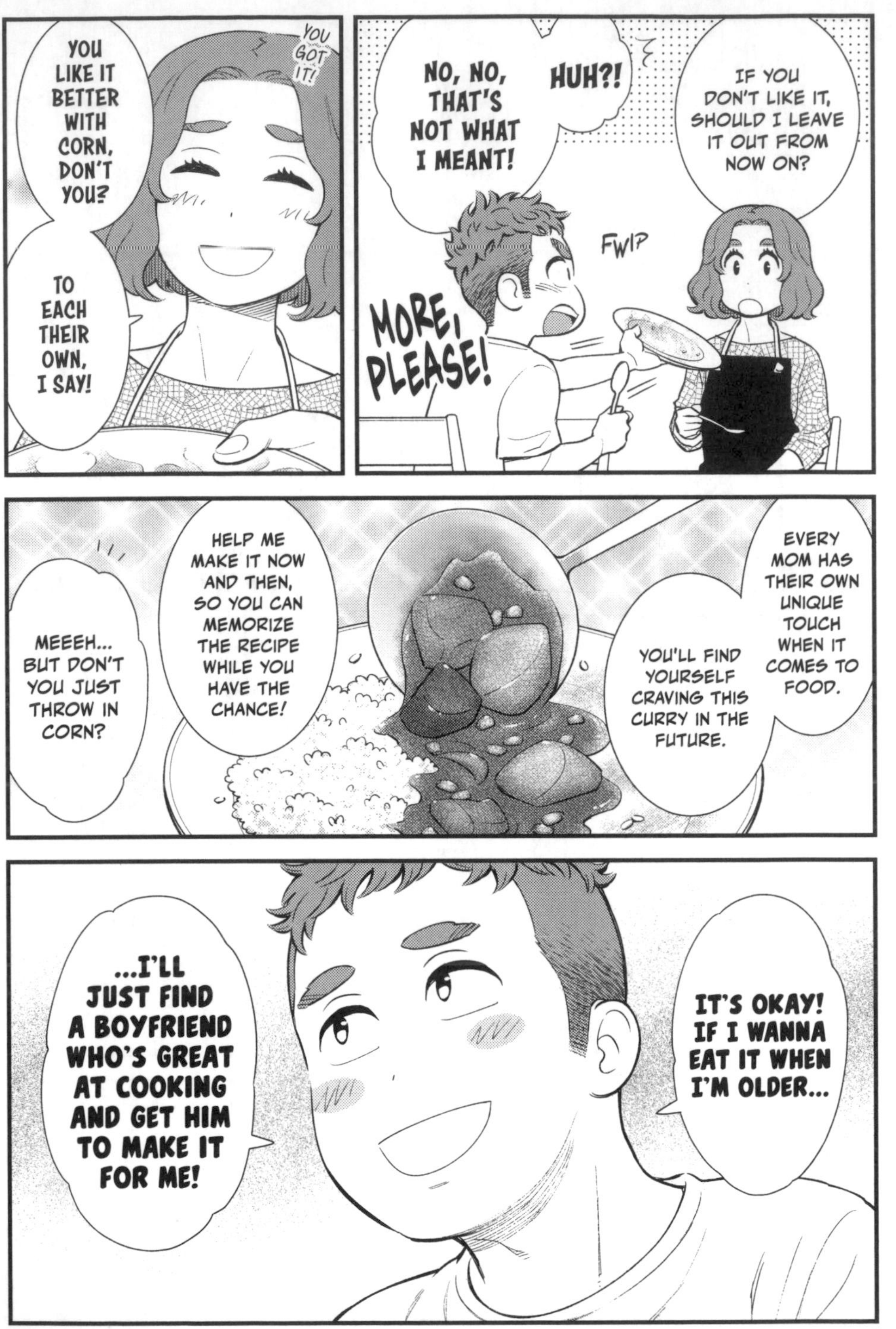

IF YOU DON'T LIKE IT, SHOULD I LEAVE IT OUT FROM NOW ON?
HUH?!
NO, NO, THAT'S NOT WHAT I MEANT!
FWIP
MORE, PLEASE!
YOU GOT IT!
YOU LIKE IT BETTER WITH CORN, DON'T YOU?
TO EACH THEIR OWN, I SAY!
EVERY MOM HAS THEIR OWN UNIQUE TOUCH WHEN IT COMES TO FOOD.
YOU'LL FIND YOURSELF CRAVING THIS CURRY IN THE FUTURE.
HELP ME MAKE IT NOW AND THEN, SO YOU CAN MEMORIZE THE RECIPE WHILE YOU HAVE THE CHANCE!
MEEEH... BUT DON'T YOU JUST THROW IN CORN?
IT'S OKAY! IF I WANNA EAT IT WHEN I'M OLDER...
...I'LL JUST FIND A BOYFRIEND WHO'S GREAT AT COOKING AND GET HIM TO MAKE IT FOR ME!

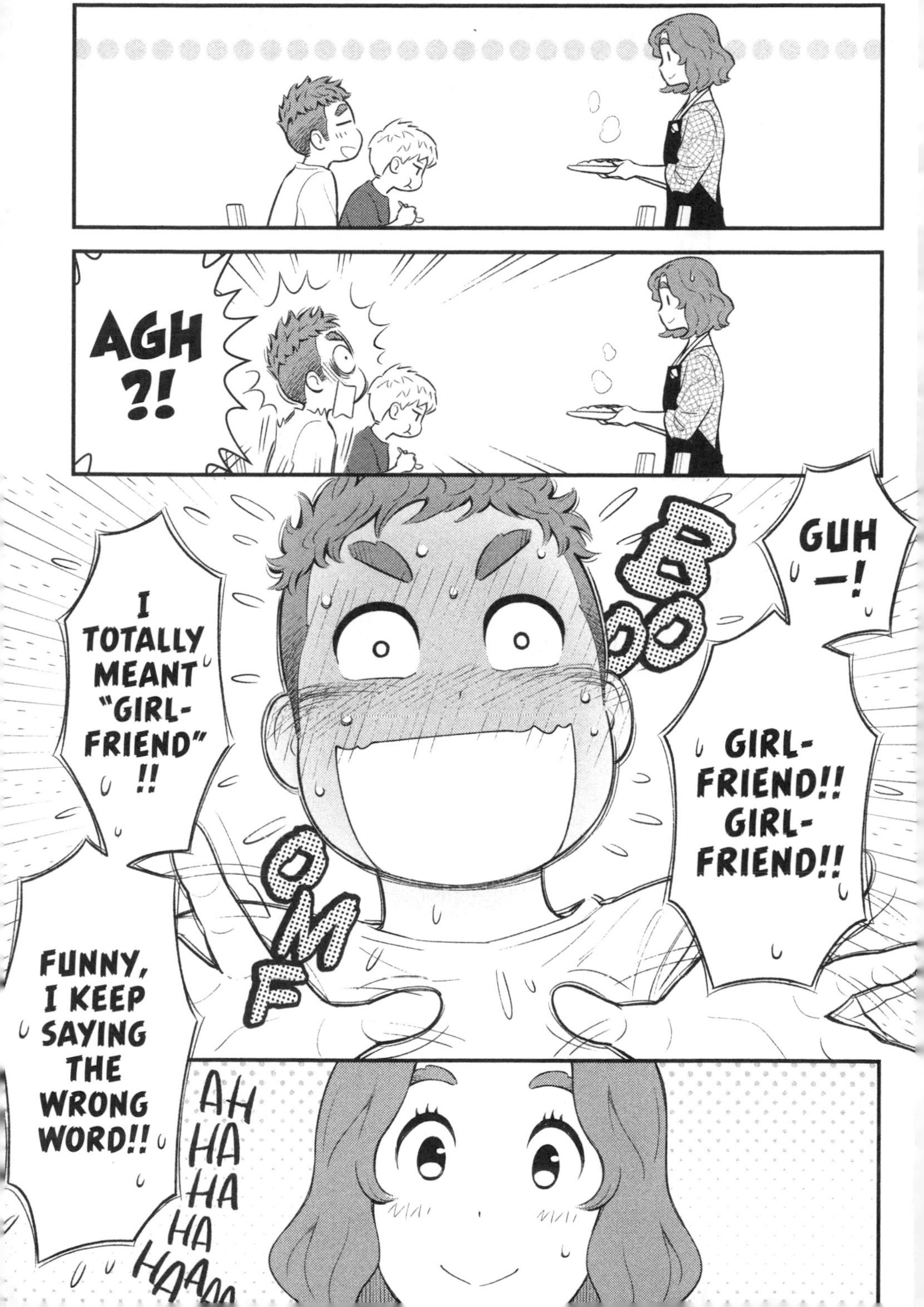
AGH ?!
GUH —!
BOO
GIRL-FRIEND!! GIRL-FRIEND!!
I TOTALLY MEANT "GIRL-FRIEND"!!
OMF
AH HA HA HA HA HAA
FUNNY, I KEEP SAYING THE WRONG WORD!!

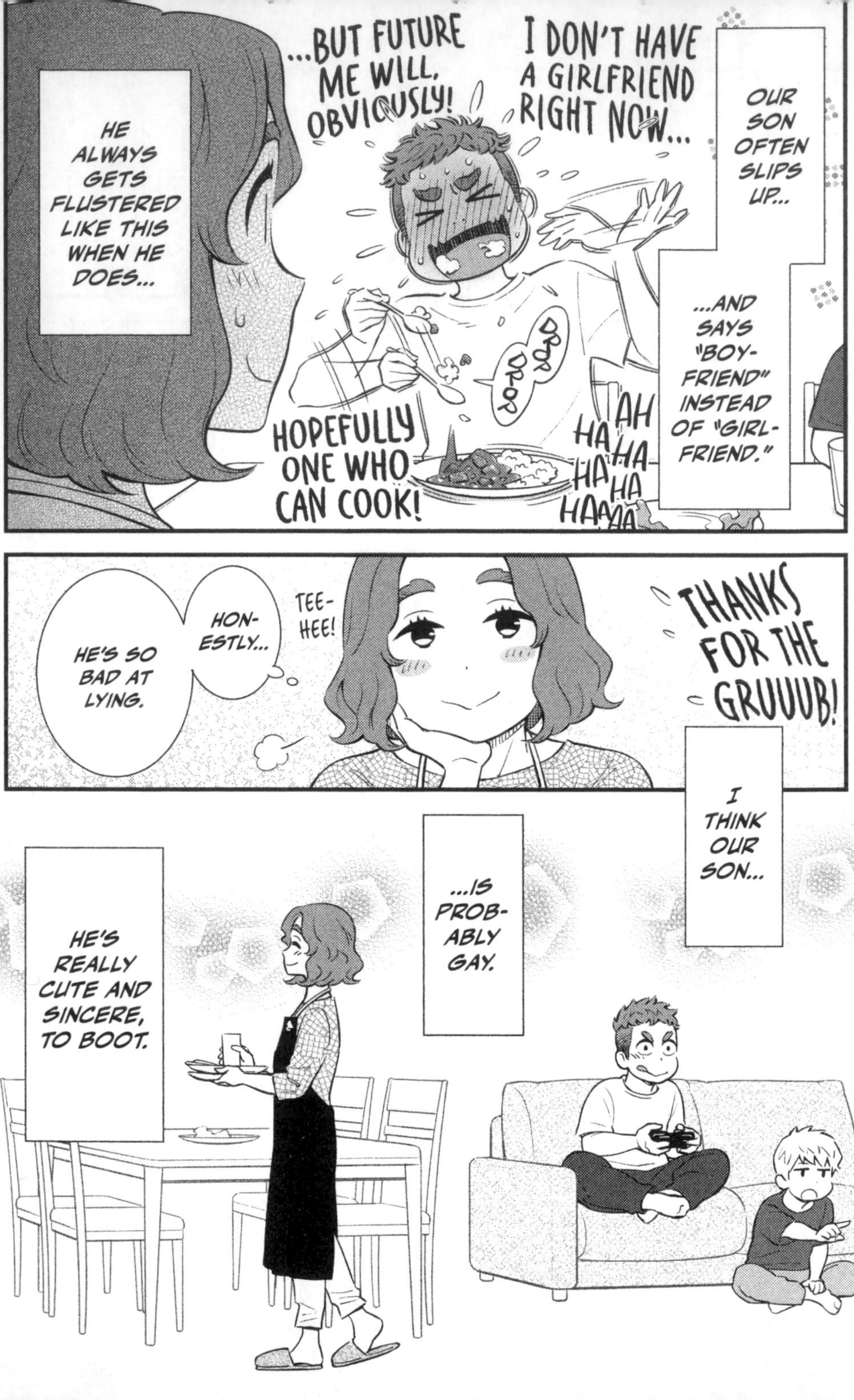
OUR SON OFTEN SLIPS UP...
...AND SAYS "BOY-FRIEND" INSTEAD OF "GIRL-FRIEND."
I DON'T HAVE A GIRLFRIEND RIGHT NOW...
...BUT FUTURE ME WILL, OBVIOUSLY!
AH HA HA HA HA HA HAAA
DROP DROP
HOPEFULLY ONE WHO CAN COOK!
HE ALWAYS GETS FLUSTERED LIKE THIS WHEN HE DOES...
THANKS FOR THE GRUUUB!
TEE-HEE!
HON-ESTLY...
HE'S SO BAD AT LYING.
I THINK OUR SON...
...IS PROBABLY GAY.
HE'S REALLY CUTE AND SINCERE, TO BOOT.

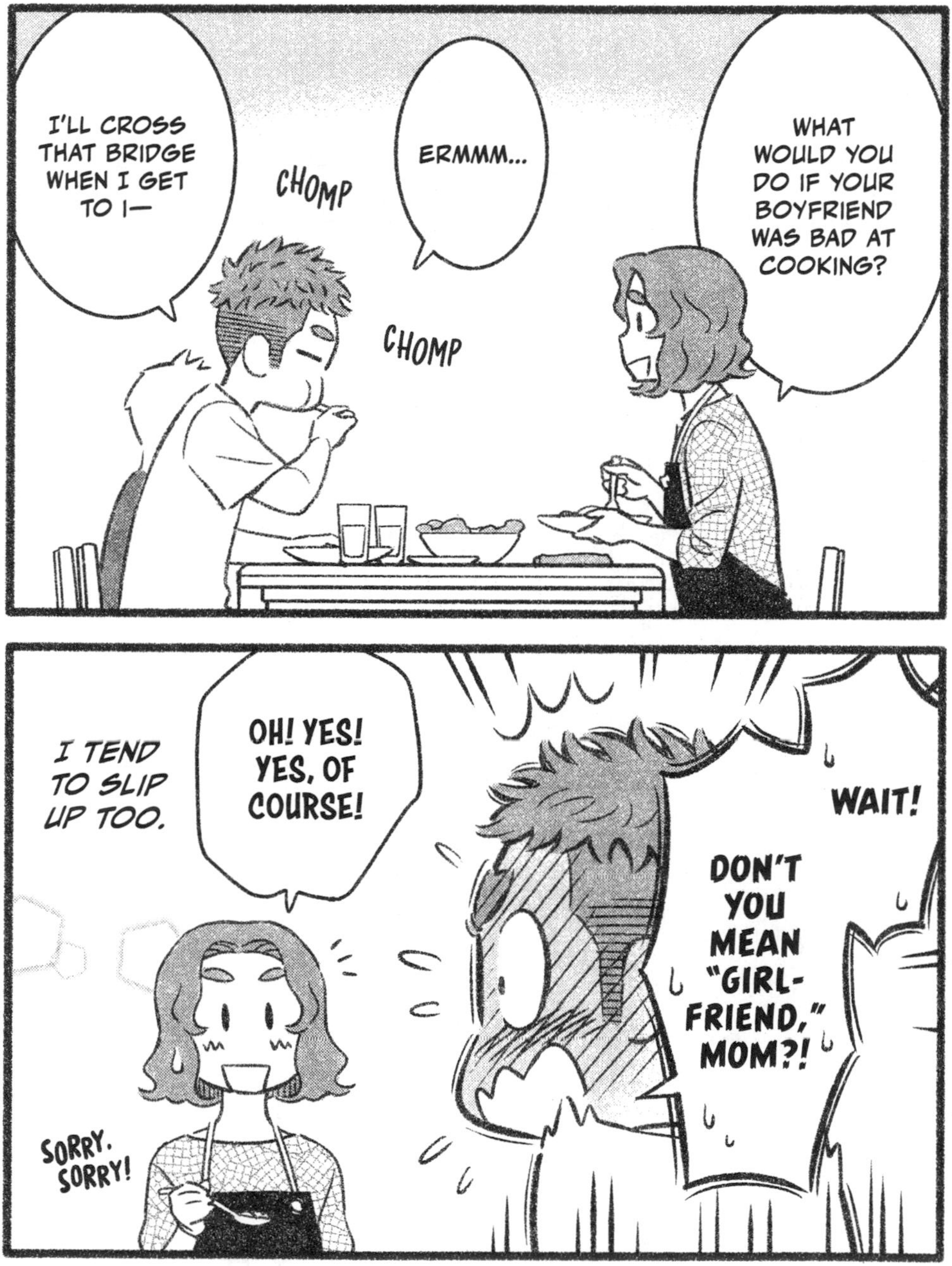
WHAT WOULD YOU DO IF YOUR BOYFRIEND WAS BAD AT COOKING?
CHOMP
ERMMM...
CHOMP
I'LL CROSS THAT BRIDGE WHEN I GET TO I—
WAIT!
DON'T YOU MEAN "GIRL-FRIEND," MOM?!
OH! YES! YES, OF COURSE!
I TEND TO SLIP UP TOO.
SORRY. SORRY!

I Think
Our Son
Is Gay

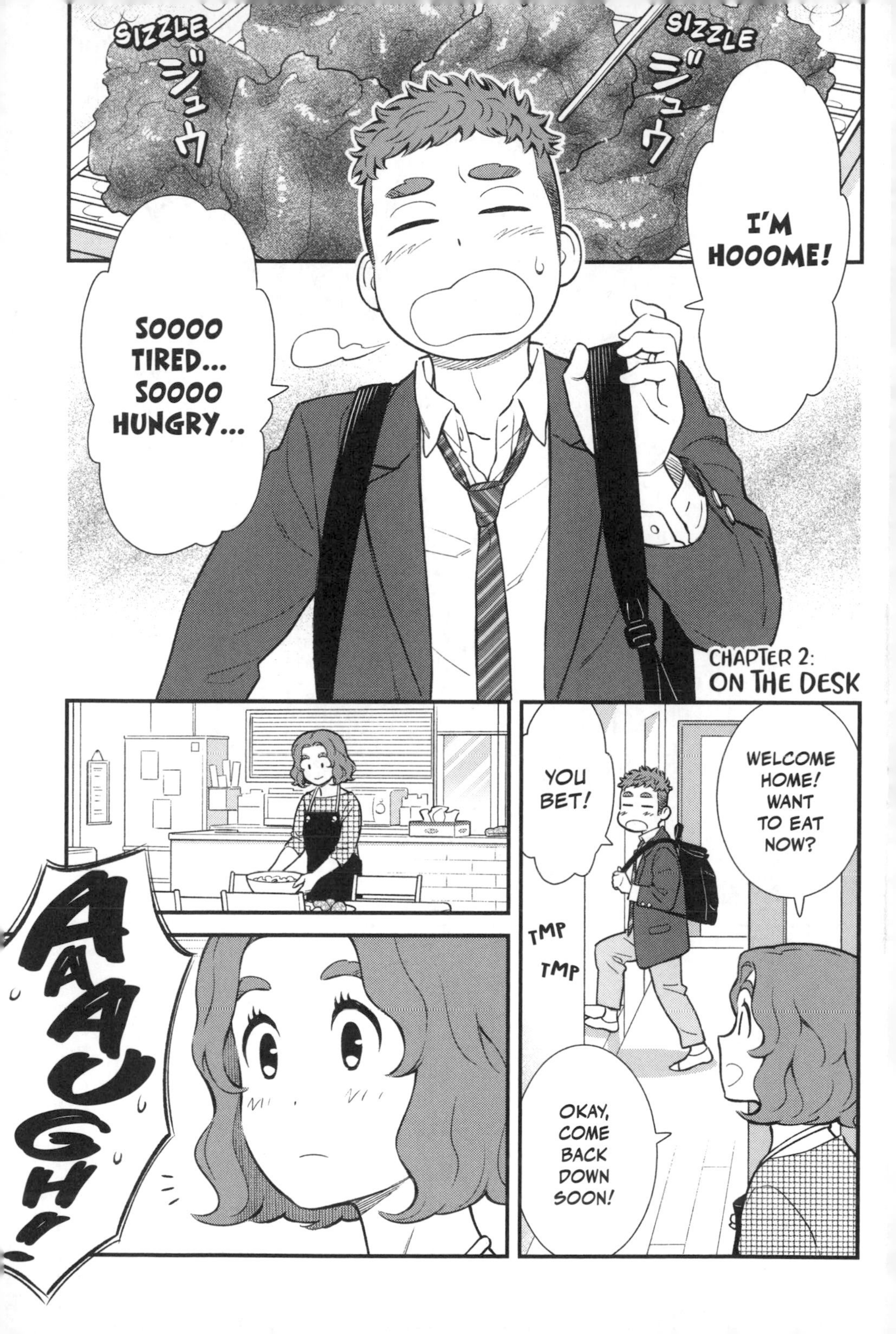
SIZZLE
ジュウ
SIZZLE
ジュウ
I'M HOOOME!
SOOOO TIRED... SOOOO HUNGRY...
CHAPTER 2: ON THE DESK
WELCOME HOME! WANT TO EAT NOW?
YOU BET!
TMP
TMP
OKAY, COME BACK DOWN SOON!
AAAUGH!!

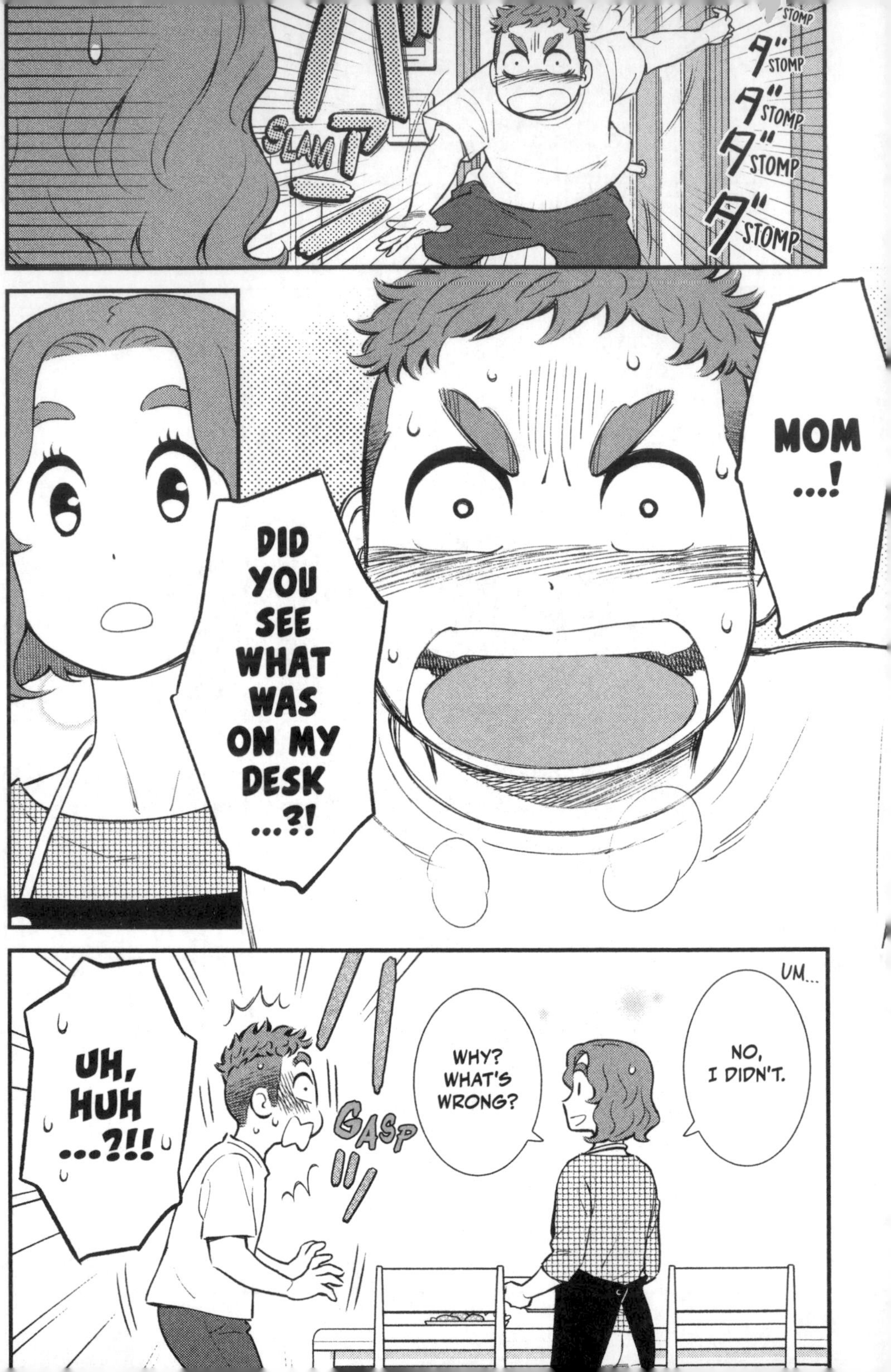
STOMP
ダ" STOMP
ダ" STOMP
ダ" STOMP
ダ" STOMP
SLAM
MOM ...!
DID YOU SEE WHAT WAS ON MY DESK ...?!
UM...
NO, I DIDN'T.
WHY? WHAT'S WRONG?
GASP
UH, HUH ...?!!

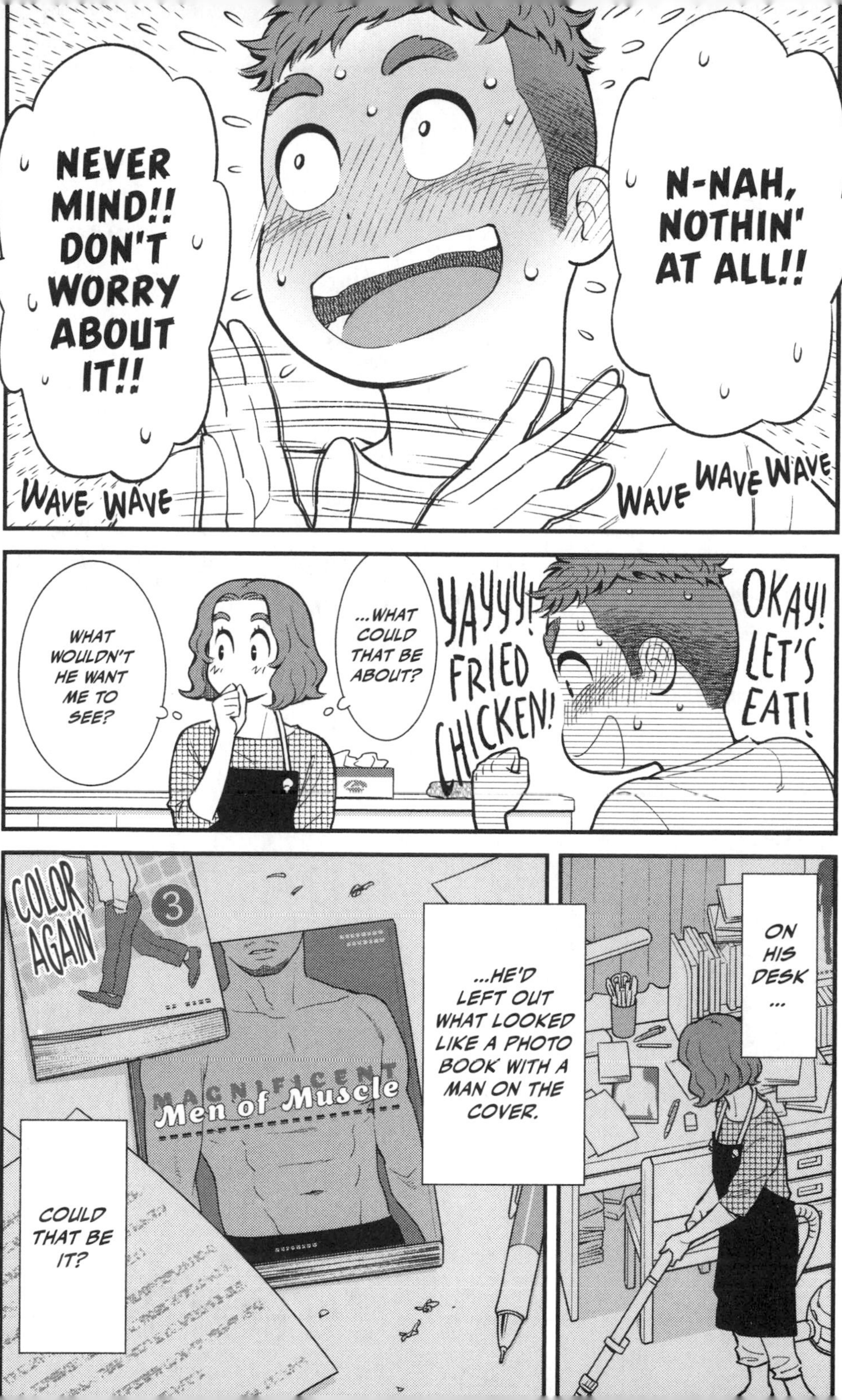
N-NAH, NOTHIN' AT ALL!!
NEVER MIND!! DON'T WORRY ABOUT IT!!
WAVE WAVE WAVE
WAVE WAVE
OKAY! LET'S EAT!
YAYYY! FRIED CHICKEN!
...WHAT COULD THAT BE ABOUT?
WHAT WOULDN'T HE WANT ME TO SEE?
ON HIS DESK ...
...HE'D LEFT OUT WHAT LOOKED LIKE A PHOTO BOOK WITH A MAN ON THE COVER.
COLOR AGAIN
3
MAGNIFICENT
Men of Muscle
COULD THAT BE IT?

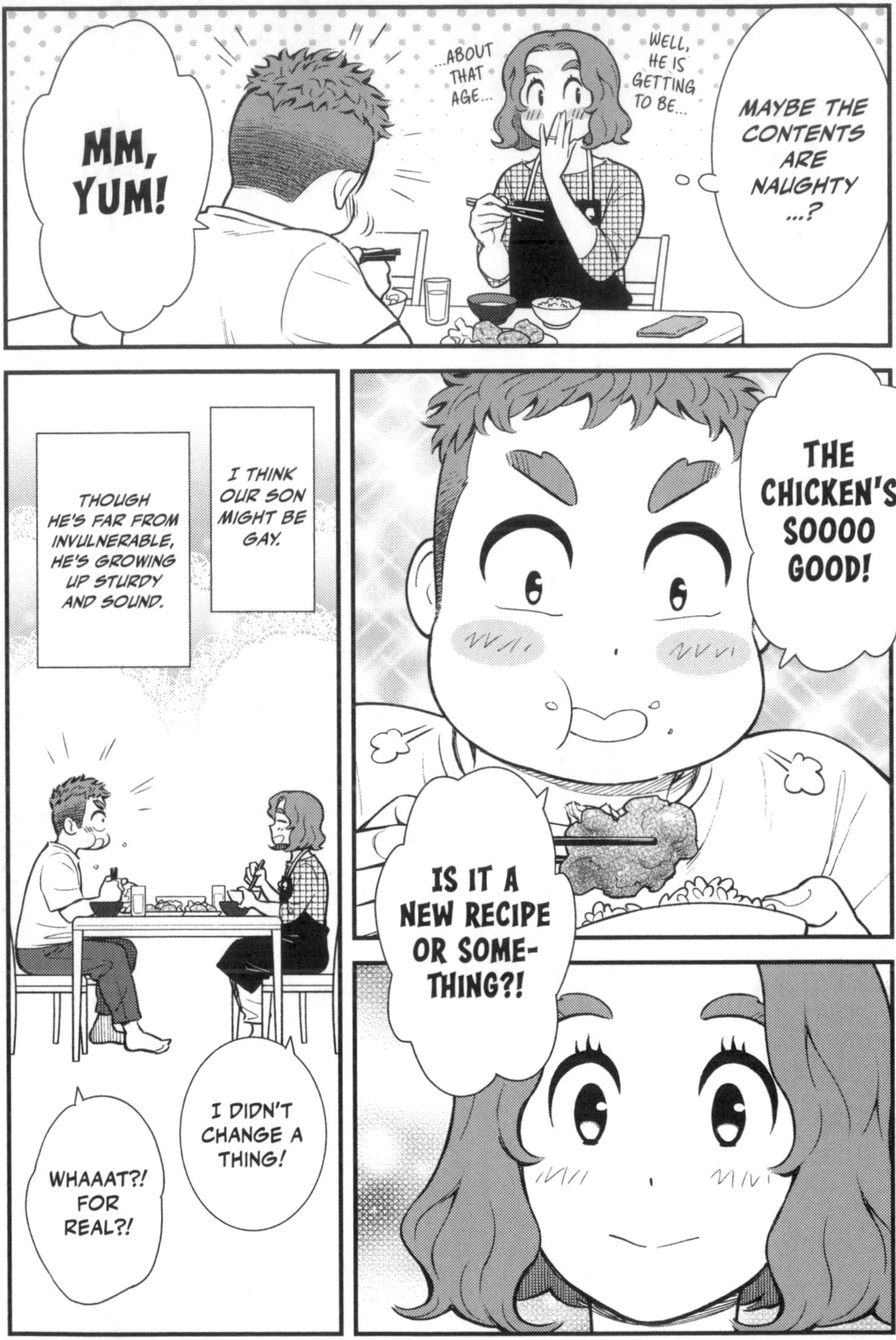
MAYBE THE CONTENTS ARE NAUGHTY ...?
WELL, HE IS GETTING TO BE...
...ABOUT THAT AGE...
MM, YUM!
THE CHICKEN'S SOOOO GOOD!
IS IT A NEW RECIPE OR SOME-THING?!
I THINK OUR SON MIGHT BE GAY.
THOUGH HE'S FAR FROM INVULNERABLE, HE'S GROWING UP STURDY AND SOUND.
I DIDN'T CHANGE A THING!
WHAAAT?! FOR REAL?!

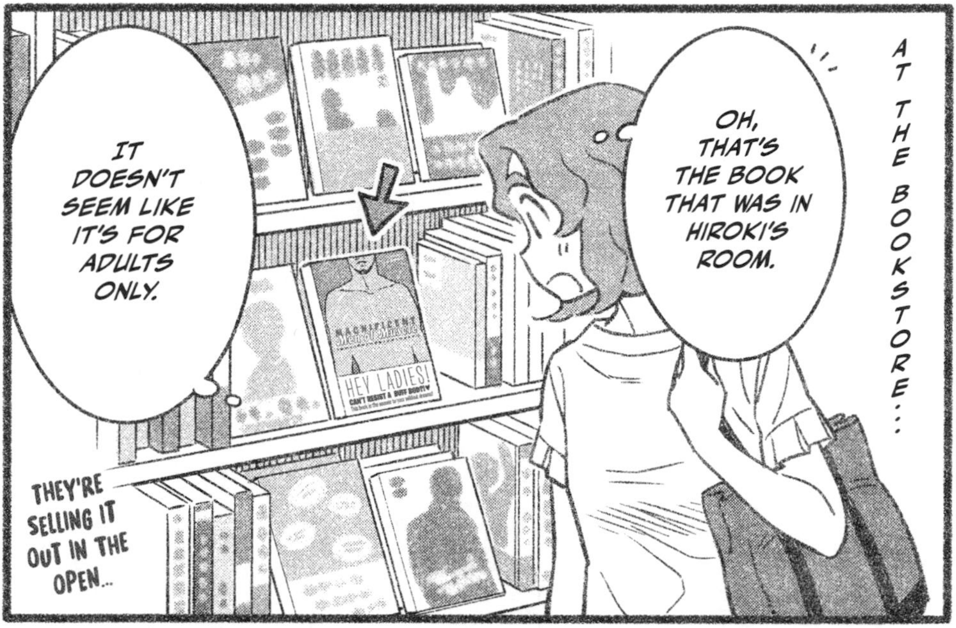
AT THE BOOKSTORE...
OH, THAT'S THE BOOK THAT WAS IN HIROKI'S ROOM.
IT DOESN'T SEEM LIKE IT'S FOR ADULTS ONLY.
THEY'RE SELLING IT OUT IN THE OPEN...
MAGNIFICENT Men of Muscle
HEY LADIES!
CAN'T RESIST A BUFF BOD?!♥
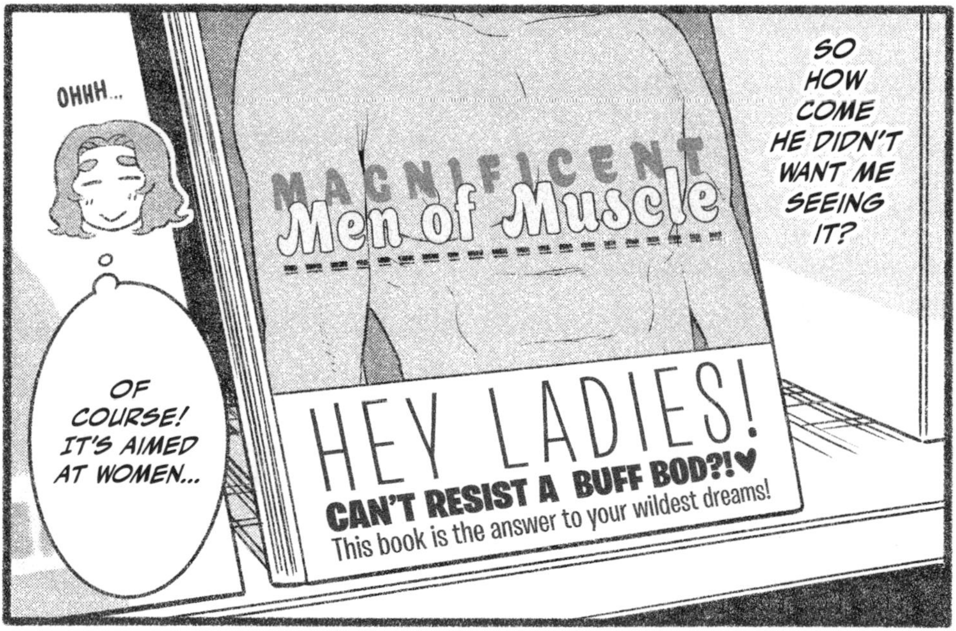
SO HOW COME HE DIDN'T WANT ME SEEING IT?
MAGNIFICENT Men of Muscle
HEY LADIES!
CAN'T RESIST A BUFF BOD?!♥
This book is the answer to your wildest dreams!
OHHH...
OF COURSE! IT'S AIMED AT WOMEN...

I Think
Our Son
Is Gay

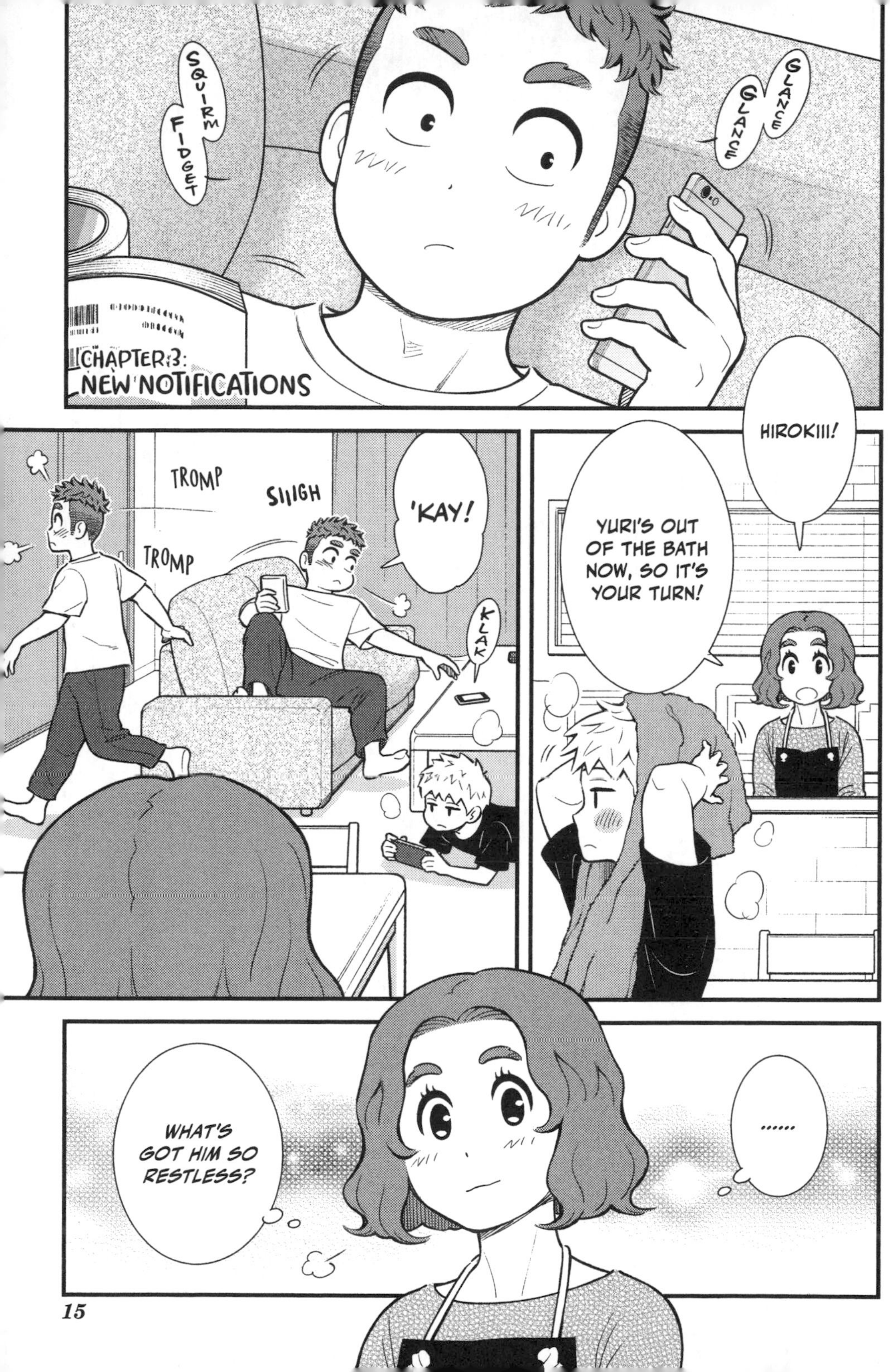
GLANCE GLANCE
SQUIRM FIDGET
CHAPTER 3: NEW NOTIFICATIONS
HIROKIII!
YURI'S OUT OF THE BATH NOW, SO IT'S YOUR TURN!
'KAY!
KLAK
SIIIGH
TROMP
TROMP
......
WHAT'S GOT HIM SO RESTLESS?

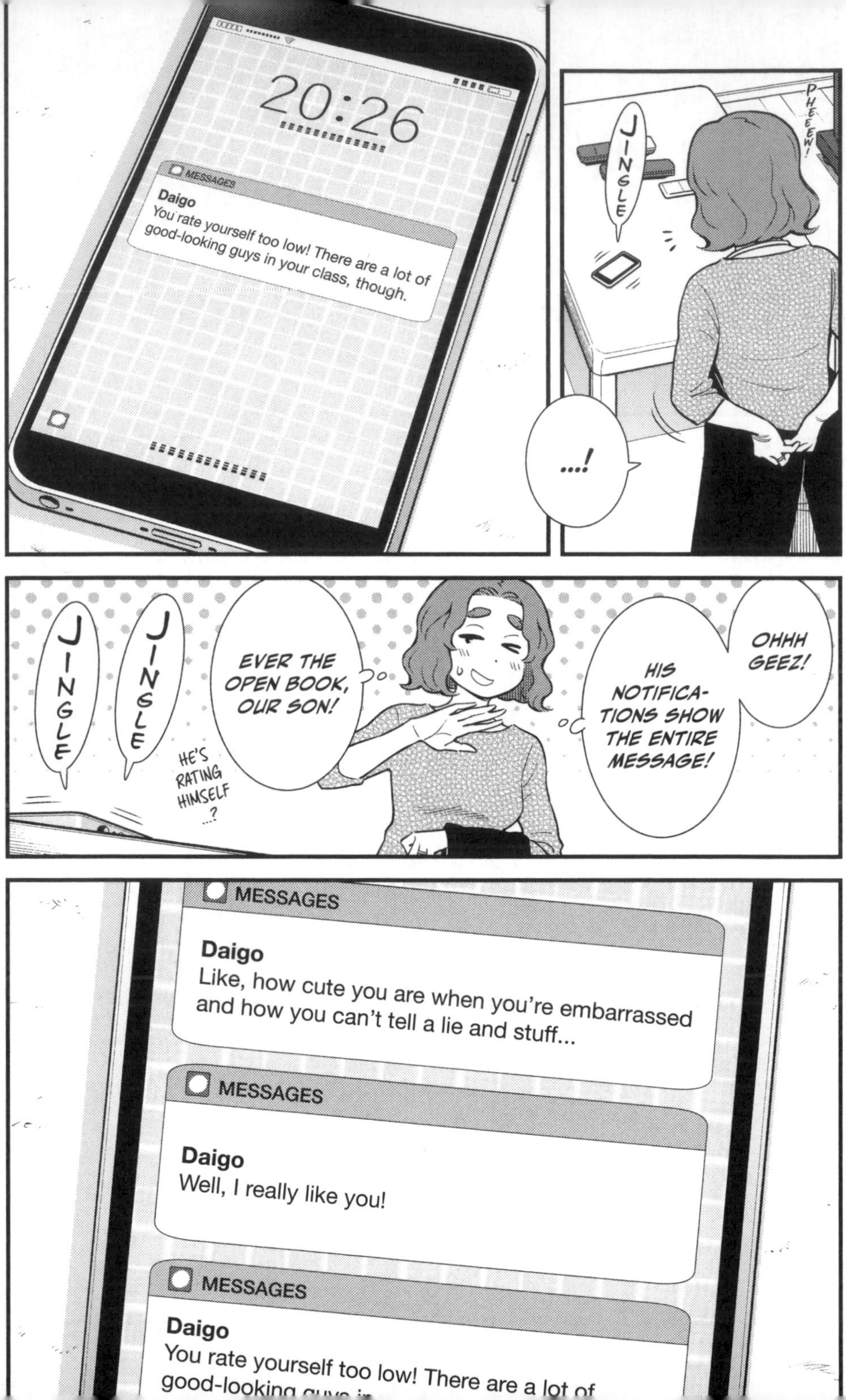
PHEEEW!
JINGLE
...!
20:26
MESSAGES
Daigo
You rate yourself too low! There are a lot of good-looking guys in your class, though.
OHHH GEEZ!
HIS NOTIFICATIONS SHOW THE ENTIRE MESSAGE!
EVER THE OPEN BOOK, OUR SON!
HE'S RATING HIMSELF ...?
JINGLE
JINGLE
MESSAGES
Daigo
Like, how cute you are when you're embarrassed and how you can't tell a lie and stuff...
MESSAGES
Daigo
Well, I really like you!
MESSAGES
Daigo
You rate yourself too low! There are a lot of
good-looking

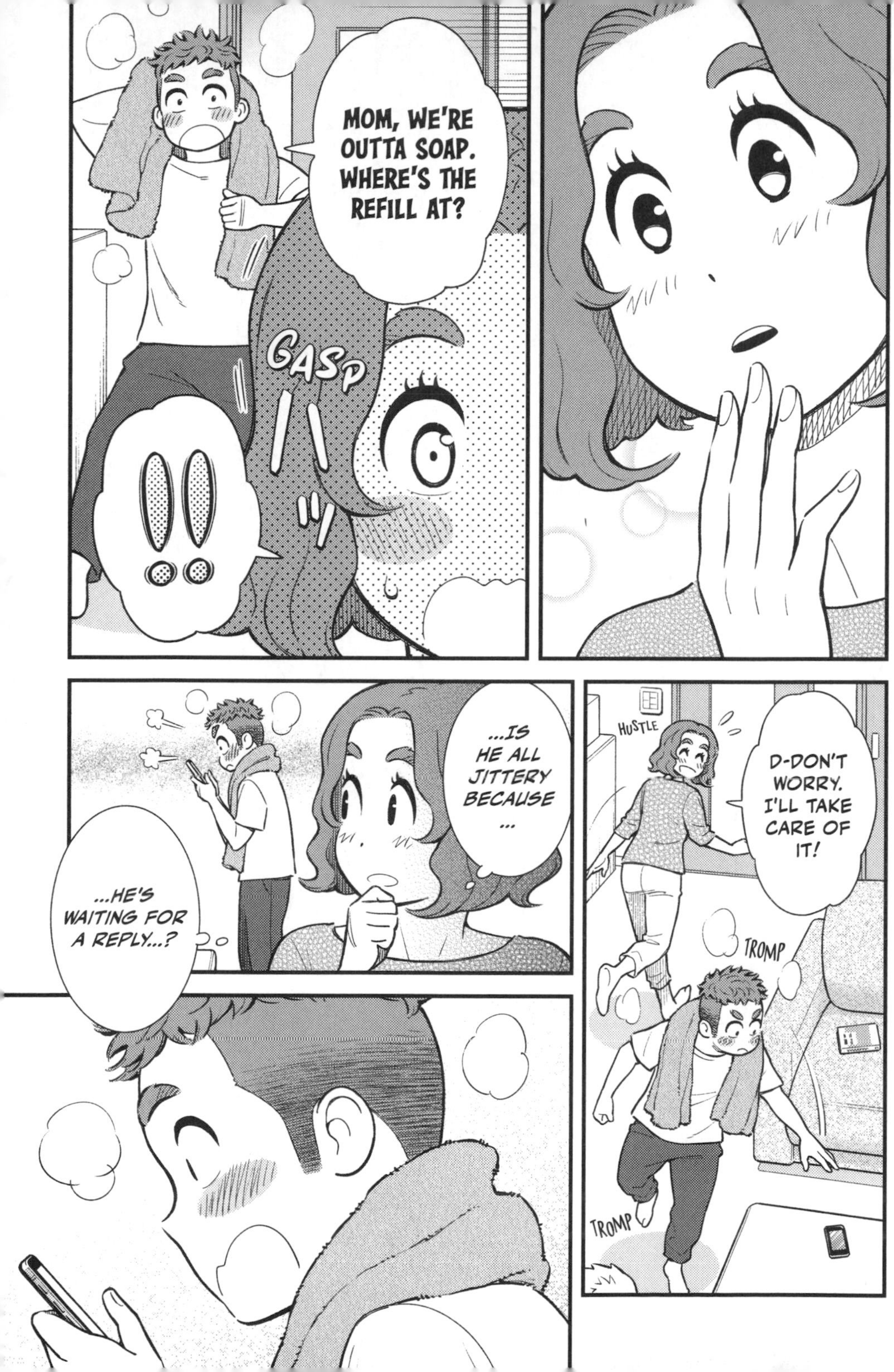
MOM, WE'RE OUTTA SOAP. WHERE'S THE REFILL AT?
GASP
!!
HUSTLE
D-DON'T WORRY. I'LL TAKE CARE OF IT!
TROMP
TROMP
...IS HE ALL JITTERY BECAUSE ...
...HE'S WAITING FOR A REPLY...?

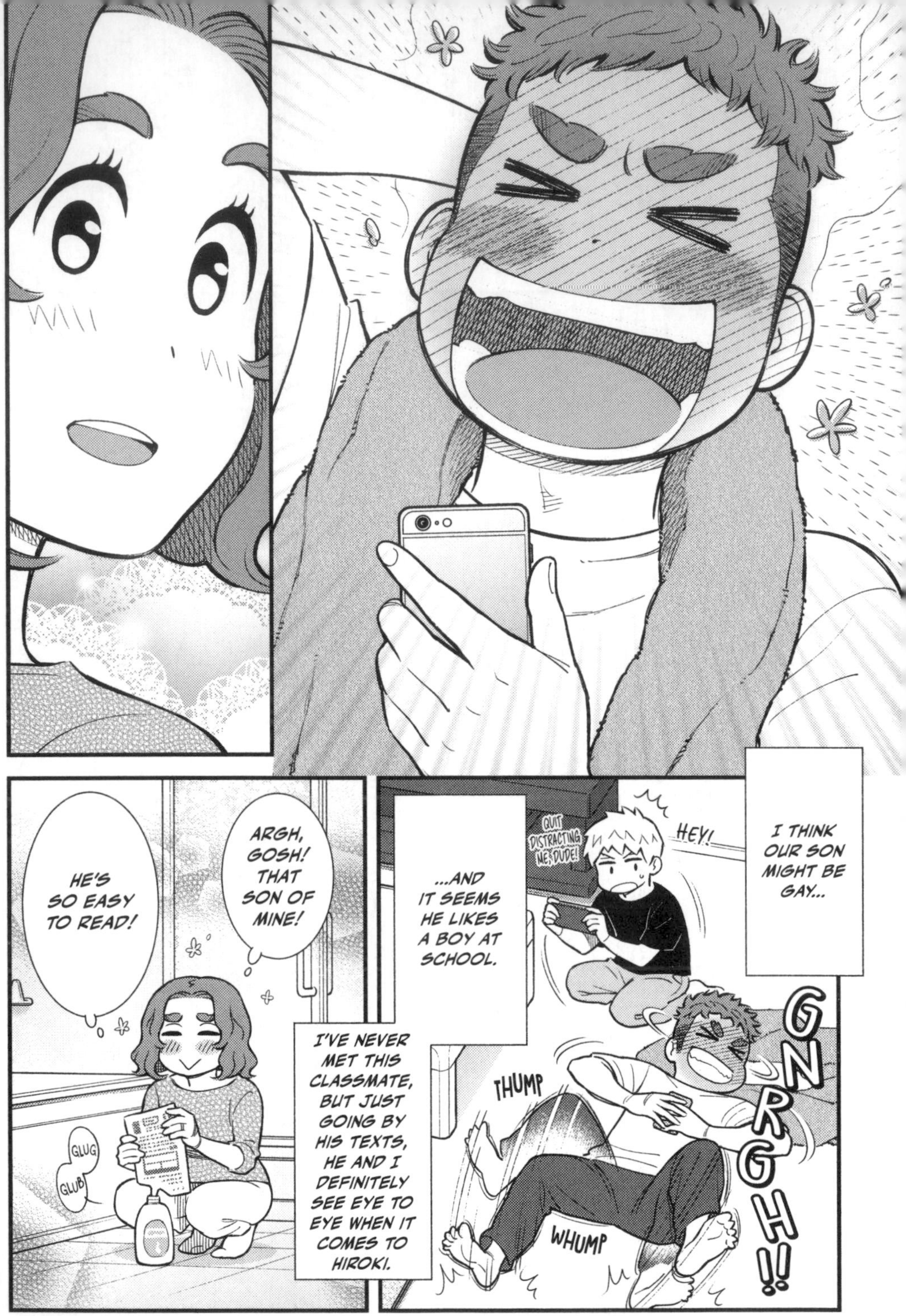
I THINK OUR SON MIGHT BE GAY...
HEY!
QUIT DISTRACTING ME, DUDE!
...AND IT SEEMS HE LIKES A BOY AT SCHOOL.
GNRGH!!
THUMP
WHUMP
I'VE NEVER MET THIS CLASSMATE, BUT JUST GOING BY HIS TEXTS, HE AND I DEFINITELY SEE EYE TO EYE WHEN IT COMES TO HIROKI.
ARGH, GOSH! THAT SON OF MINE!
HE'S SO EASY TO READ!
GLUG
GLUB

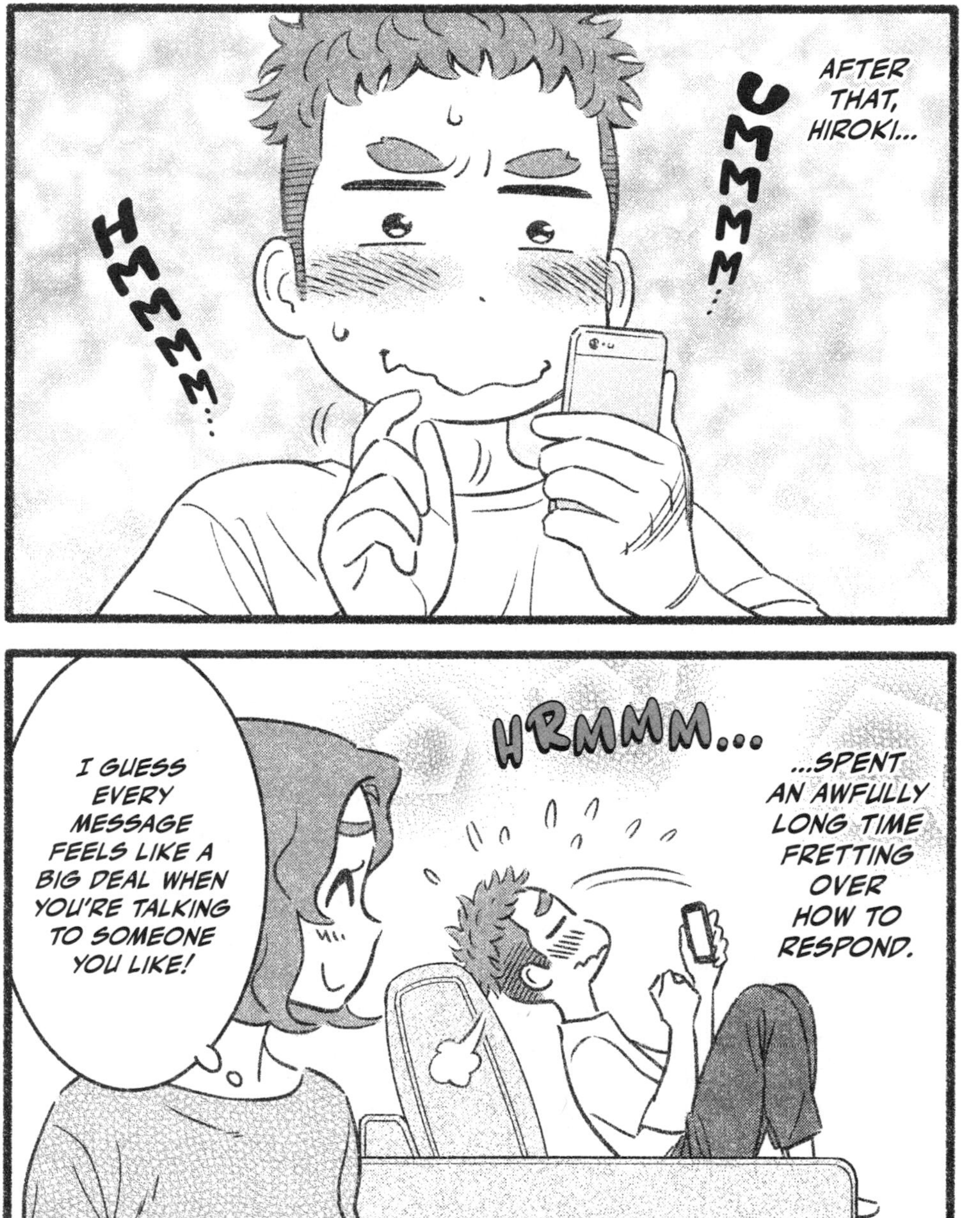
AFTER THAT, HIROKI...
UMMMM...
HMMMM...
...SPENT AN AWFULLY LONG TIME FRETTING OVER HOW TO RESPOND.
HRMMM...
I GUESS EVERY MESSAGE FEELS LIKE A BIG DEAL WHEN YOU'RE TALKING TO SOMEONE YOU LIKE!

I Think
Our Son
Is Gay

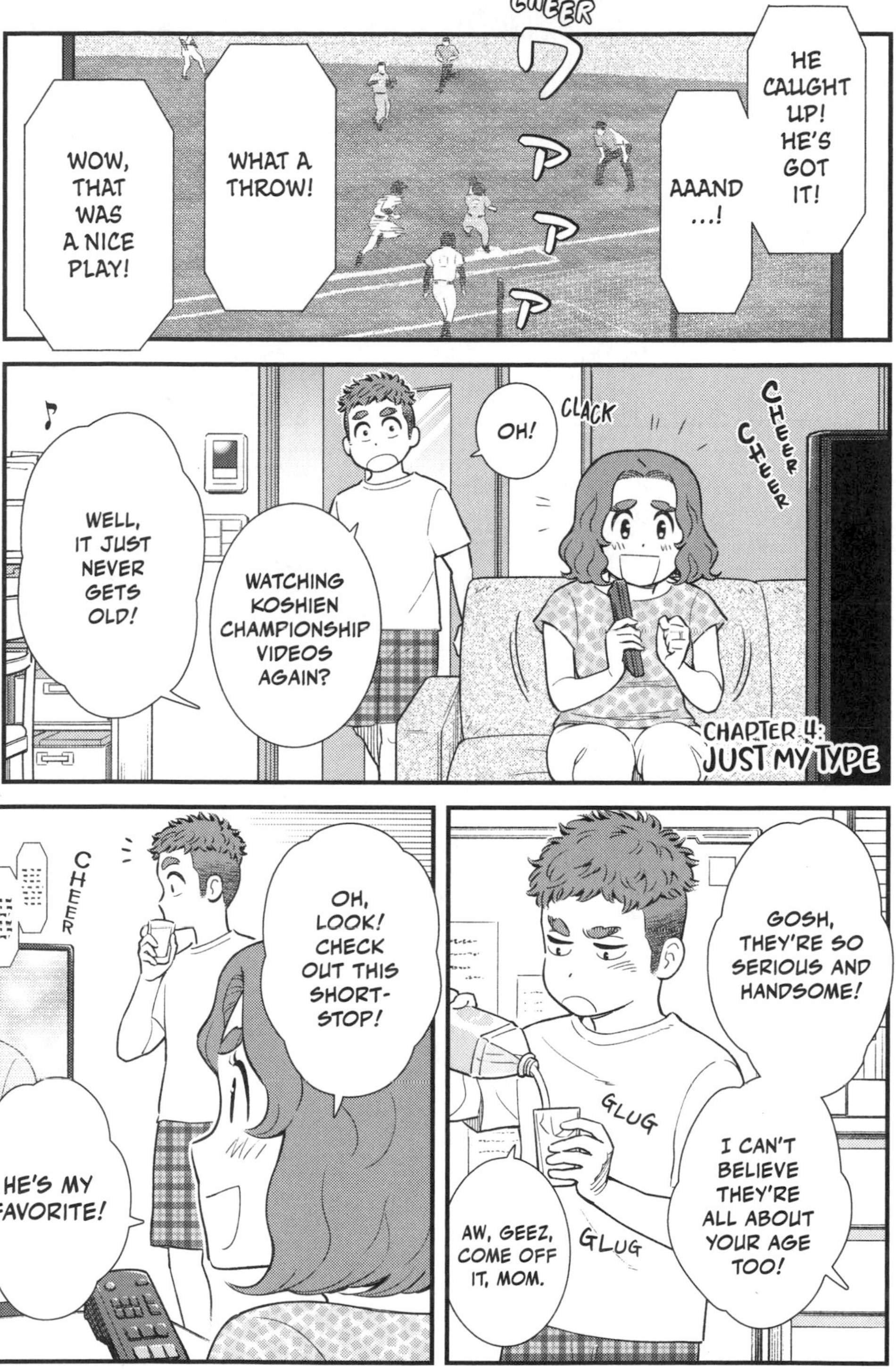

CHEER
HE CAUGHT UP! HE'S GOT IT!
AAAND ...!
WHAT A THROW!
WOW, THAT WAS A NICE PLAY!
CHEER CHEER
CLACK
OH!
WATCHING KOSHIEN CHAMPIONSHIP VIDEOS AGAIN?
WELL, IT JUST NEVER GETS OLD!
CHAPTER 4: JUST MY TYPE
GOSH, THEY'RE SO SERIOUS AND HANDSOME!
I CAN'T BELIEVE THEY'RE ALL ABOUT YOUR AGE TOO!
GLUG
GLUG
AW, GEEZ, COME OFF IT, MOM.
OH, LOOK! CHECK OUT THIS SHORT-STOP!
CHEER
CHEER
HE'S MY FAVORITE!

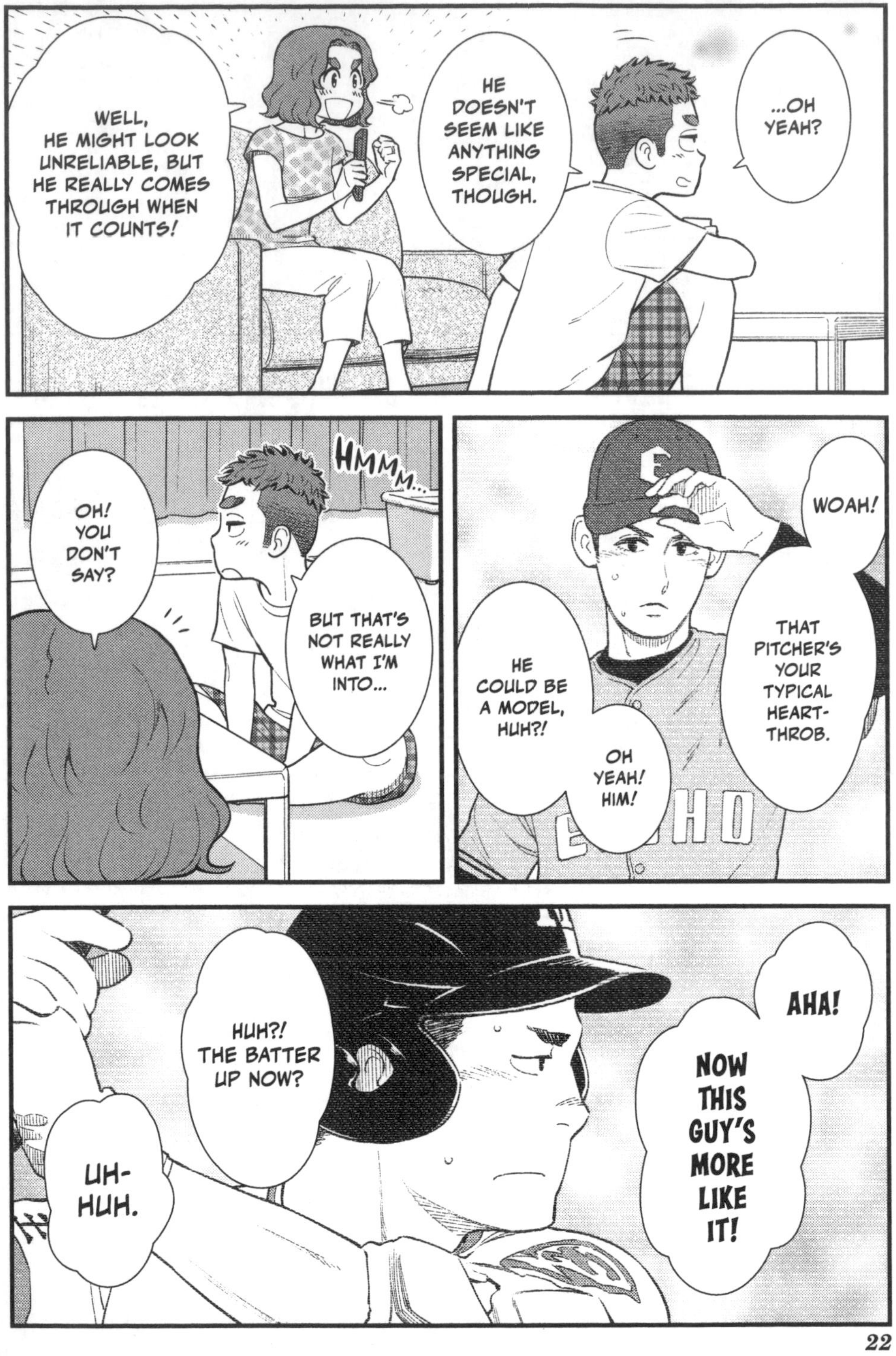
...OH YEAH?
HE DOESN'T SEEM LIKE ANYTHING SPECIAL, THOUGH.
WELL, HE MIGHT LOOK UNRELIABLE, BUT HE REALLY COMES THROUGH WHEN IT COUNTS!
WOAH!
THAT PITCHER'S YOUR TYPICAL HEART-THROB.
HE COULD BE A MODEL, HUH?!
OH YEAH! HIM!
HMMM...
OH! YOU DON'T SAY?
BUT THAT'S NOT REALLY WHAT I'M INTO...
AHA!
NOW THIS GUY'S MORE LIKE IT!
HUH?! THE BATTER UP NOW?
UH-HUH.

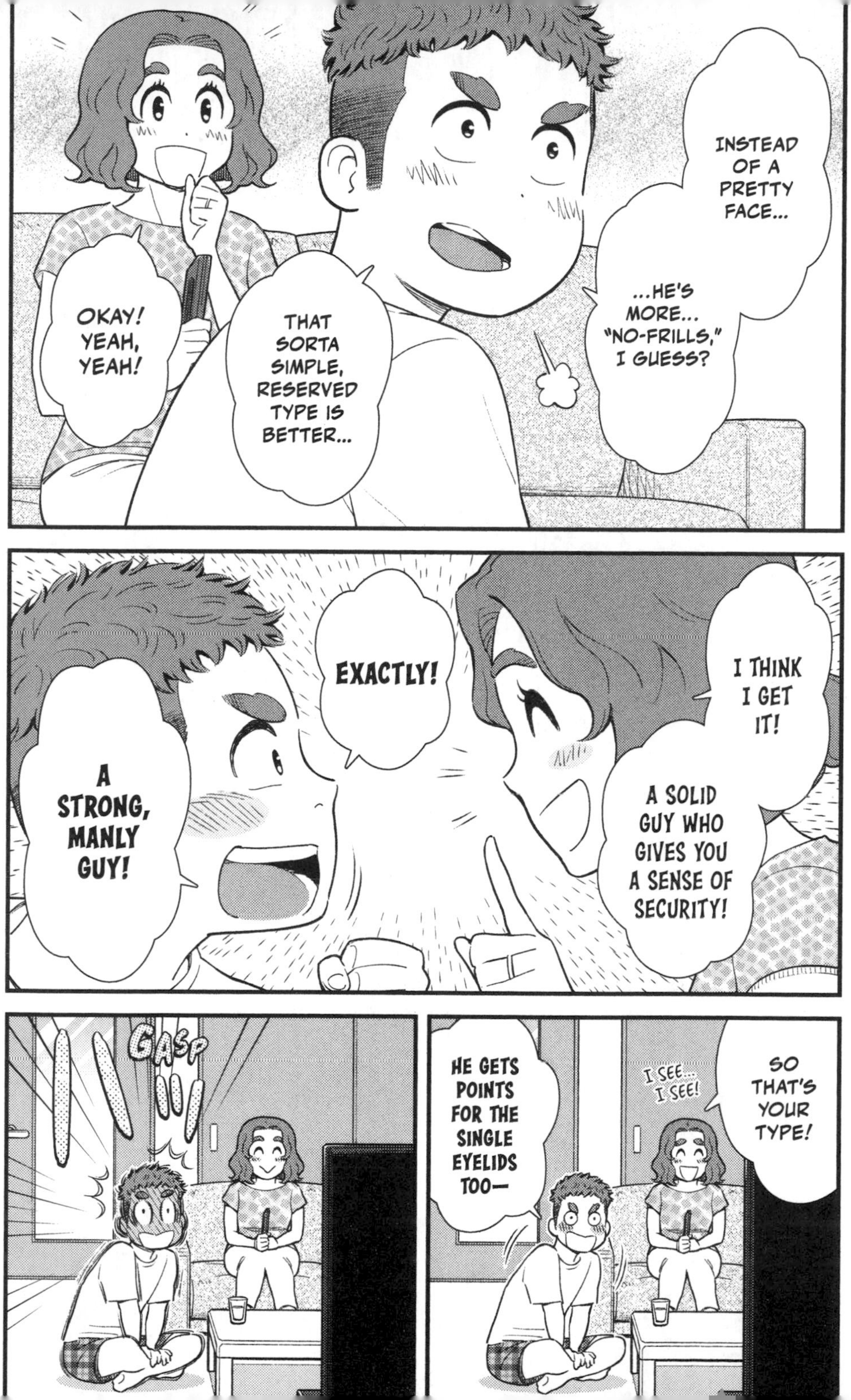
INSTEAD OF A PRETTY FACE...
...HE'S MORE... "NO-FRILLS," I GUESS?
THAT SORTA SIMPLE, RESERVED TYPE IS BETTER...
OKAY! YEAH, YEAH!
I THINK I GET IT!
EXACTLY!
A SOLID GUY WHO GIVES YOU A SENSE OF SECURITY!
A STRONG, MANLY GUY!
SO THAT'S YOUR TYPE!
I SEE... I SEE!
HE GETS POINTS FOR THE SINGLE EYELIDS TOO—
GASP

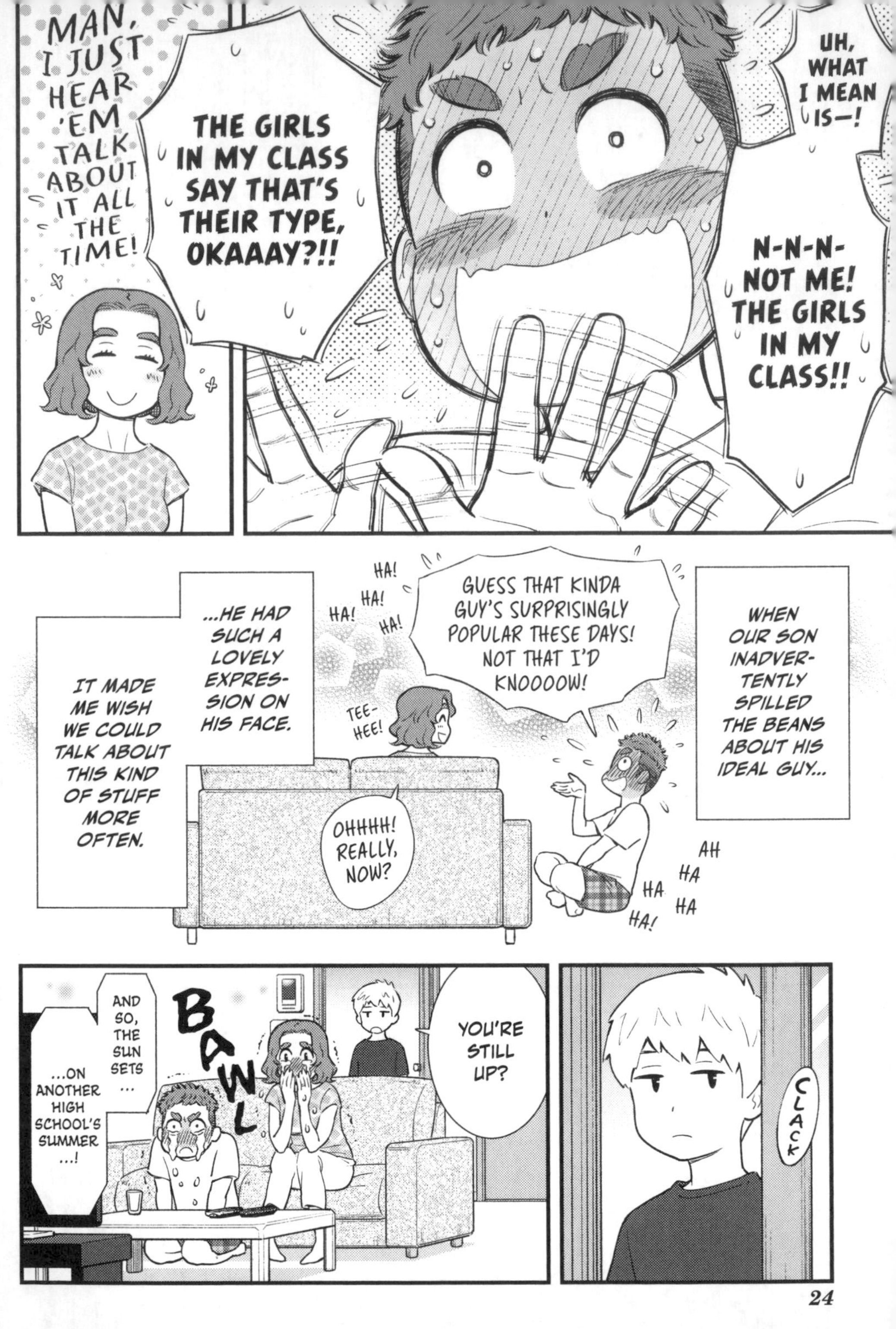
UH, WHAT I MEAN IS—!
N-N-N-NOT ME! THE GIRLS IN MY CLASS!!
THE GIRLS IN MY CLASS SAY THAT'S THEIR TYPE, OKAAAY?!!
MAN, I JUST HEAR 'EM TALK ABOUT IT ALL THE TIME!
WHEN OUR SON INADVERTENTLY SPILLED THE BEANS ABOUT HIS IDEAL GUY...
GUESS THAT KINDA GUY'S SURPRISINGLY POPULAR THESE DAYS! NOT THAT I'D KNOOOOW!
HA! HA! HA! HA!
TEE-HEE!
OHHHH! REALLY, NOW?
AH HA HA HA HA!
...HE HAD SUCH A LOVELY EXPRESSION ON HIS FACE.
IT MADE ME WISH WE COULD TALK ABOUT THIS KIND OF STUFF MORE OFTEN.
CLACK
YOU'RE STILL UP?
BAWL
AND SO, THE SUN SETS...
...ON ANOTHER HIGH SCHOOL'S SUMMER...!

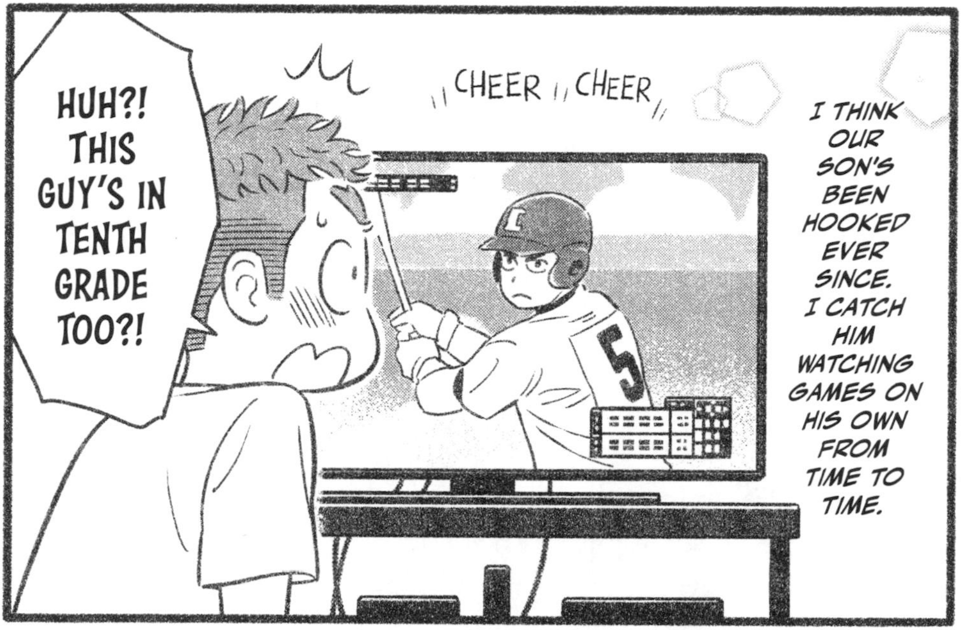
I THINK OUR SON'S BEEN HOOKED EVER SINCE. I CATCH HIM WATCHING GAMES ON HIS OWN FROM TIME TO TIME.
CHEER CHEER
HUH?! THIS GUY'S IN TENTH GRADE TOO?!

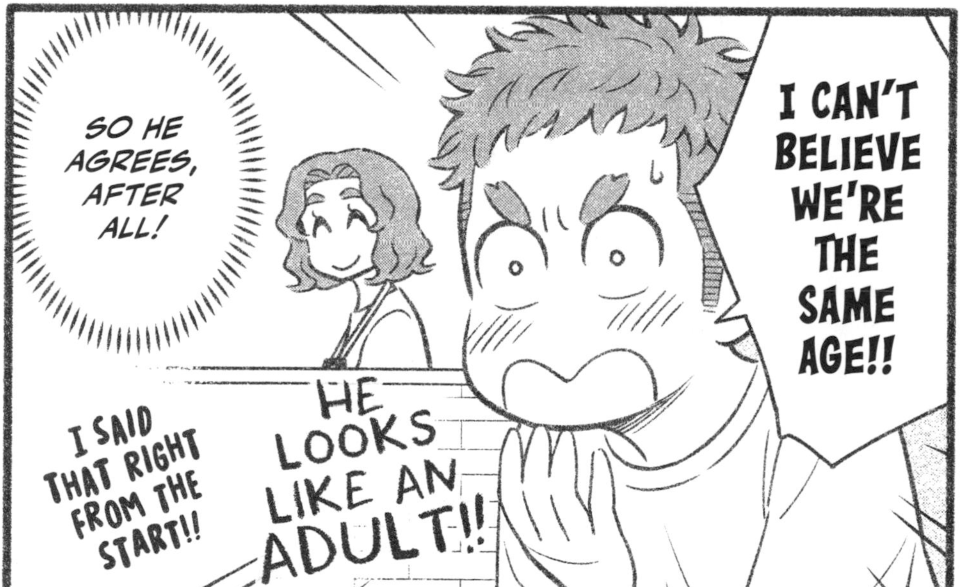
I CAN'T BELIEVE WE'RE THE SAME AGE!!
SO HE AGREES, AFTER ALL!
HE LOOKS LIKE AN ADULT!!
I SAID THAT RIGHT FROM THE START!!

I Think Our Son Is Gay

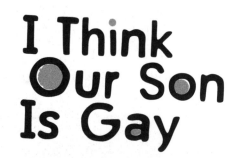

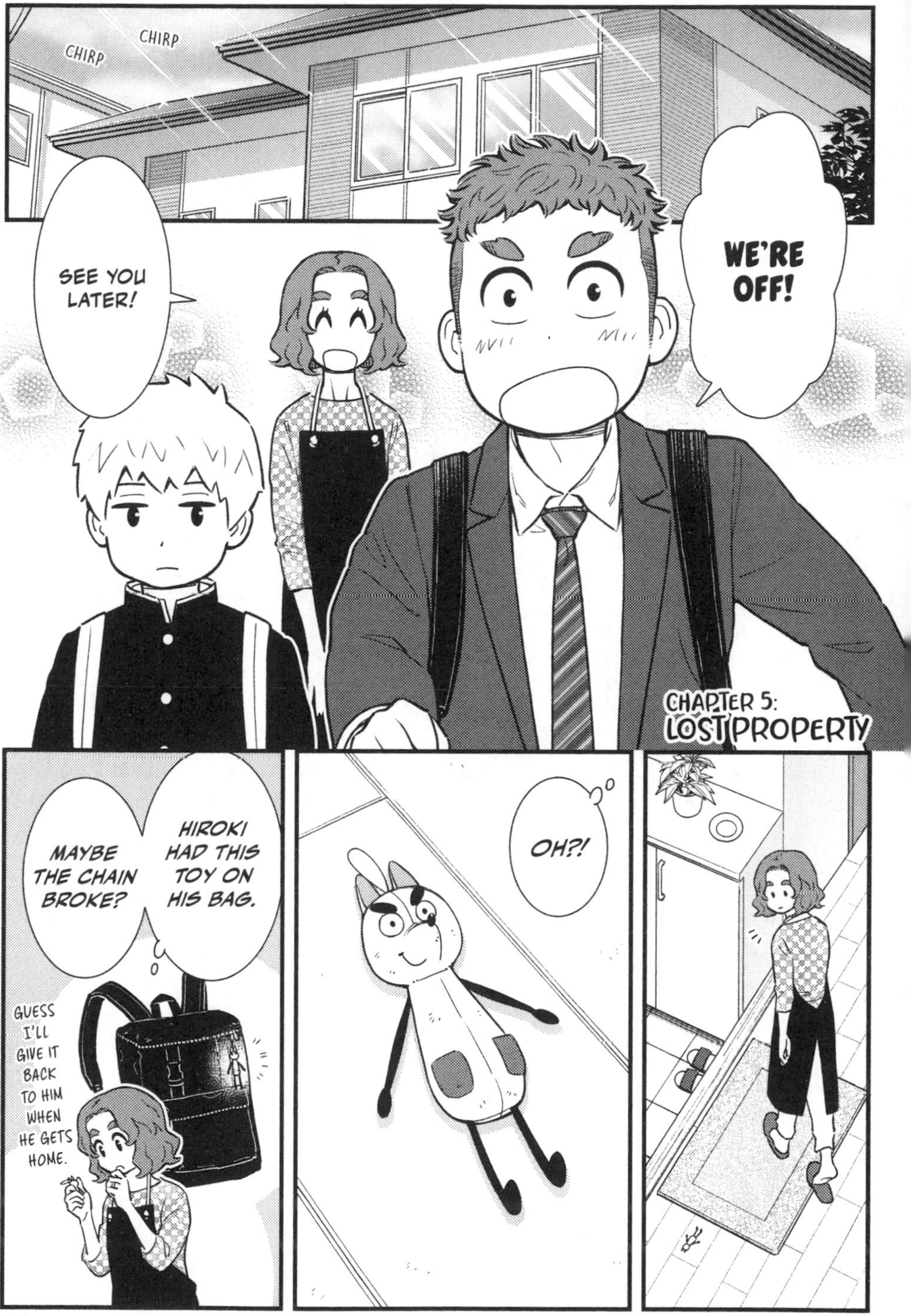
CHIRP
CHIRP
WE'RE OFF!
SEE YOU LATER!
CHAPTER 5: LOST PROPERTY
OH?!
HIROKI HAD THIS TOY ON HIS BAG.
MAYBE THE CHAIN BROKE?
GUESS I'LL GIVE IT BACK TO HIM WHEN HE GETS HOME.

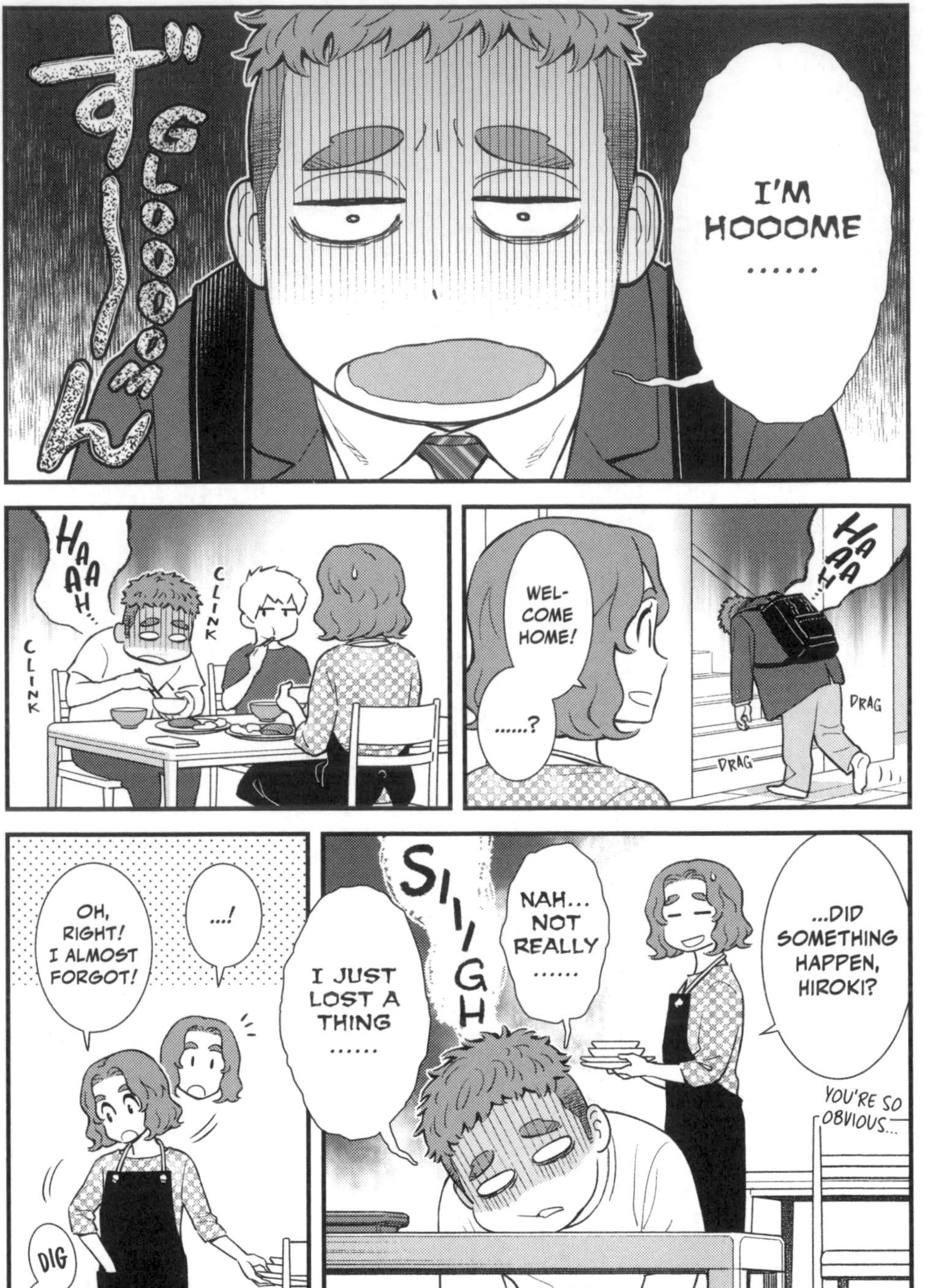
ずーん
GLOOOOOM
I'M HOOOME ......
WEL-COME HOME!
......?
HAAAH...
DRAG
DRAG
HAAAH...
CLINK
CLINK
...DID SOMETHING HAPPEN, HIROKI?
YOU'RE SO OBVIOUS...
NAH... NOT REALLY ......
SIIIGH
I JUST LOST A THING ......
...!
OH, RIGHT! I ALMOST FORGOT!
DIG
DIG

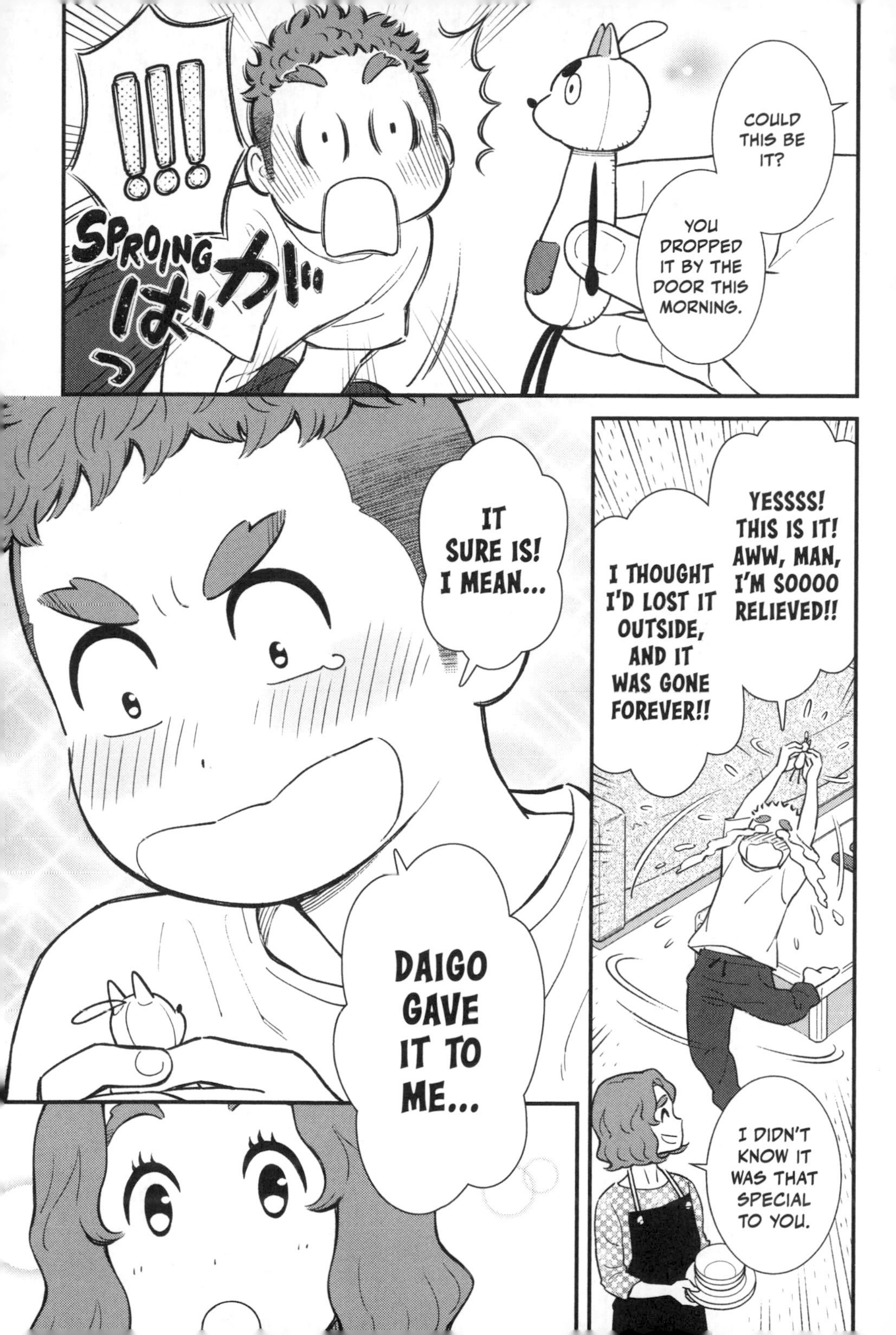
COULD THIS BE IT?
YOU DROPPED IT BY THE DOOR THIS MORNING.
!!!
SPROING
YESSSS! THIS IS IT! AWW, MAN, I'M SOOOO RELIEVED!!
I THOUGHT I'D LOST IT OUTSIDE, AND IT WAS GONE FOREVER!!
I DIDN'T KNOW IT WAS THAT SPECIAL TO YOU.
IT SURE IS! I MEAN...
DAIGO GAVE IT TO ME...

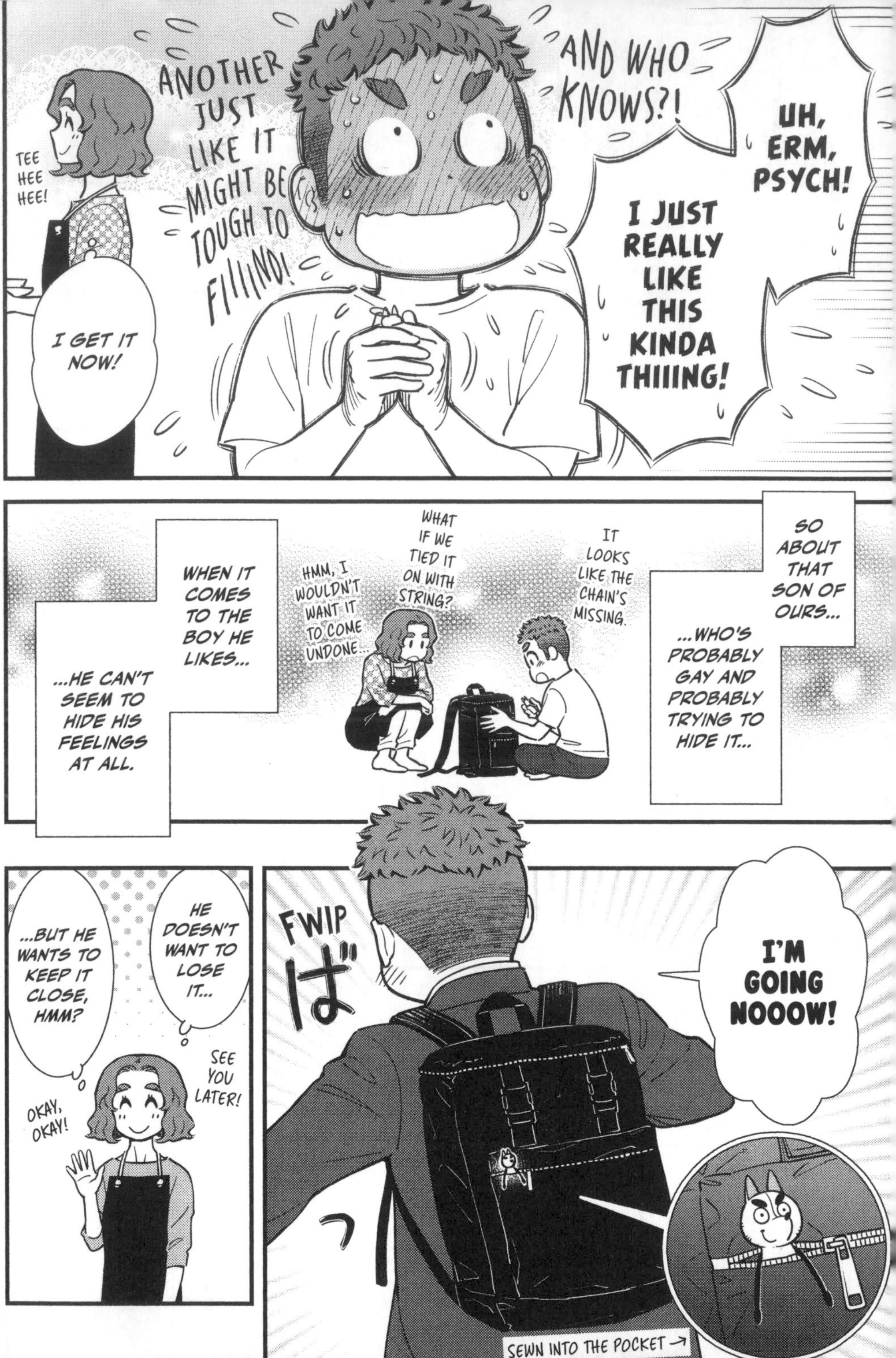
UH, ERM, PSYCH!
I JUST REALLY LIKE THIS KINDA THIIING!
AND WHO KNOWS?!
ANOTHER JUST LIKE IT MIGHT BE TOUGH TO FIIIIND!
TEE HEE HEE!
I GET IT NOW!
SO ABOUT THAT SON OF OURS...
...WHO'S PROBABLY GAY AND PROBABLY TRYING TO HIDE IT...
IT LOOKS LIKE THE CHAIN'S MISSING.
WHAT IF WE TIED IT ON WITH STRING?
HMM, I WOULDN'T WANT IT TO COME UNDONE...
WHEN IT COMES TO THE BOY HE LIKES...
...HE CAN'T SEEM TO HIDE HIS FEELINGS AT ALL.
I'M GOING NOOOW!
FWIP
ば
SEWN INTO THE POCKET →
HE DOESN'T WANT TO LOSE IT...
...BUT HE WANTS TO KEEP IT CLOSE, HMM?
SEE YOU LATER!
OKAY, OKAY!

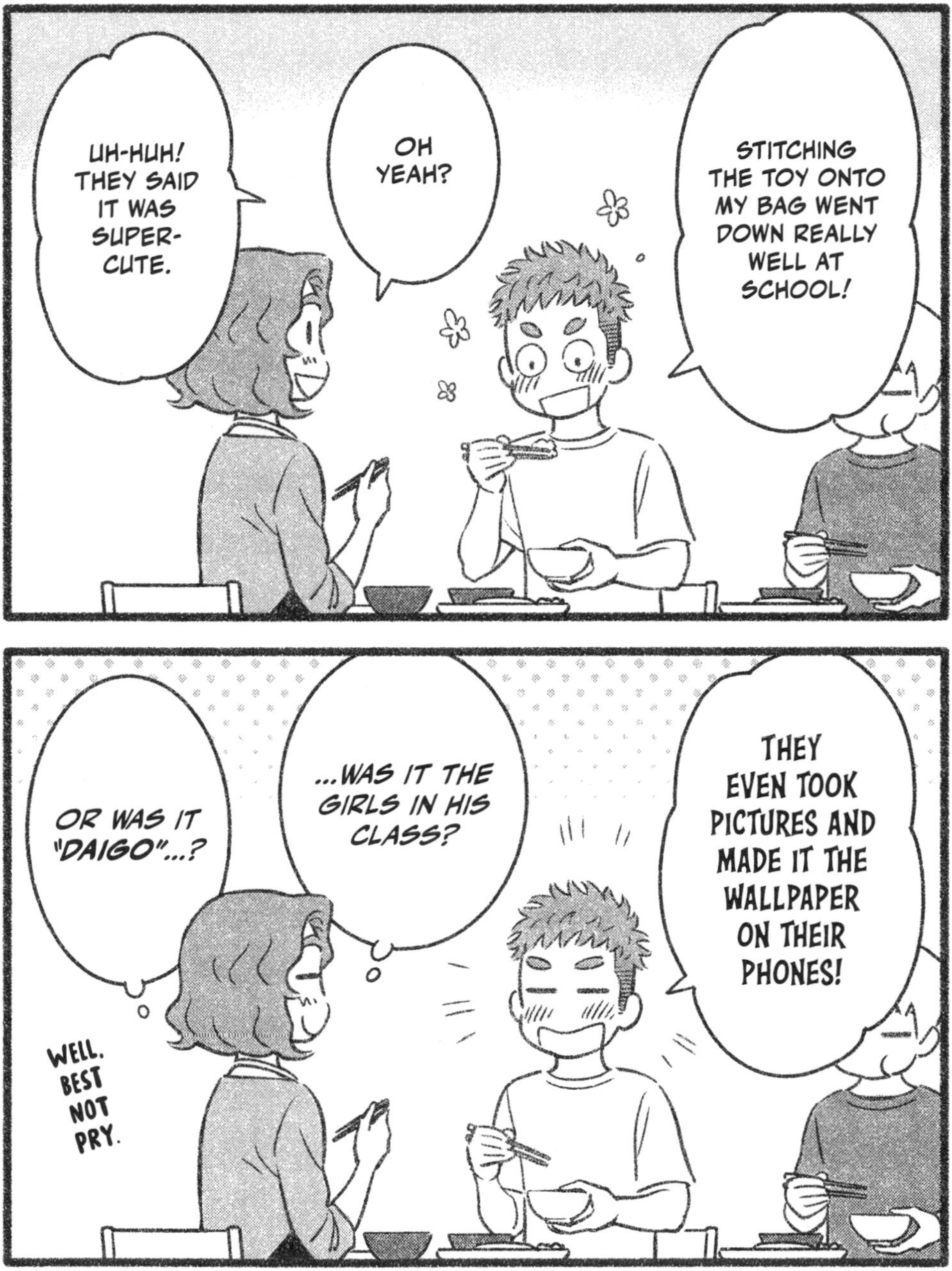
STITCHING THE TOY ONTO MY BAG WENT DOWN REALLY WELL AT SCHOOL!
OH YEAH?
UH-HUH! THEY SAID IT WAS SUPER-CUTE.
THEY EVEN TOOK PICTURES AND MADE IT THE WALLPAPER ON THEIR PHONES!
...WAS IT THE GIRLS IN HIS CLASS?
OR WAS IT "DAIGO"...?
WELL. BEST NOT PRY.

I Think
Our Son
Is Gay

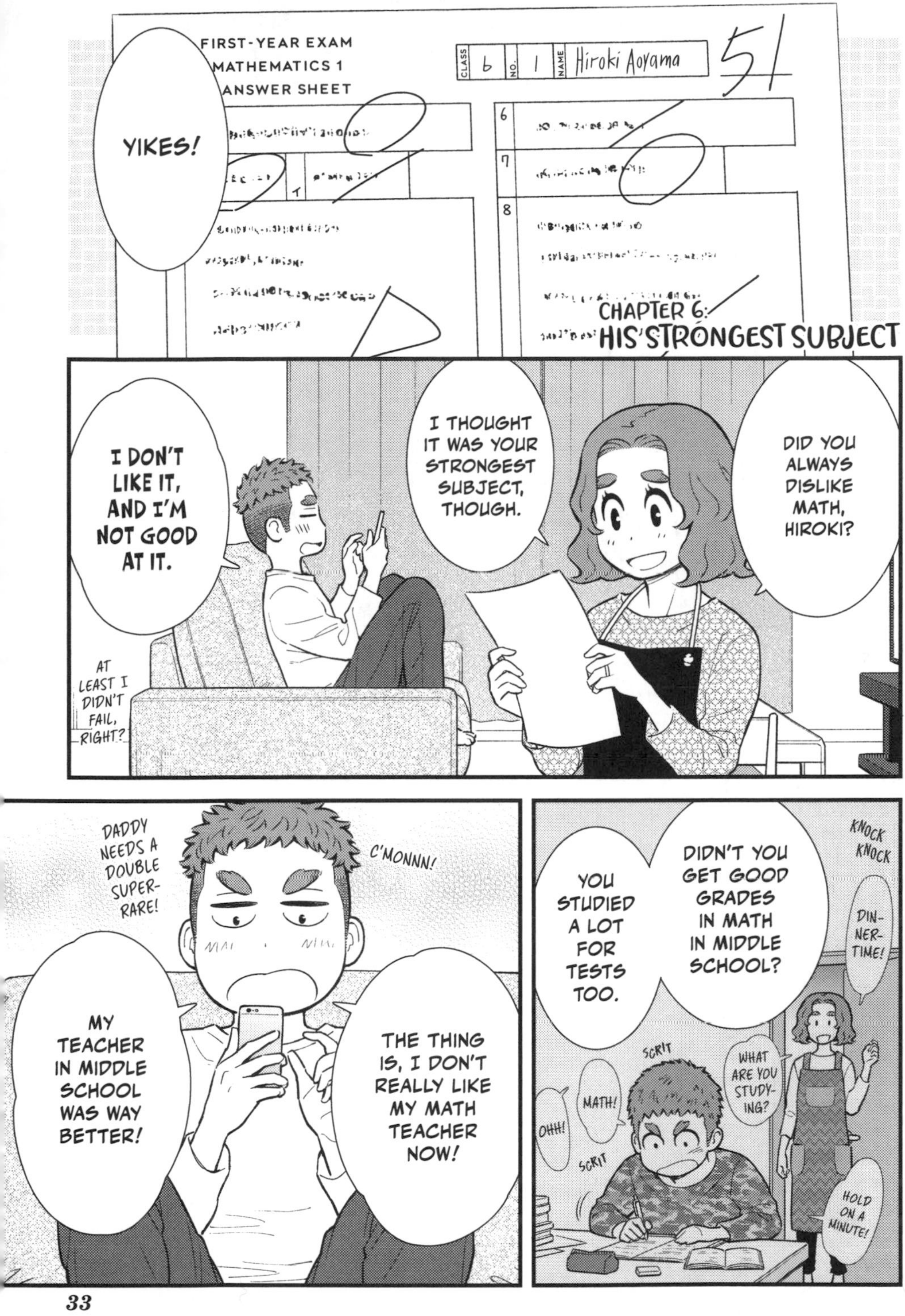
FIRST-YEAR EXAM
MATHEMATICS 1
ANSWER SHEET
CLASS 6 NO. 1 NAME Hiroki Aoyama
51
YIKES!
CHAPTER 6: HIS STRONGEST SUBJECT
DID YOU ALWAYS DISLIKE MATH, HIROKI?
I THOUGHT IT WAS YOUR STRONGEST SUBJECT, THOUGH.
I DON'T LIKE IT, AND I'M NOT GOOD AT IT.
AT LEAST I DIDN'T FAIL, RIGHT?
KNOCK KNOCK
DIDN'T YOU GET GOOD GRADES IN MATH IN MIDDLE SCHOOL?
YOU STUDIED A LOT FOR TESTS TOO.
DINNERTIME!
WHAT ARE YOU STUDYING?
SCRIT
MATH!
OHH!
SCRIT
HOLD ON A MINUTE!
C'MONNN!
DADDY NEEDS A DOUBLE SUPER-RARE!
THE THING IS, I DON'T REALLY LIKE MY MATH TEACHER NOW!
MY TEACHER IN MIDDLE SCHOOL WAS WAY BETTER!

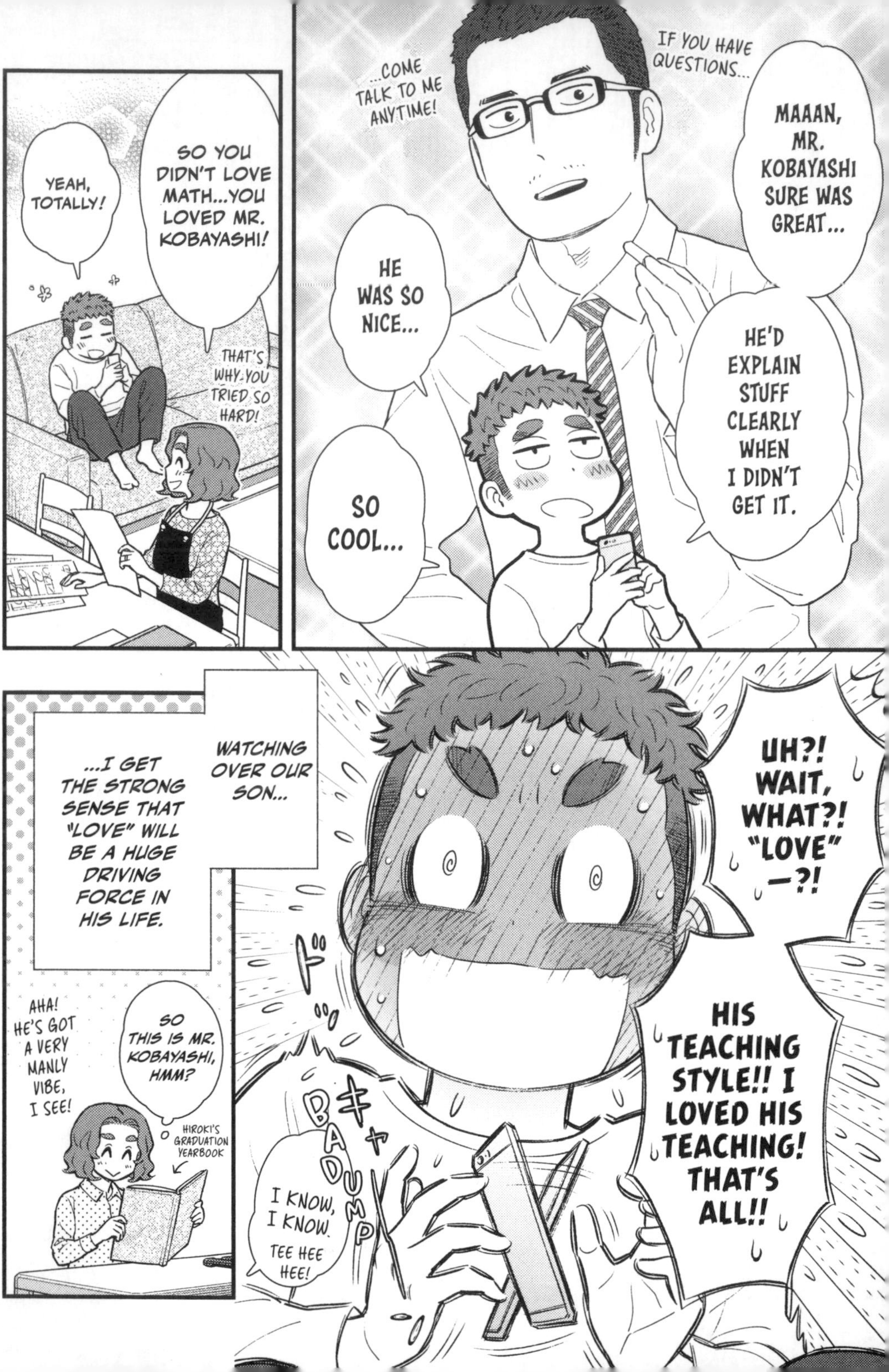
IF YOU HAVE QUESTIONS...
...COME TALK TO ME ANYTIME!
MAAAN, MR. KOBAYASHI SURE WAS GREAT...
HE'D EXPLAIN STUFF CLEARLY WHEN I DIDN'T GET IT.
HE WAS SO NICE...
SO COOL...
SO YOU DIDN'T LOVE MATH...YOU LOVED MR. KOBAYASHI!
YEAH, TOTALLY!
THAT'S WHY YOU TRIED SO HARD!
UH?! WAIT, WHAT?! "LOVE" —?!
HIS TEACHING STYLE!! I LOVED HIS TEACHING! THAT'S ALL!!
BADUMP
I KNOW, I KNOW. TEE HEE HEE!
WATCHING OVER OUR SON...
...I GET THE STRONG SENSE THAT "LOVE" WILL BE A HUGE DRIVING FORCE IN HIS LIFE.
SO THIS IS MR. KOBAYASHI, HMM?
AHA! HE'S GOT A VERY MANLY VIBE, I SEE!
HIROKI'S GRADUATION YEARBOOK

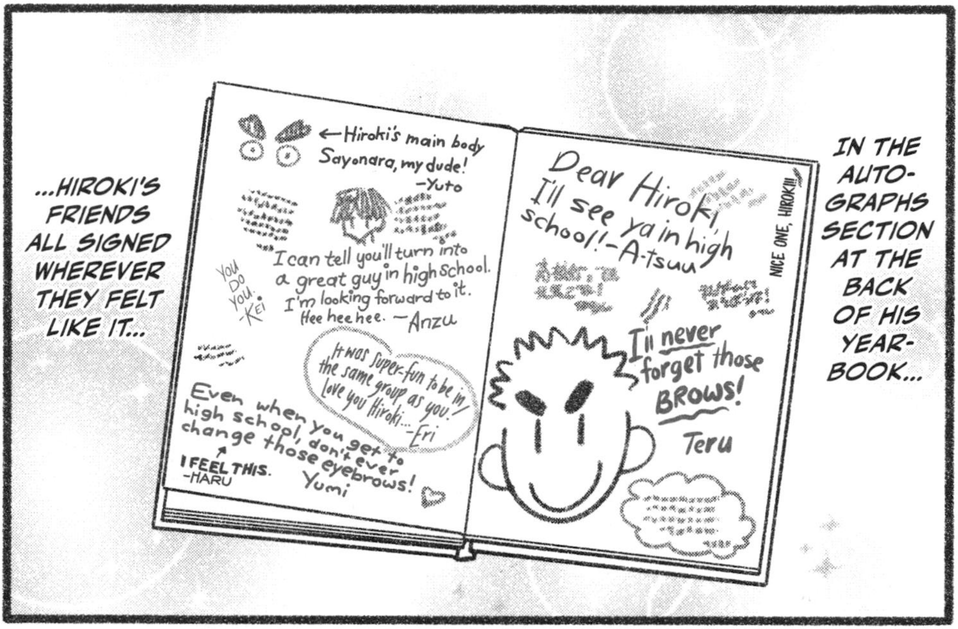
IN THE AUTOGRAPHS SECTION AT THE BACK OF HIS YEARBOOK...
...HIROKI'S FRIENDS ALL SIGNED WHEREVER THEY FELT LIKE IT...
Dear Hiroki, I'll see ya in high school!! -A-tsuu
NICE ONE, HIROKI!!!
I'll never forget those BROWS! Teru
← Hiroki's main body
Sayonara, my dude! -Yuto
I can tell you'll turn into a great guy in high school. I'm looking forward to it. Hee hee hee. —Anzu
YOU DO YOU. -KEI
It was super-fun to be in the same group as you! Love you Hiroki... -Eri
Even when you get to high school, don't ever change those eyebrows! Yumi
I FEEL THIS. -HARU

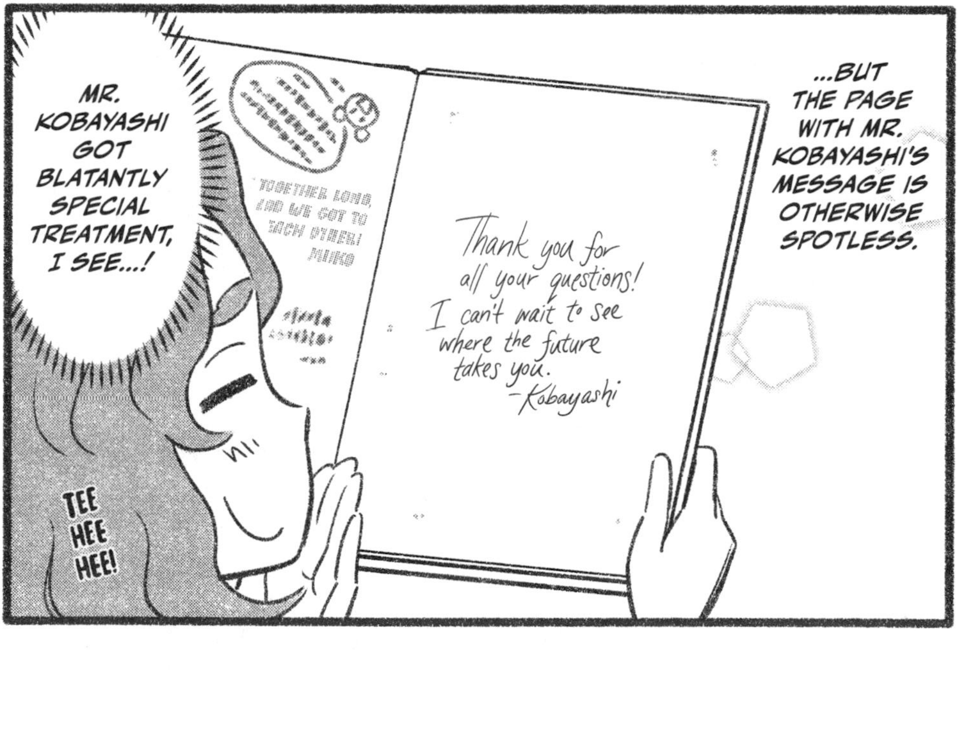
...BUT THE PAGE WITH MR. KOBAYASHI'S MESSAGE IS OTHERWISE SPOTLESS.
MR. KOBAYASHI GOT BLATANTLY SPECIAL TREATMENT, I SEE...!
Thank you for all your questions! I can't wait to see where the future takes you. -Kobayashi
TEE HEE HEE!

I Think
Our Son
Is Gay

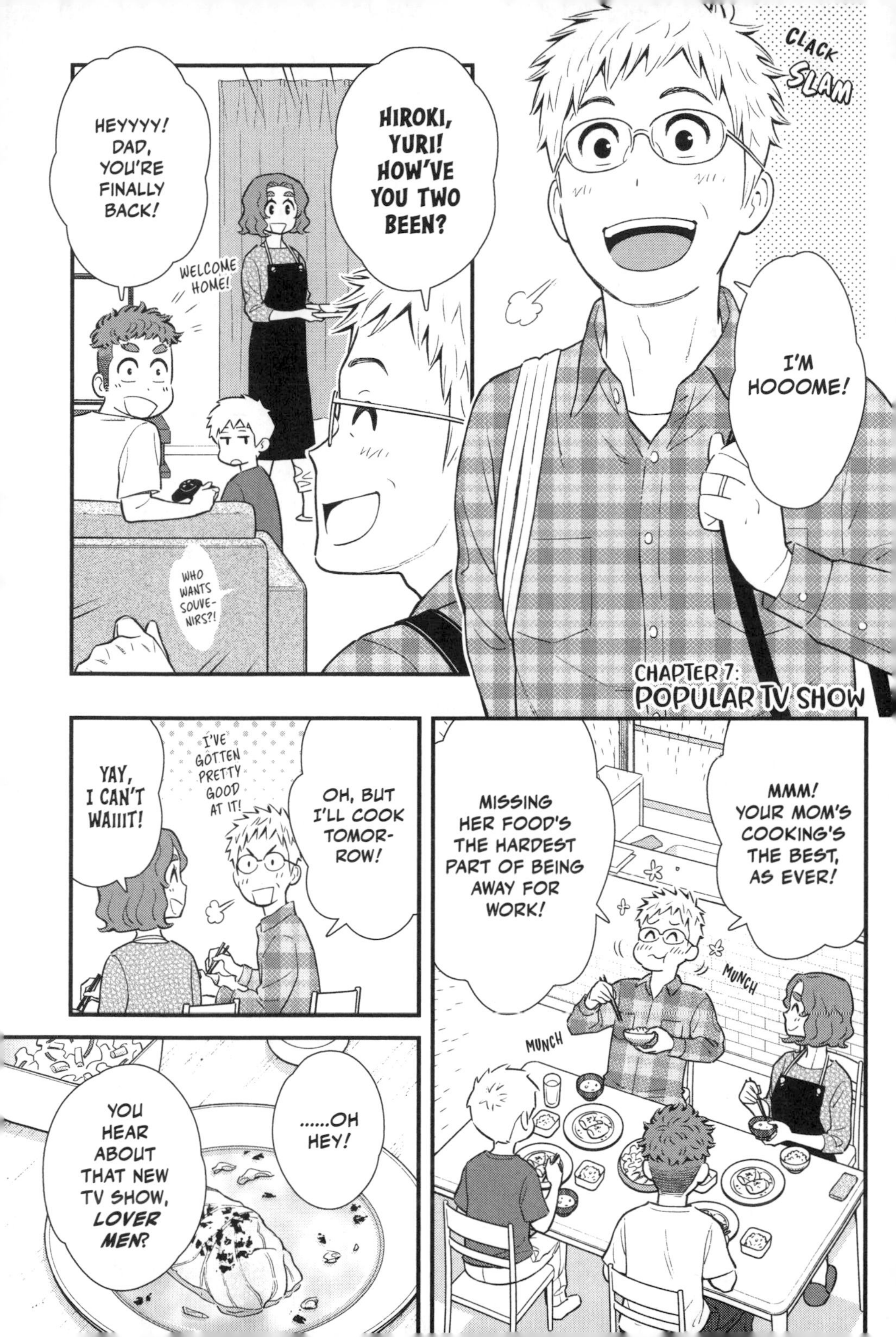
CLACK
SLAM
I'M HOOOME!
CHAPTER 7:
POPULAR TV SHOW
HIROKI, YURI! HOW'VE YOU TWO BEEN?
HEYYYY! DAD, YOU'RE FINALLY BACK!
WELCOME HOME!
WHO WANTS SOUVENIRS?!
MMM! YOUR MOM'S COOKING'S THE BEST, AS EVER!
MISSING HER FOOD'S THE HARDEST PART OF BEING AWAY FOR WORK!
MUNCH
MUNCH
OH, BUT I'LL COOK TOMORROW!
I'VE GOTTEN PRETTY GOOD AT IT!
YAY, I CAN'T WAIIIT!
......OH HEY!
YOU HEAR ABOUT THAT NEW TV SHOW, LOVER MEN?

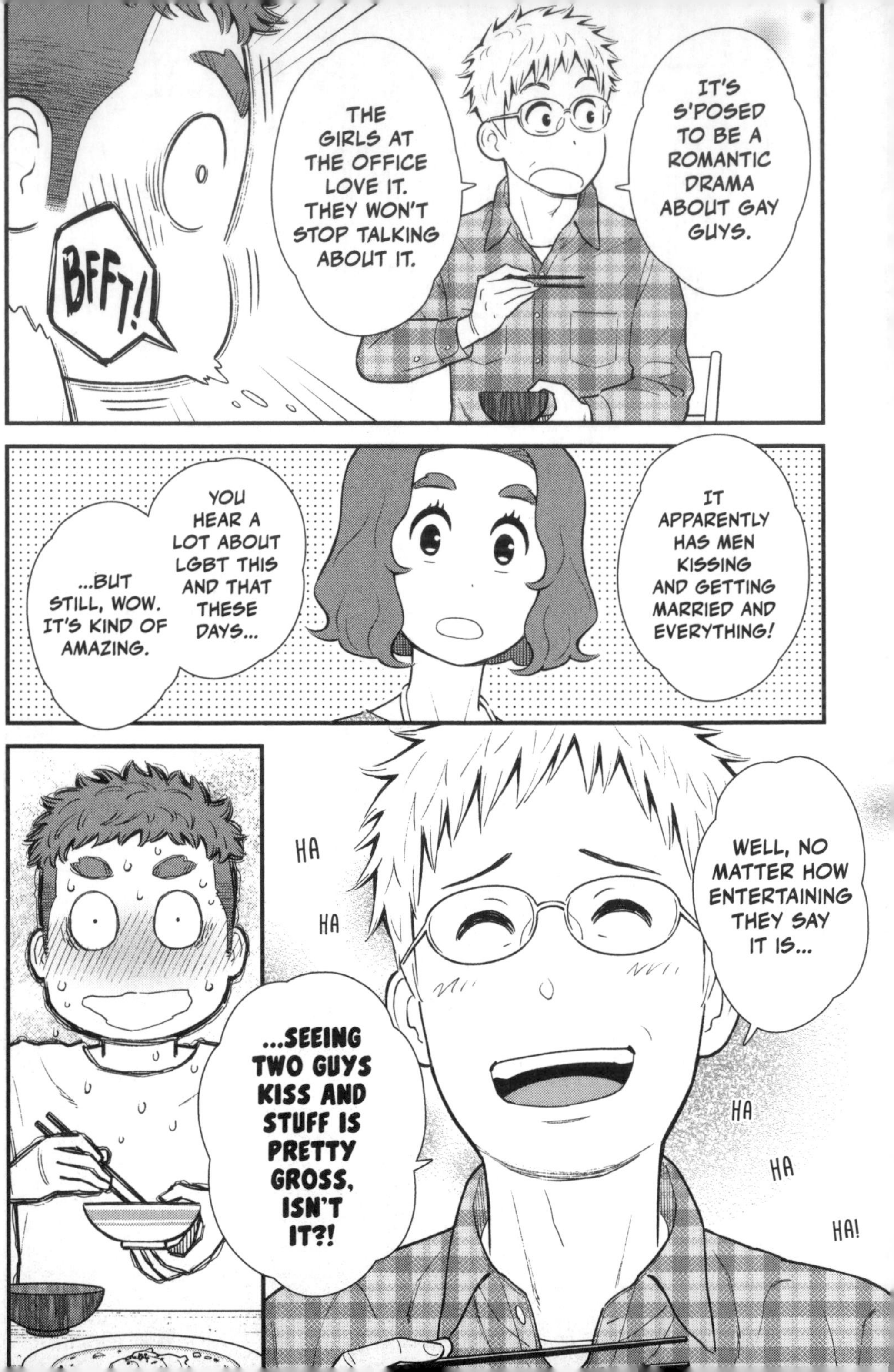
IT'S S'POSED TO BE A ROMANTIC DRAMA ABOUT GAY GUYS.
THE GIRLS AT THE OFFICE LOVE IT. THEY WON'T STOP TALKING ABOUT IT.
BFFT!!
IT APPARENTLY HAS MEN KISSING AND GETTING MARRIED AND EVERYTHING!
YOU HEAR A LOT ABOUT LGBT THIS AND THAT THESE DAYS...
...BUT STILL, WOW. IT'S KIND OF AMAZING.
WELL, NO MATTER HOW ENTERTAINING THEY SAY IT IS...
HA
HA
...SEEING TWO GUYS KISS AND STUFF IS PRETTY GROSS, ISN'T IT?!
HA
HA
HA!

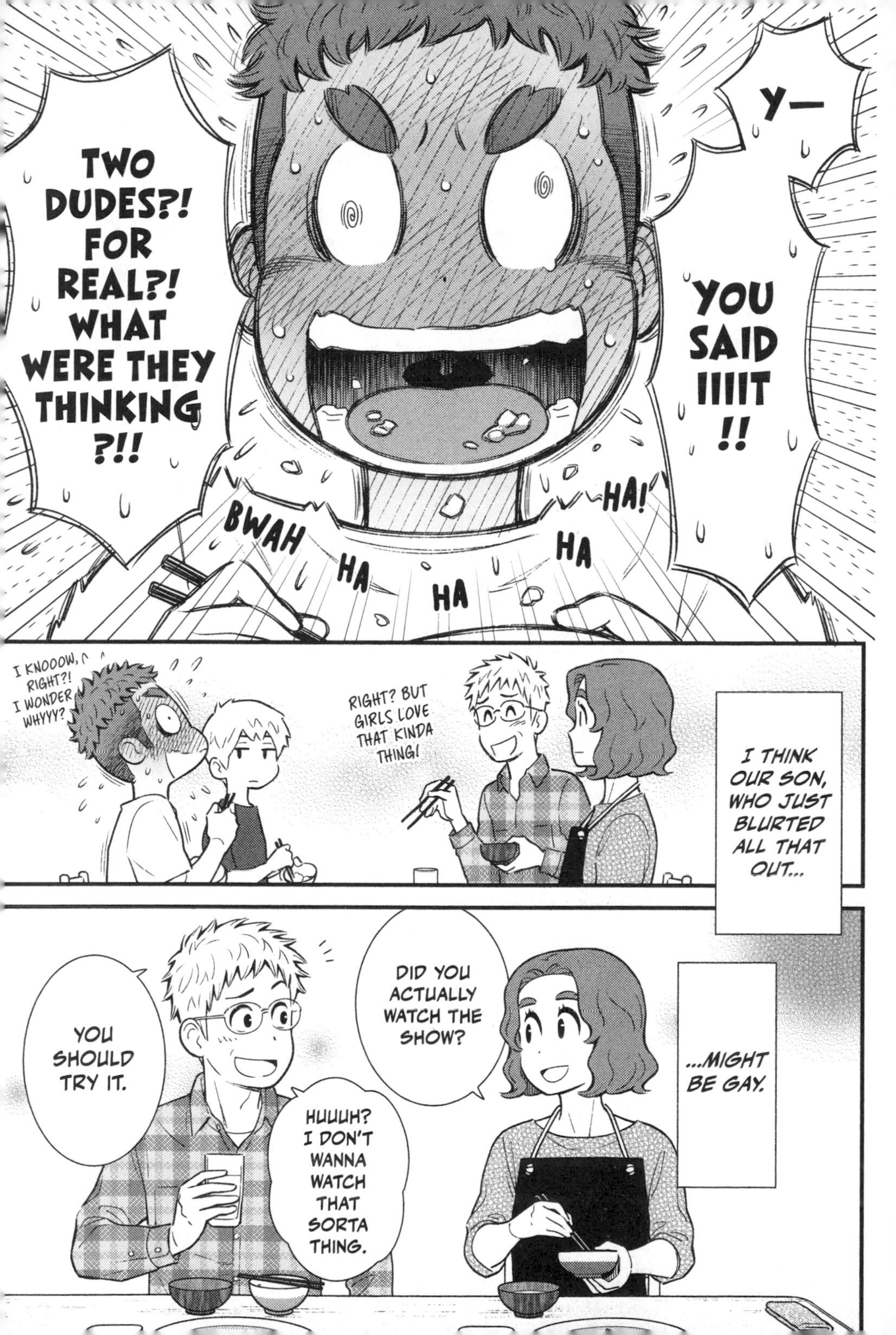

Y—
YOU SAID IIIIT !!
TWO DUDES?! FOR REAL?! WHAT WERE THEY THINKING ?!!
BWAH HA HA HA HA!
I THINK OUR SON, WHO JUST BLURTED ALL THAT OUT...
RIGHT? BUT GIRLS LOVE THAT KINDA THING!
I KNOOOW, RIGHT?! I WONDER WHYYY?
...MIGHT BE GAY.
DID YOU ACTUALLY WATCH THE SHOW?
YOU SHOULD TRY IT.
HUUUH? I DON'T WANNA WATCH THAT SORTA THING.

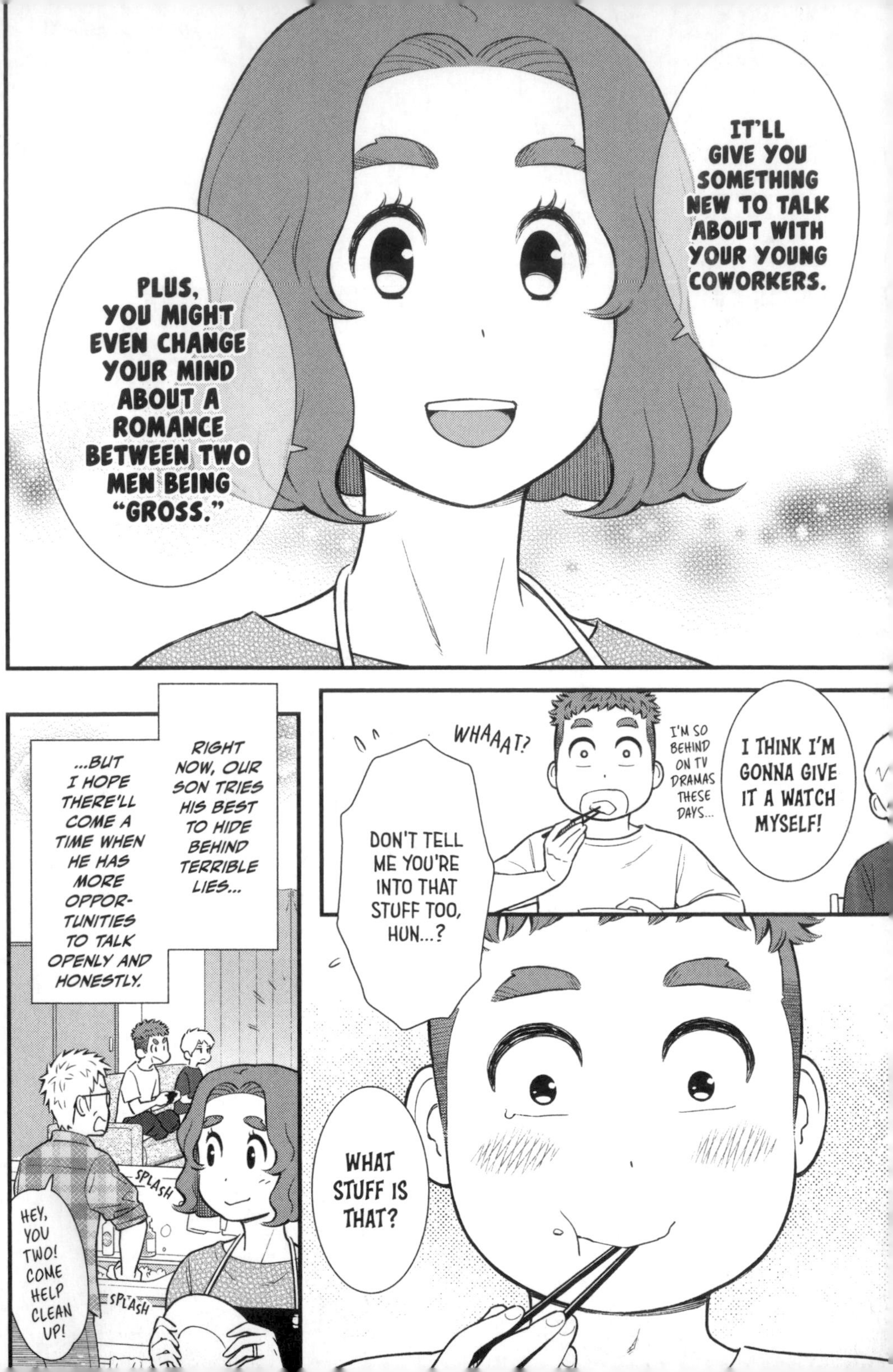
IT'LL GIVE YOU SOMETHING NEW TO TALK ABOUT WITH YOUR YOUNG COWORKERS.
PLUS, YOU MIGHT EVEN CHANGE YOUR MIND ABOUT A ROMANCE BETWEEN TWO MEN BEING "GROSS."
I THINK I'M GONNA GIVE IT A WATCH MYSELF!
I'M SO BEHIND ON TV DRAMAS THESE DAYS...
WHAAAT?
DON'T TELL ME YOU'RE INTO THAT STUFF TOO, HUN...?
WHAT STUFF IS THAT?
RIGHT NOW, OUR SON TRIES HIS BEST TO HIDE BEHIND TERRIBLE LIES...
...BUT I HOPE THERE'LL COME A TIME WHEN HE HAS MORE OPPOR-TUNITIES TO TALK OPENLY AND HONESTLY.
SPLASH
HEY, YOU TWO! COME HELP CLEAN UP!
SPLASH

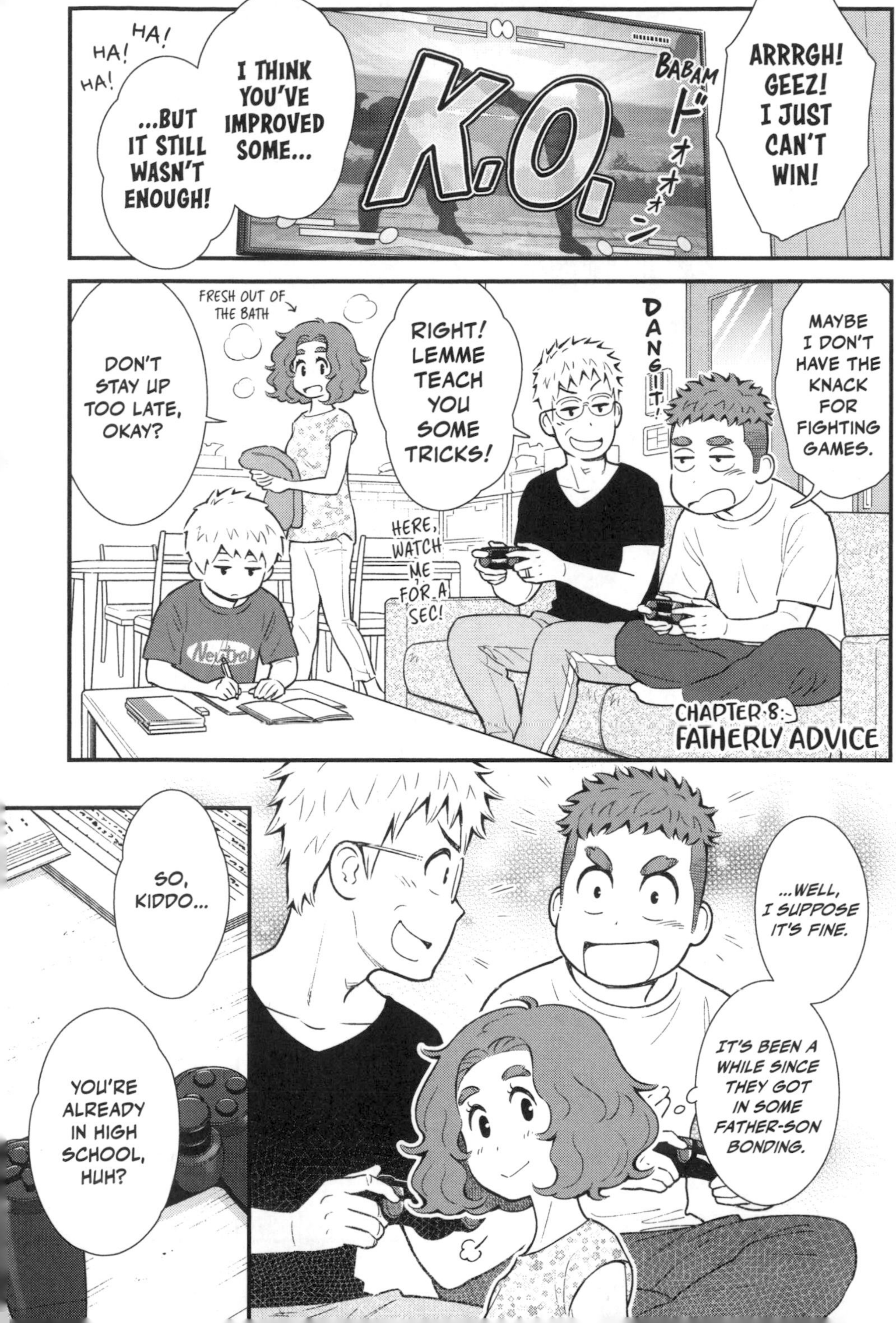
ARRRGH! GEEZ! I JUST CAN'T WIN!
BABAM
I THINK YOU'VE IMPROVED SOME...
...BUT IT STILL WASN'T ENOUGH!
HA! HA! HA!
MAYBE I DON'T HAVE THE KNACK FOR FIGHTING GAMES.
DANG IT!
RIGHT! LEMME TEACH YOU SOME TRICKS!
HERE, WATCH ME FOR A SEC!
FRESH OUT OF THE BATH
DON'T STAY UP TOO LATE, OKAY?
CHAPTER 8: FATHERLY ADVICE
...WELL, I SUPPOSE IT'S FINE.
IT'S BEEN A WHILE SINCE THEY GOT IN SOME FATHER-SON BONDING.
SO, KIDDO...
YOU'RE ALREADY IN HIGH SCHOOL, HUH?

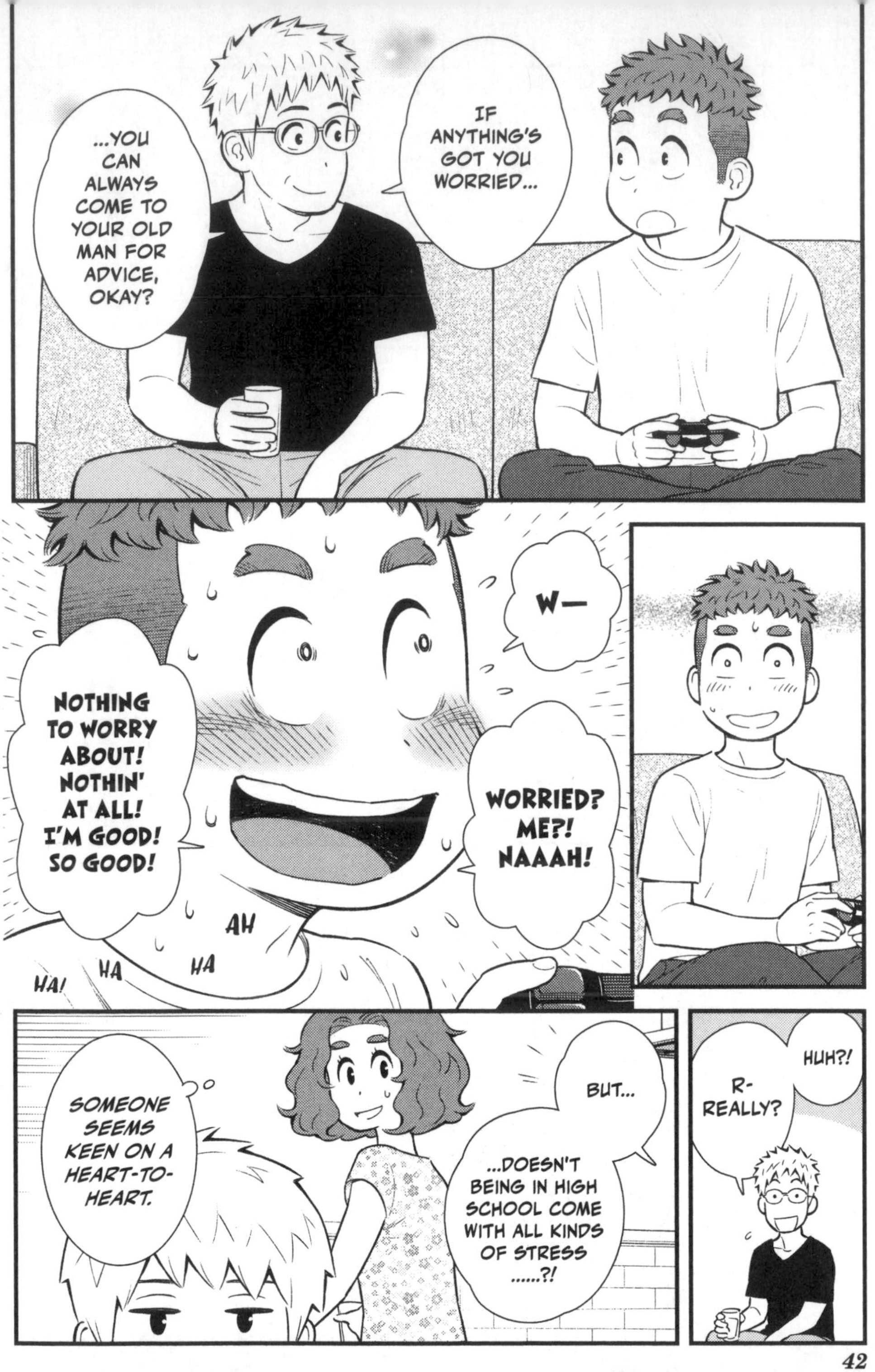
IF ANYTHING'S GOT YOU WORRIED...
...YOU CAN ALWAYS COME TO YOUR OLD MAN FOR ADVICE, OKAY?
W—
WORRIED? ME?! NAAAH!
NOTHING TO WORRY ABOUT! NOTHIN' AT ALL! I'M GOOD! SO GOOD!
AH HA HA HA!
HUH?!
R-REALLY?
BUT...
...DOESN'T BEING IN HIGH SCHOOL COME WITH ALL KINDS OF STRESS ......?!
SOMEONE SEEMS KEEN ON A HEART-TO-HEART.

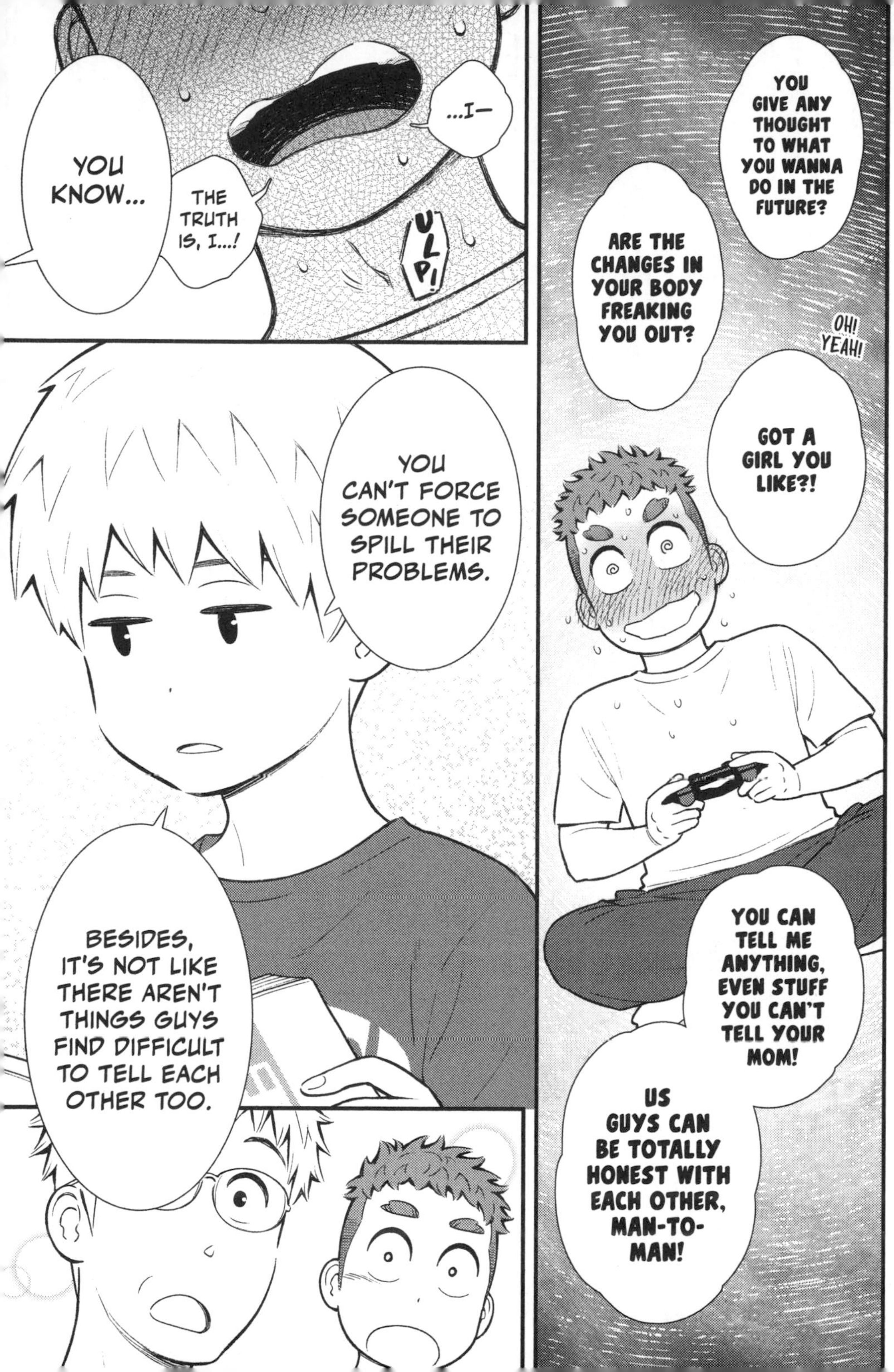
YOU GIVE ANY THOUGHT TO WHAT YOU WANNA DO IN THE FUTURE?
ARE THE CHANGES IN YOUR BODY FREAKING YOU OUT?
OH! YEAH!
GOT A GIRL YOU LIKE?!
YOU CAN TELL ME ANYTHING, EVEN STUFF YOU CAN'T TELL YOUR MOM!
US GUYS CAN BE TOTALLY HONEST WITH EACH OTHER, MAN-TO-MAN!
...I—
THE TRUTH IS, I...!
ULP!
YOU KNOW...
YOU CAN'T FORCE SOMEONE TO SPILL THEIR PROBLEMS.
BESIDES, IT'S NOT LIKE THERE AREN'T THINGS GUYS FIND DIFFICULT TO TELL EACH OTHER TOO.

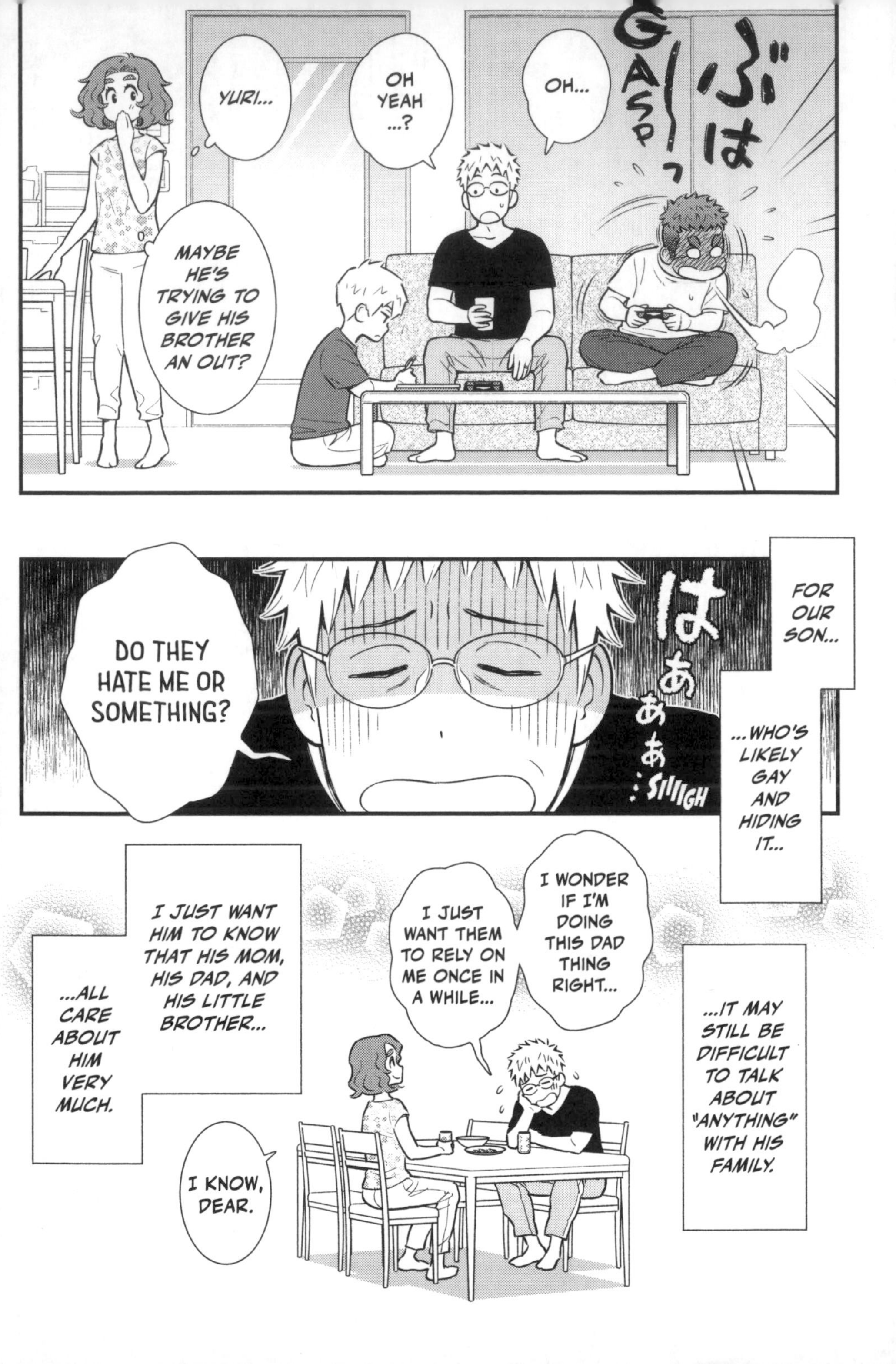

ぶはっ
GASP
OH...
OH YEAH ...?
YURI...
MAYBE HE'S TRYING TO GIVE HIS BROTHER AN OUT?
FOR OUR SON...
はあぁぁ
SIIIGH
DO THEY HATE ME OR SOMETHING?
...WHO'S LIKELY GAY AND HIDING IT...
...IT MAY STILL BE DIFFICULT TO TALK ABOUT "ANYTHING" WITH HIS FAMILY.
I WONDER IF I'M DOING THIS DAD THING RIGHT...
I JUST WANT THEM TO RELY ON ME ONCE IN A WHILE...
I KNOW, DEAR.
I JUST WANT HIM TO KNOW THAT HIS MOM, HIS DAD, AND HIS LITTLE BROTHER...
...ALL CARE ABOUT HIM VERY MUCH.

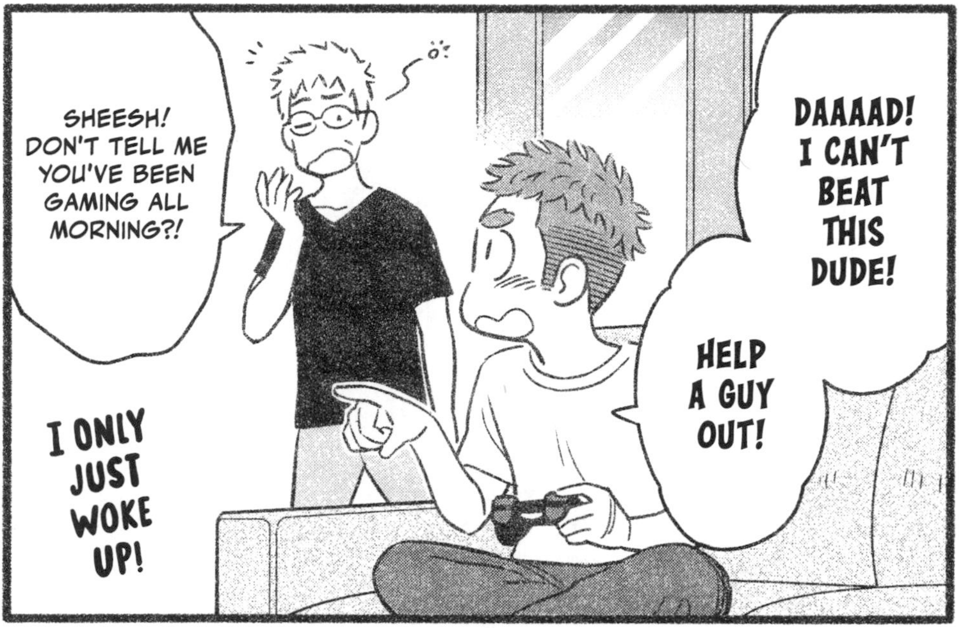
DAAAAD! I CAN'T BEAT THIS DUDE!
HELP A GUY OUT!
SHEESH! DON'T TELL ME YOU'VE BEEN GAMING ALL MORNING?!
I ONLY JUST WOKE UP!

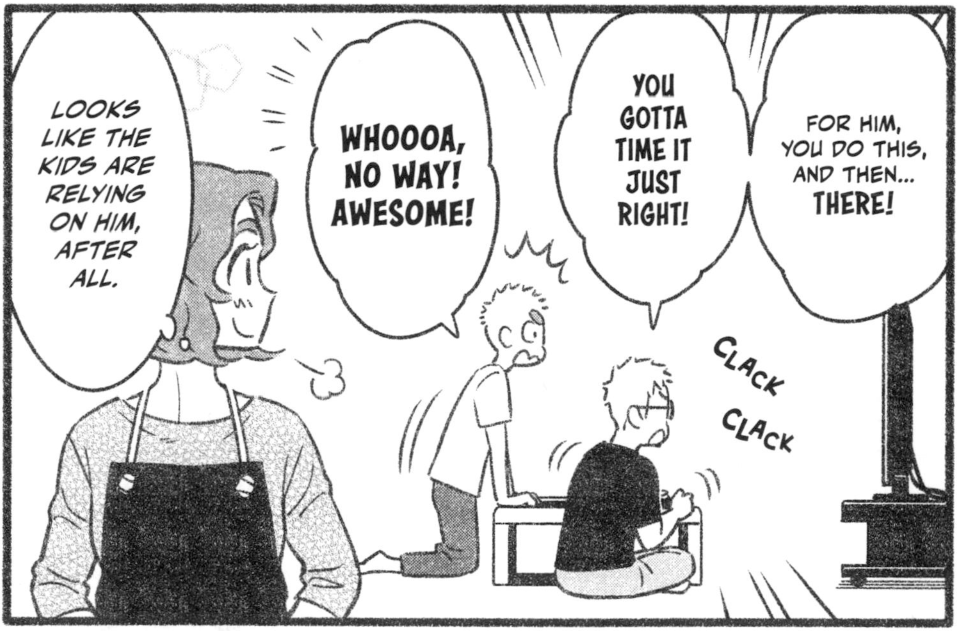
FOR HIM, YOU DO THIS, AND THEN... THERE!
YOU GOTTA TIME IT JUST RIGHT!
CLACK
CLACK
WHOOOA, NO WAY! AWESOME!
LOOKS LIKE THE KIDS ARE RELYING ON HIM, AFTER ALL.

I Think
Our Son
Is Gay

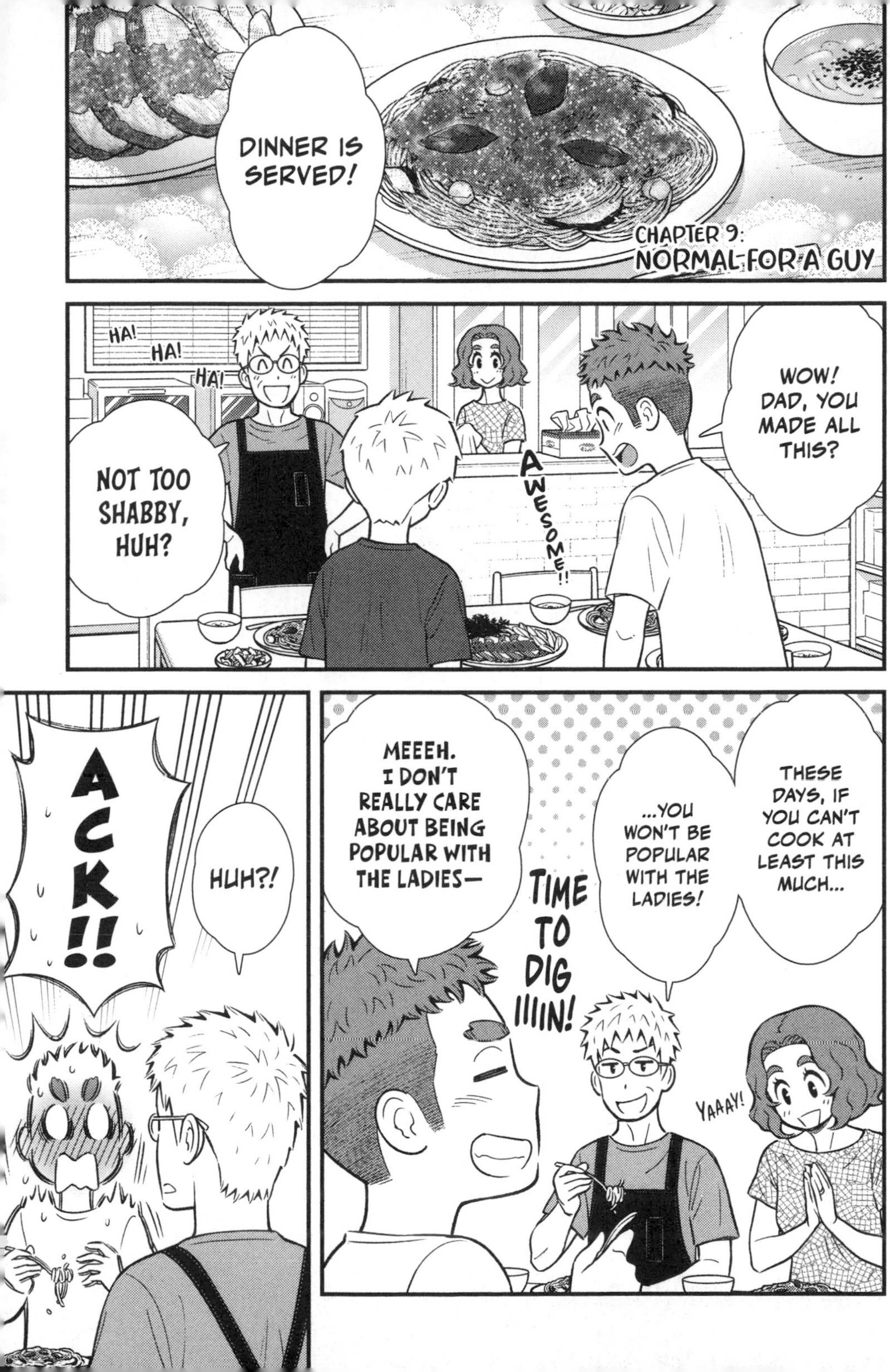
DINNER IS SERVED!
CHAPTER 9: NORMAL FOR A GUY
WOW! DAD, YOU MADE ALL THIS?
AWESOME!!
HA! HA! HA!
NOT TOO SHABBY, HUH?
THESE DAYS, IF YOU CAN'T COOK AT LEAST THIS MUCH...
...YOU WON'T BE POPULAR WITH THE LADIES!
YAAAY!
TIME TO DIG IIIIN!
MEEEH. I DON'T REALLY CARE ABOUT BEING POPULAR WITH THE LADIES—
HUH?!
ACK!!

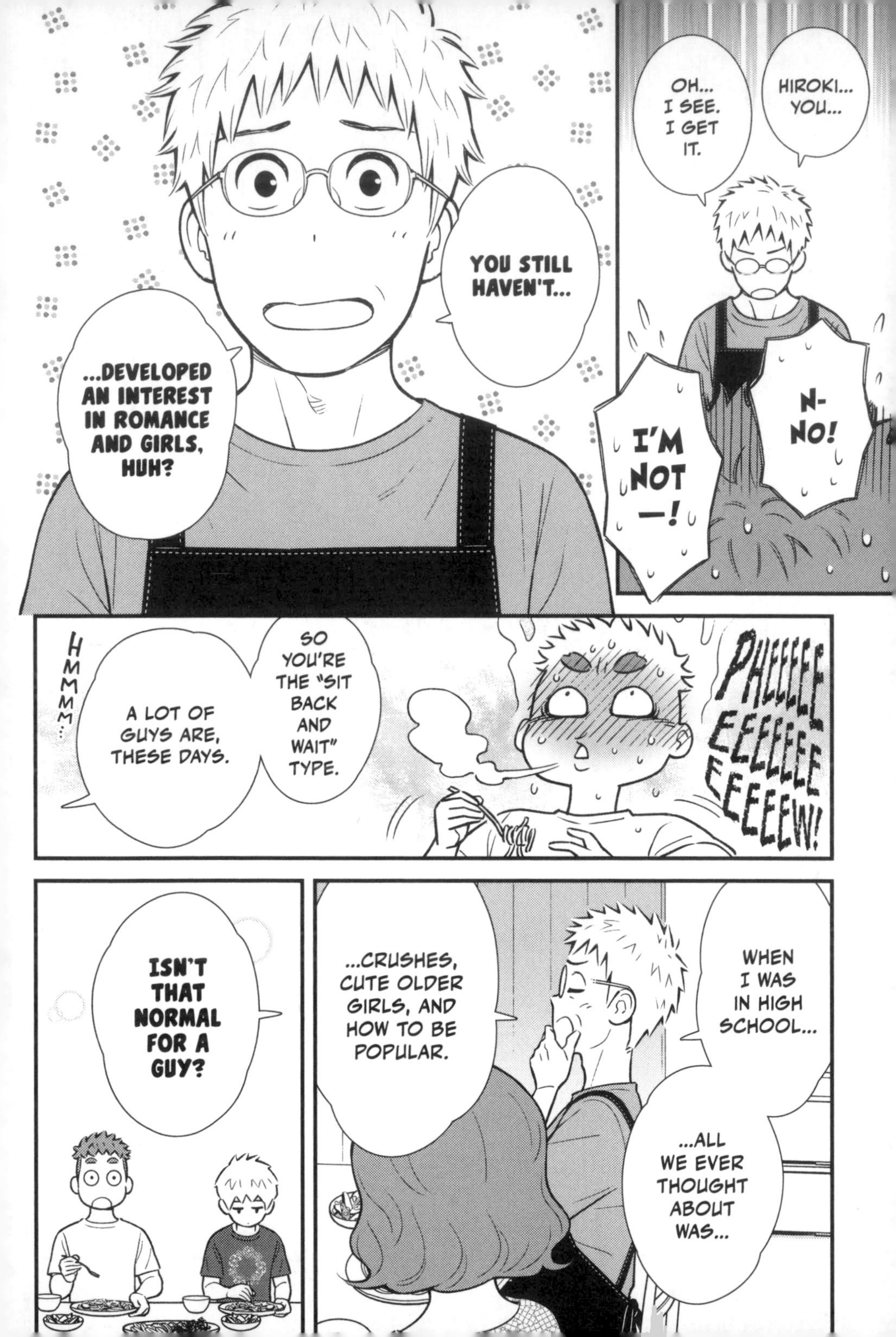
HIROKI... YOU...
OH... I SEE. I GET IT.
N-NO!
I'M NOT—!
YOU STILL HAVEN'T...
...DEVELOPED AN INTEREST IN ROMANCE AND GIRLS, HUH?
PHEEEEEEEEEEEEEEEEEW!
SO YOU'RE THE "SIT BACK AND WAIT" TYPE.
A LOT OF GUYS ARE, THESE DAYS.
HMMMM...
WHEN I WAS IN HIGH SCHOOL...
...ALL WE EVER THOUGHT ABOUT WAS...
...CRUSHES, CUTE OLDER GIRLS, AND HOW TO BE POPULAR.
ISN'T THAT NORMAL FOR A GUY?

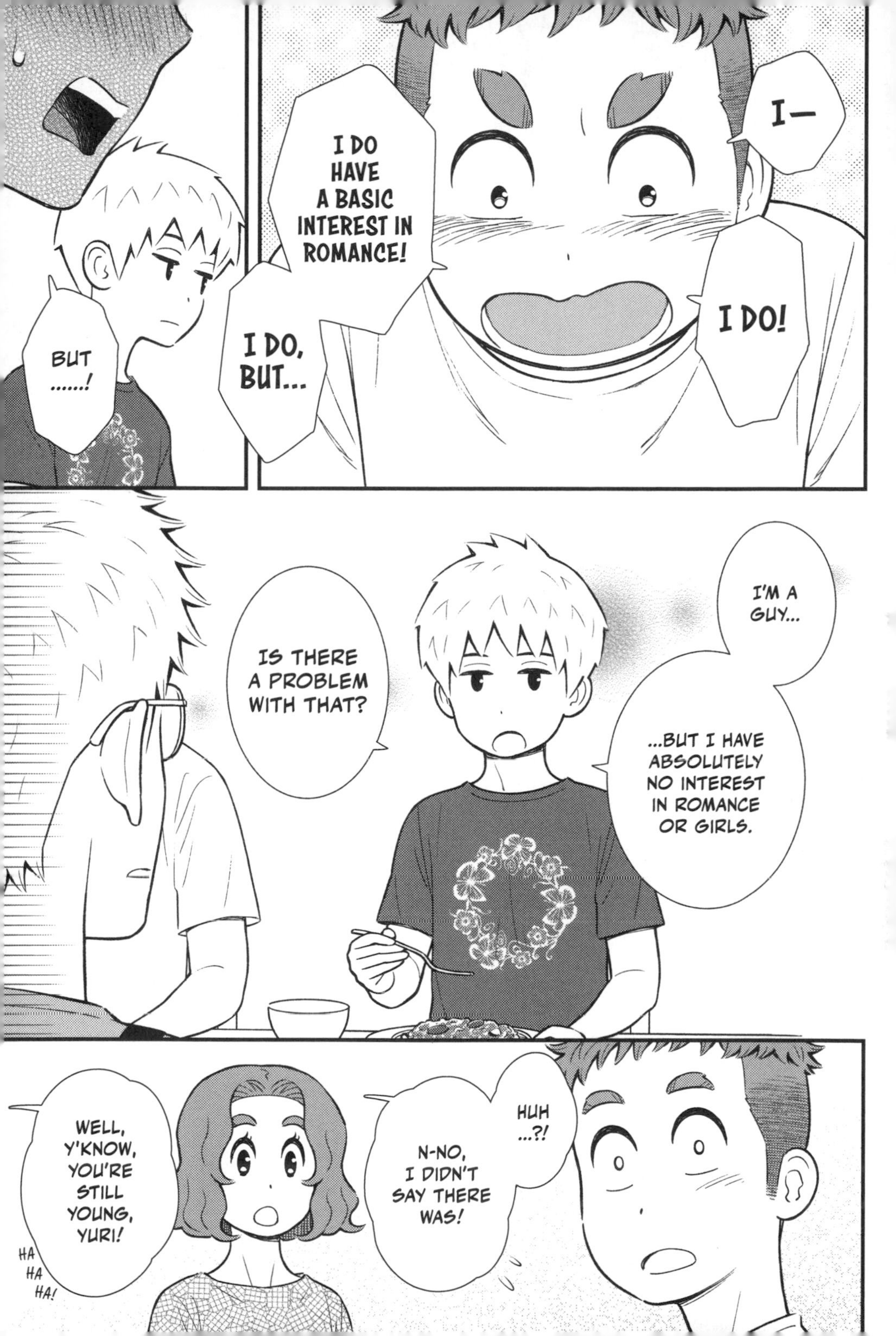
I—
I DO!
I DO HAVE A BASIC INTEREST IN ROMANCE!
I DO, BUT...
BUT ......!
I'M A GUY...
...BUT I HAVE ABSOLUTELY NO INTEREST IN ROMANCE OR GIRLS.
IS THERE A PROBLEM WITH THAT?
HUH ...?!
N-NO, I DIDN'T SAY THERE WAS!
WELL, Y'KNOW, YOU'RE STILL YOUNG, YURI!
HA HA HA!

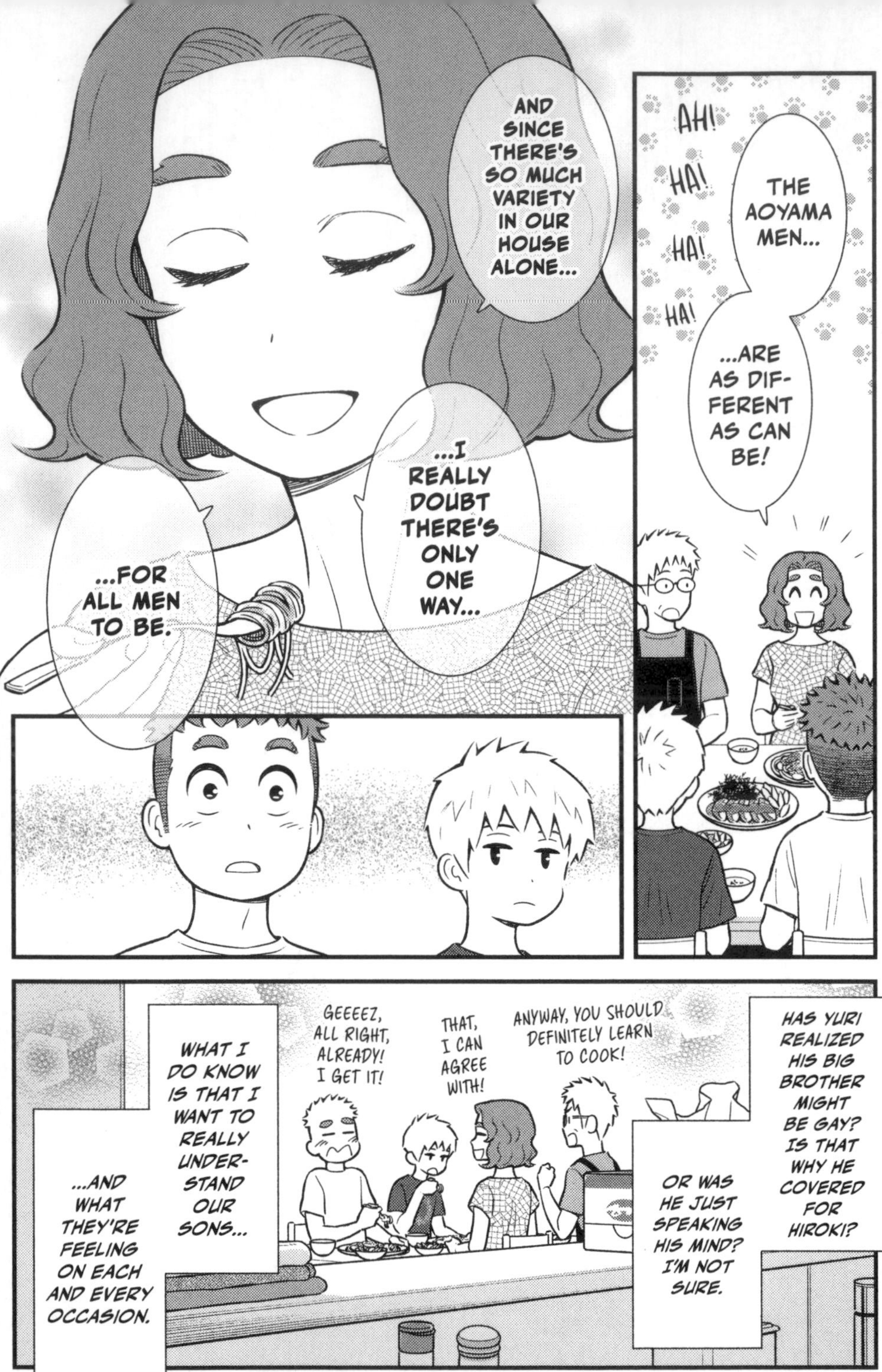
AH! HA! HA! HA!
THE AOYAMA MEN...
...ARE AS DIF-FERENT AS CAN BE!
AND SINCE THERE'S SO MUCH VARIETY IN OUR HOUSE ALONE...
...I REALLY DOUBT THERE'S ONLY ONE WAY...
...FOR ALL MEN TO BE.
HAS YURI REALIZED HIS BIG BROTHER MIGHT BE GAY? IS THAT WHY HE COVERED FOR HIROKI?
OR WAS HE JUST SPEAKING HIS MIND? I'M NOT SURE.
ANYWAY, YOU SHOULD DEFINITELY LEARN TO COOK!
THAT, I CAN AGREE WITH!
GEEEEZ, ALL RIGHT, ALREADY! I GET IT!
WHAT I DO KNOW IS THAT I WANT TO REALLY UNDER-STAND OUR SONS...
...AND WHAT THEY'RE FEELING ON EACH AND EVERY OCCASION.

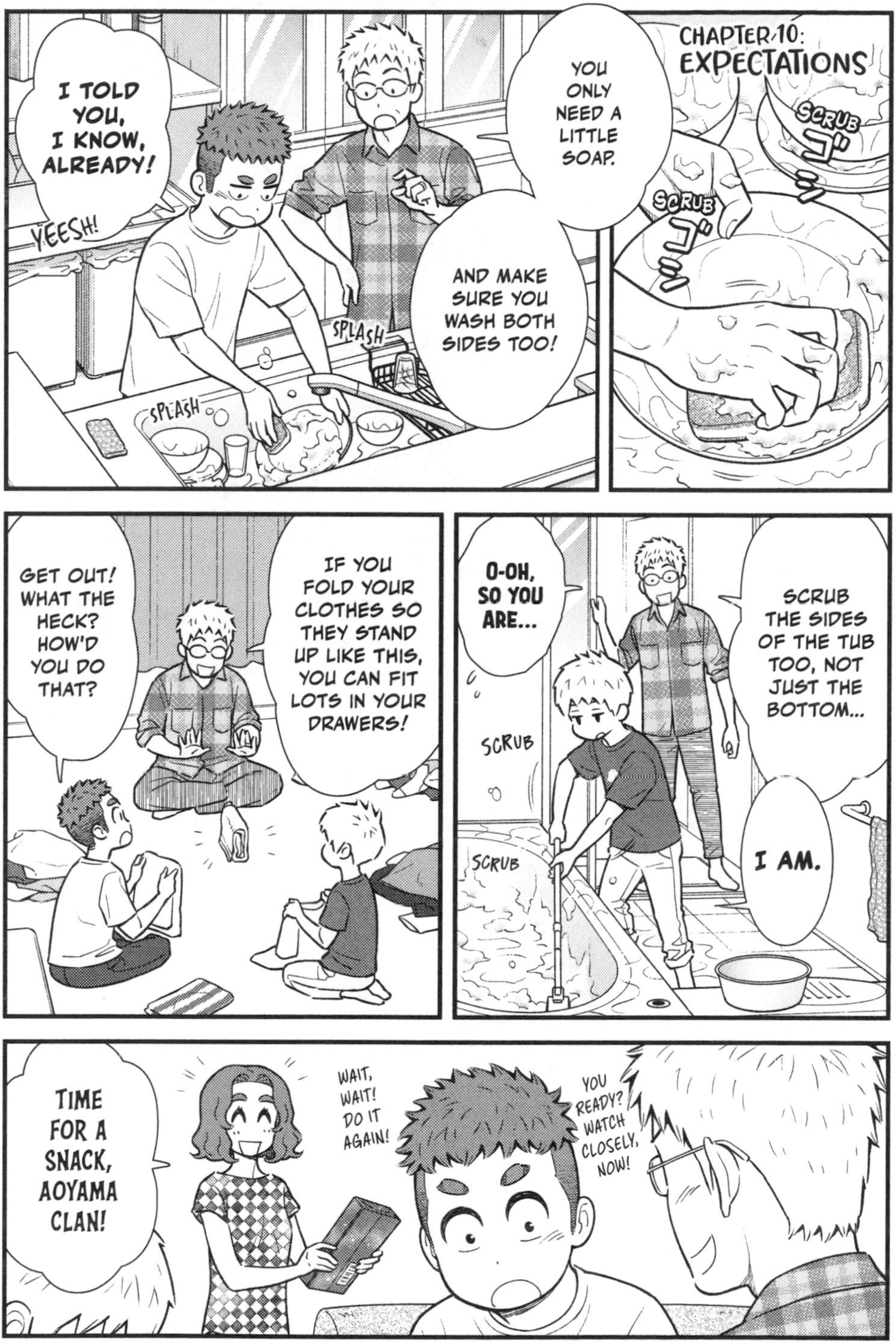
CHAPTER 10: EXPECTATIONS
SCRUB ゴシ
SCRUB ゴシ
YOU ONLY NEED A LITTLE SOAP.
AND MAKE SURE YOU WASH BOTH SIDES TOO!
I TOLD YOU, I KNOW, ALREADY!
YEESH!
SPLASH
SPLASH
SCRUB THE SIDES OF THE TUB TOO, NOT JUST THE BOTTOM...
I AM.
O-OH, SO YOU ARE...
SCRUB
SCRUB
IF YOU FOLD YOUR CLOTHES SO THEY STAND UP LIKE THIS, YOU CAN FIT LOTS IN YOUR DRAWERS!
GET OUT! WHAT THE HECK? HOW'D YOU DO THAT?
YOU READY? WATCH CLOSELY, NOW!
WAIT, WAIT! DO IT AGAIN!
TIME FOR A SNACK, AOYAMA CLAN!

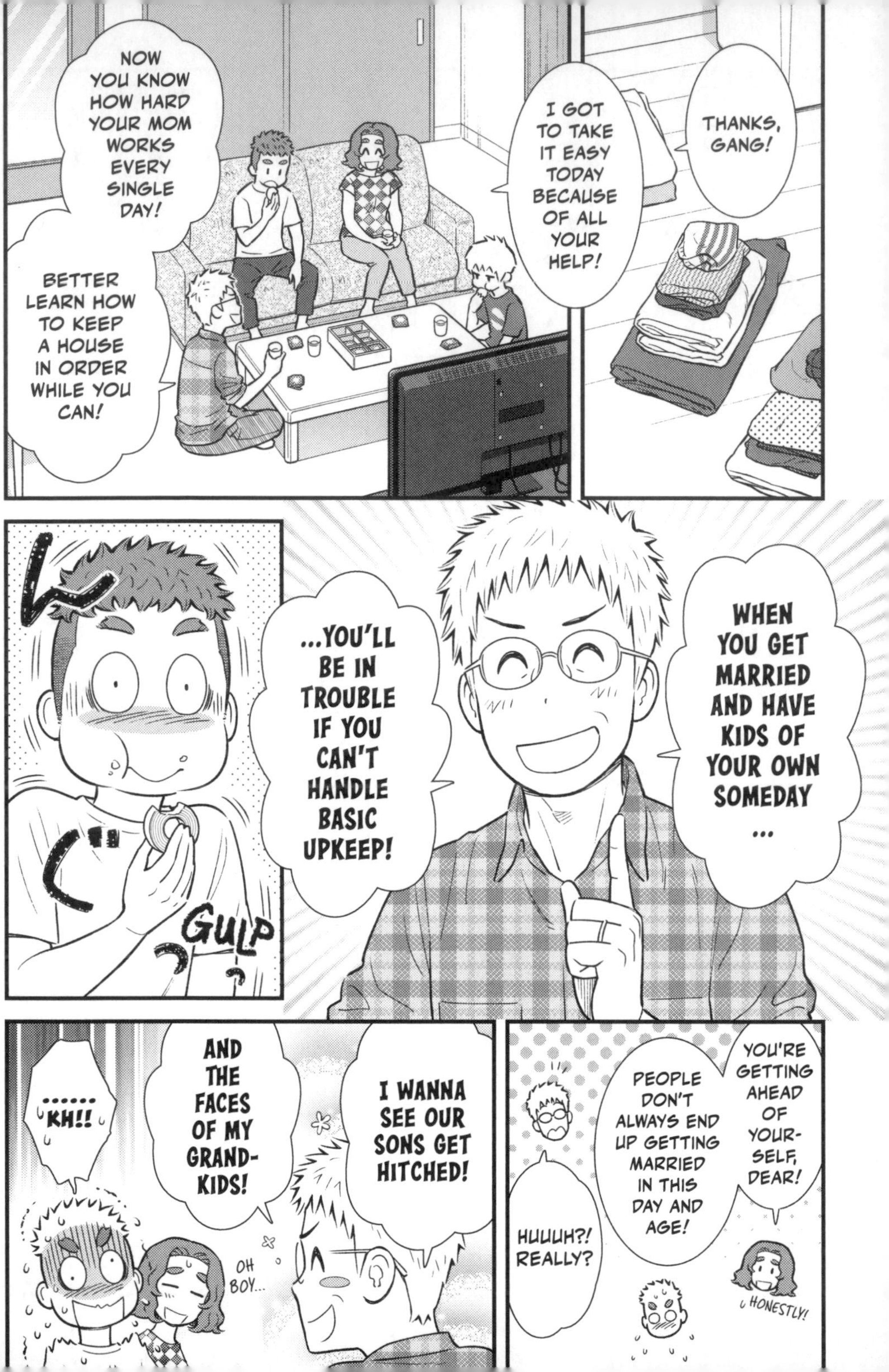
THANKS, GANG!
I GOT TO TAKE IT EASY TODAY BECAUSE OF ALL YOUR HELP!
NOW YOU KNOW HOW HARD YOUR MOM WORKS EVERY SINGLE DAY!
BETTER LEARN HOW TO KEEP A HOUSE IN ORDER WHILE YOU CAN!
WHEN YOU GET MARRIED AND HAVE KIDS OF YOUR OWN SOMEDAY ...
...YOU'LL BE IN TROUBLE IF YOU CAN'T HANDLE BASIC UPKEEP!
GULP
YOU'RE GETTING AHEAD OF YOUR-SELF, DEAR!
PEOPLE DON'T ALWAYS END UP GETTING MARRIED IN THIS DAY AND AGE!
HUUUH?! REALLY?
HONESTLY!
I WANNA SEE OUR SONS GET HITCHED!
AND THE FACES OF MY GRAND-KIDS!
......KH!!
OH BOY...

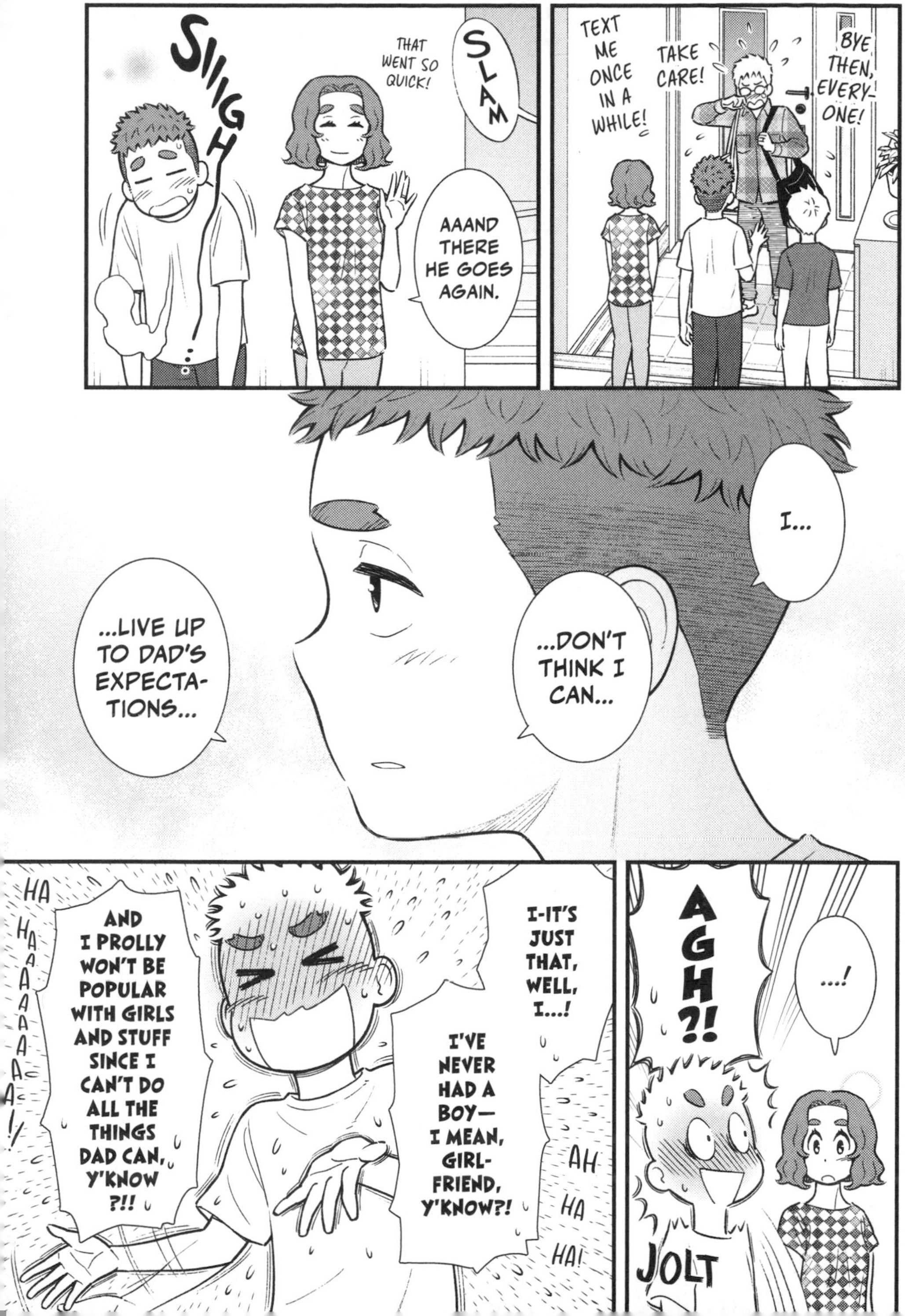
BYE THEN, EVERYONE!
TAKE CARE!
TEXT ME ONCE IN A WHILE!
SLAM
THAT WENT SO QUICK!
AAAND THERE HE GOES AGAIN.
SIIIGH
...
I...
...DON'T THINK I CAN...
...LIVE UP TO DAD'S EXPECTATIONS...
AGH?!
...!
JOLT
I-IT'S JUST THAT, WELL, I...!
I'VE NEVER HAD A BOY— I MEAN, GIRLFRIEND, Y'KNOW?!
AH HA HA!
AND I PROLLY WON'T BE POPULAR WITH GIRLS AND STUFF SINCE I CAN'T DO ALL THE THINGS DAD CAN, Y'KNOW?!!
HA HAAAAAAAA!

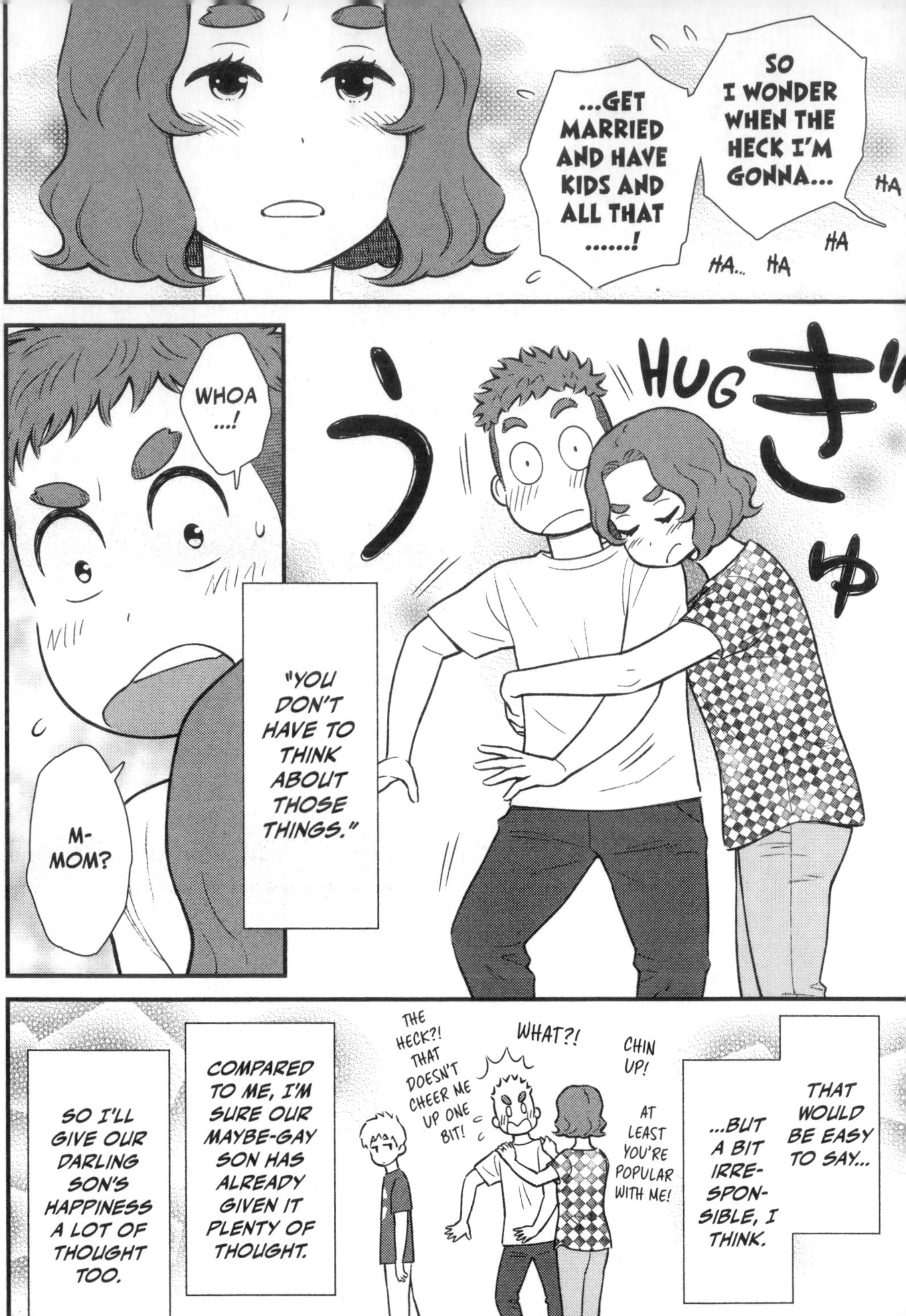
SO I WONDER WHEN THE HECK I'M GONNA...
...GET MARRIED AND HAVE KIDS AND ALL THAT ......!
HA HA
HA... HA
HUG
ぎゅう
"YOU DON'T HAVE TO THINK ABOUT THOSE THINGS."
WHOA ...!
M-MOM?
THAT WOULD BE EASY TO SAY...
...BUT A BIT IRRE-SPON-SIBLE, I THINK.
CHIN UP!
AT LEAST YOU'RE POPULAR WITH ME!
WHAT?!
THE HECK?! THAT DOESN'T CHEER ME UP ONE BIT!
COMPARED TO ME, I'M SURE OUR MAYBE-GAY SON HAS ALREADY GIVEN IT PLENTY OF THOUGHT.
SO I'LL GIVE OUR DARLING SON'S HAPPINESS A LOT OF THOUGHT TOO.

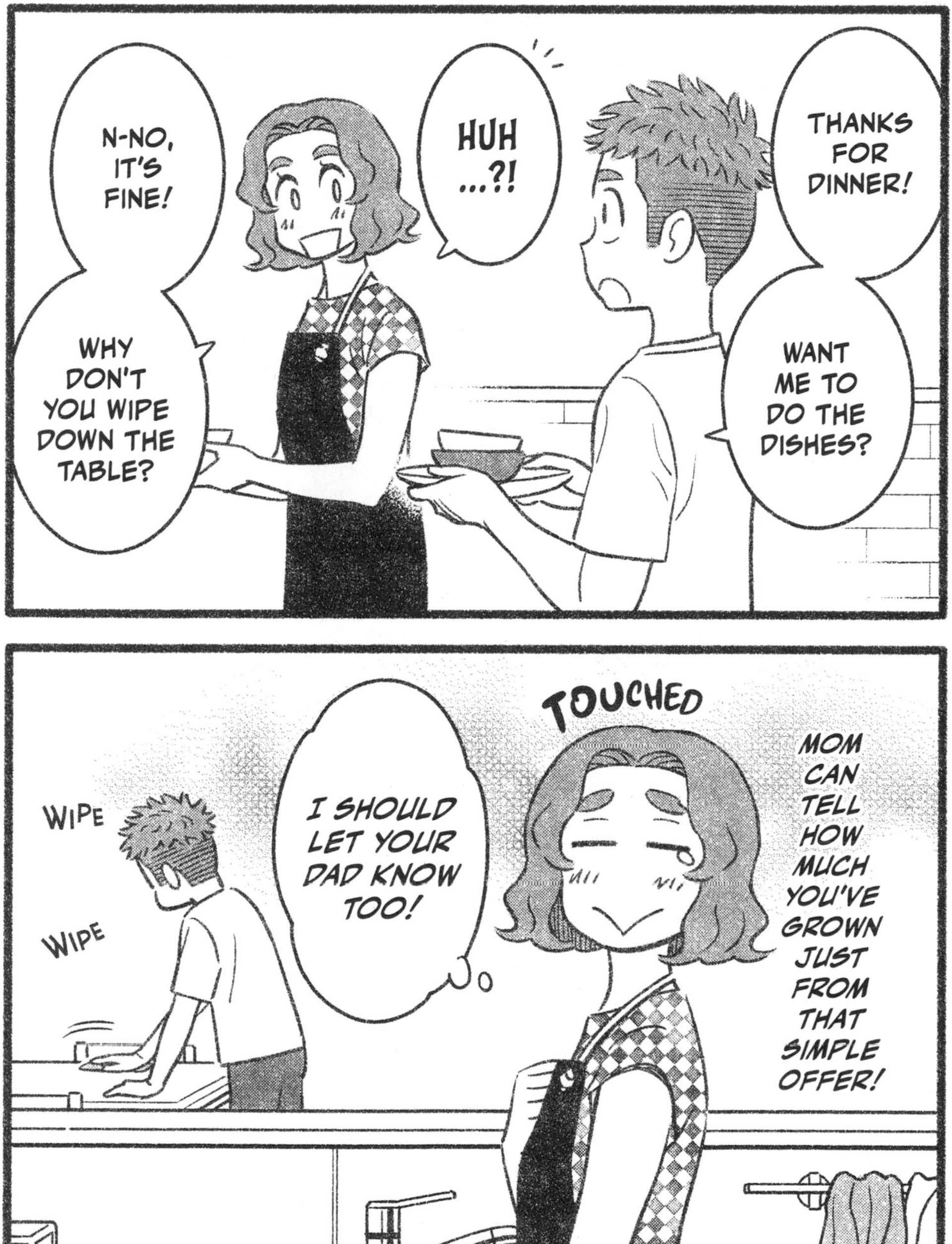
THANKS FOR DINNER!
WANT ME TO DO THE DISHES?
HUH ...?!
N-NO, IT'S FINE!
WHY DON'T YOU WIPE DOWN THE TABLE?
TOUCHED
MOM CAN TELL HOW MUCH YOU'VE GROWN JUST FROM THAT SIMPLE OFFER!
I SHOULD LET YOUR DAD KNOW TOO!
WIPE
WIPE

I Think
Our Son
Is Gay

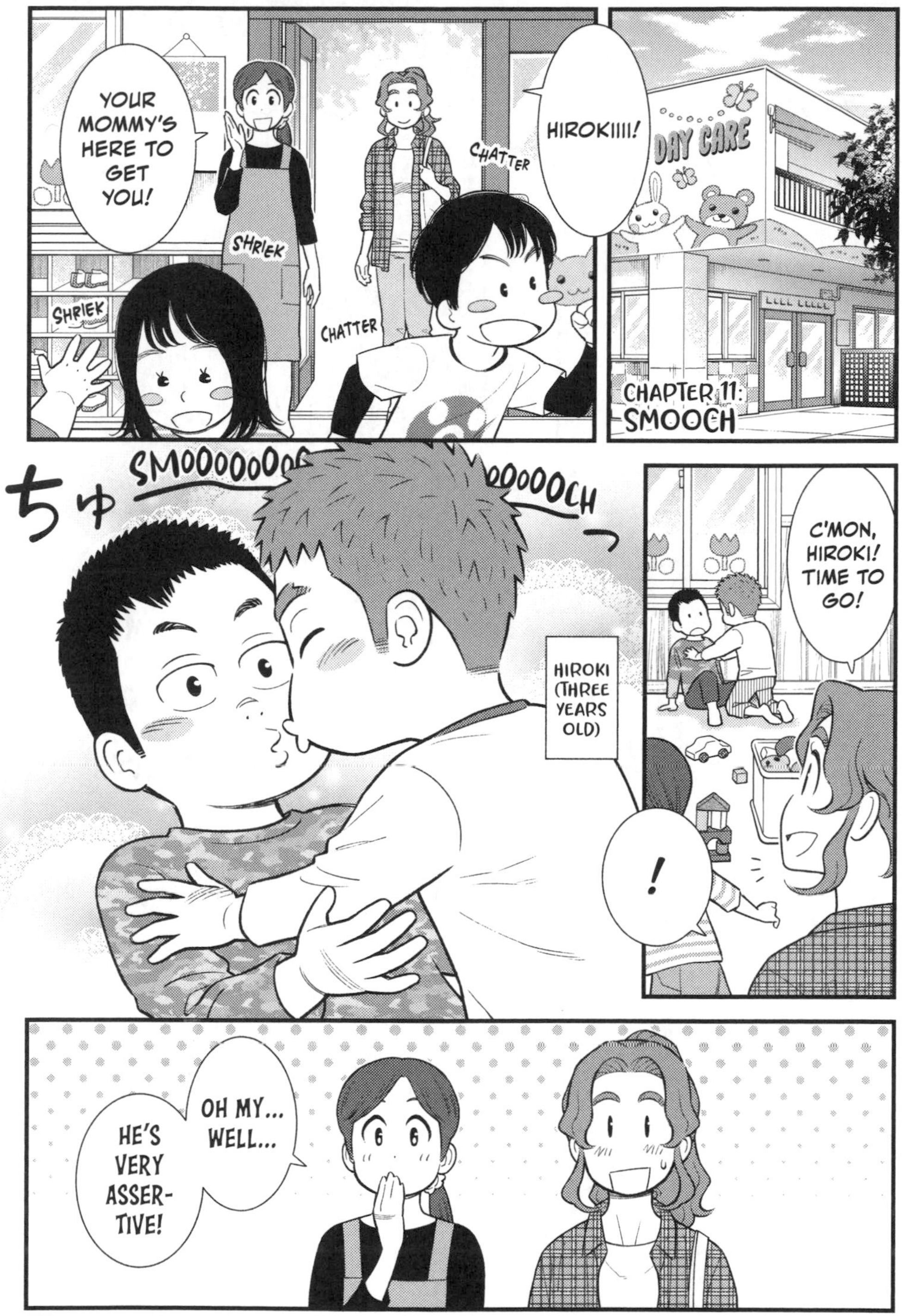
DAY CARE
CHAPTER 11: SMOOCH
HIROKIIII!
CHATTER
YOUR MOMMY'S HERE TO GET YOU!
SHRIEK
SHRIEK
CHATTER
C'MON, HIROKI! TIME TO GO!
!
HIROKI (THREE YEARS OLD)
ちゅ
SMOOOOOOO
OOOOOOCH
OH MY... WELL...
HE'S VERY ASSER-TIVE!

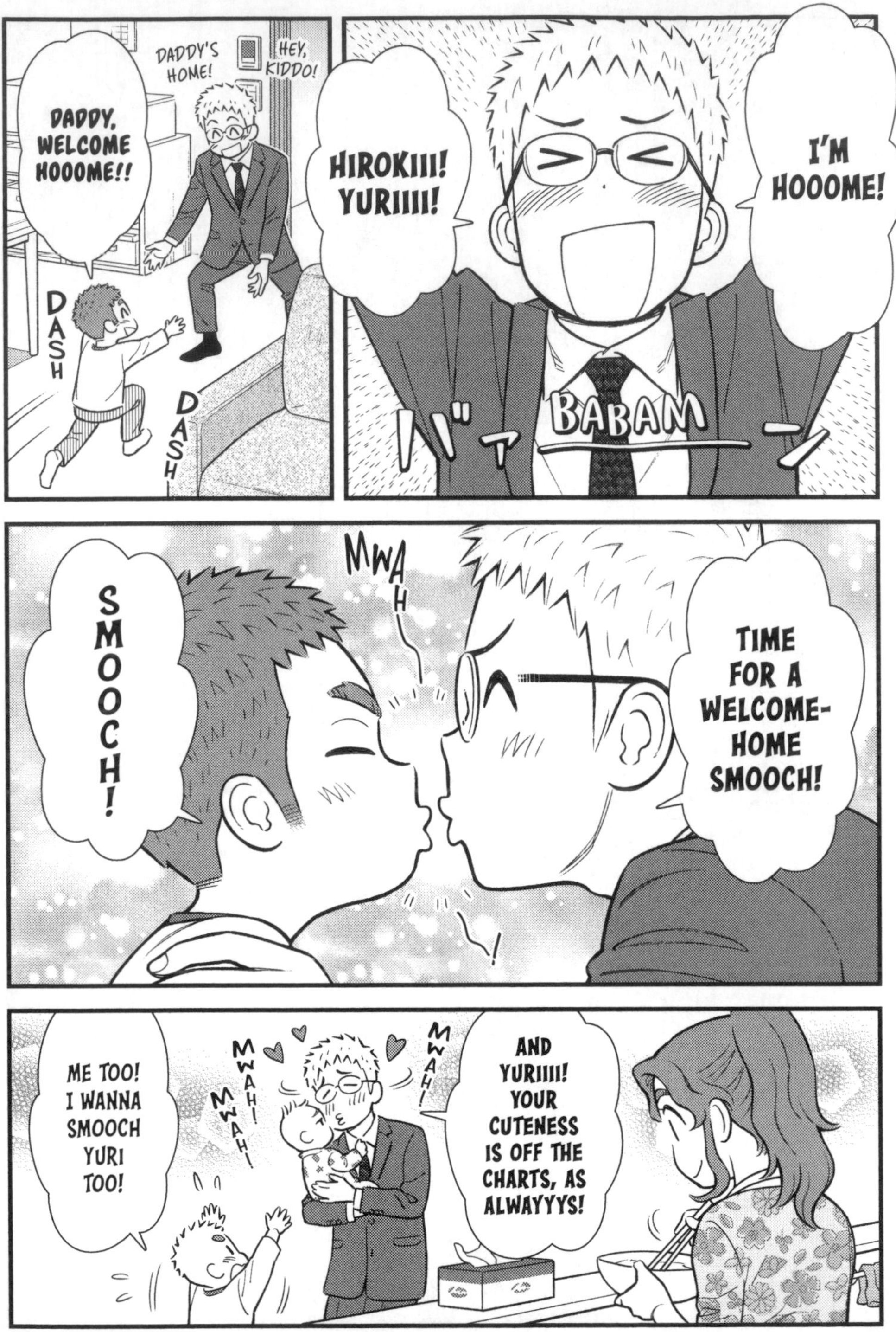
I'M HOOOME!
HIROKIII! YURIIII!
BABAM
HEY, KIDDO!
DADDY'S HOME!
DADDY, WELCOME HOOOME!!
DASH
DASH
TIME FOR A WELCOME-HOME SMOOCH!
MWAH
SMOOCH!
AND YURIIII! YOUR CUTENESS IS OFF THE CHARTS, AS ALWAYYYS!
MWAH!
MWAH!
MWAH!
ME TOO! I WANNA SMOOCH YURI TOO!

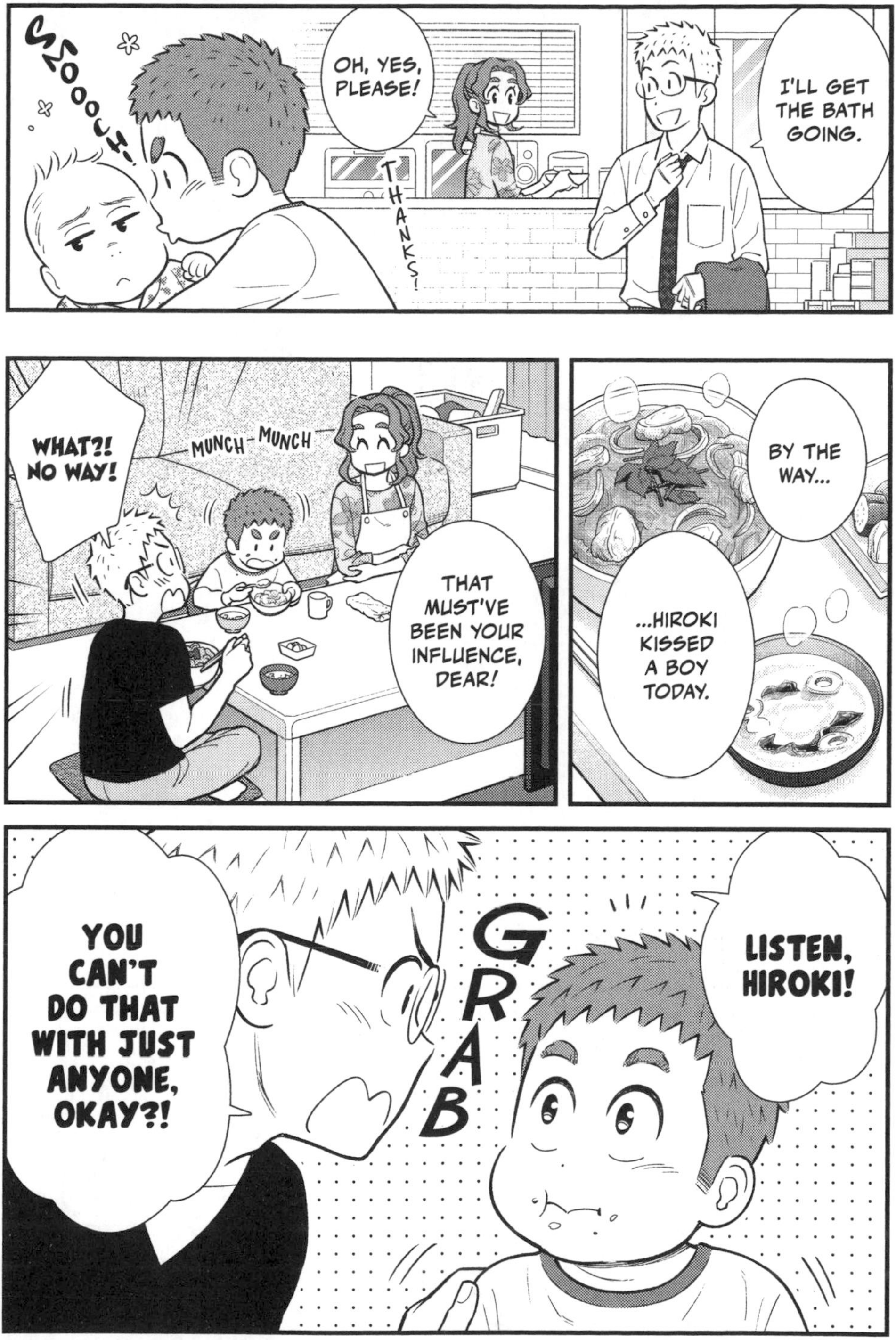
I'LL GET THE BATH GOING.
OH, YES, PLEASE!
THANKS!
SMOOOCH!
BY THE WAY...
...HIROKI KISSED A BOY TODAY.
THAT MUST'VE BEEN YOUR INFLUENCE, DEAR!
MUNCH MUNCH
WHAT?! NO WAY!
LISTEN, HIROKI!
GRAB
YOU CAN'T DO THAT WITH JUST ANYONE, OKAY?!

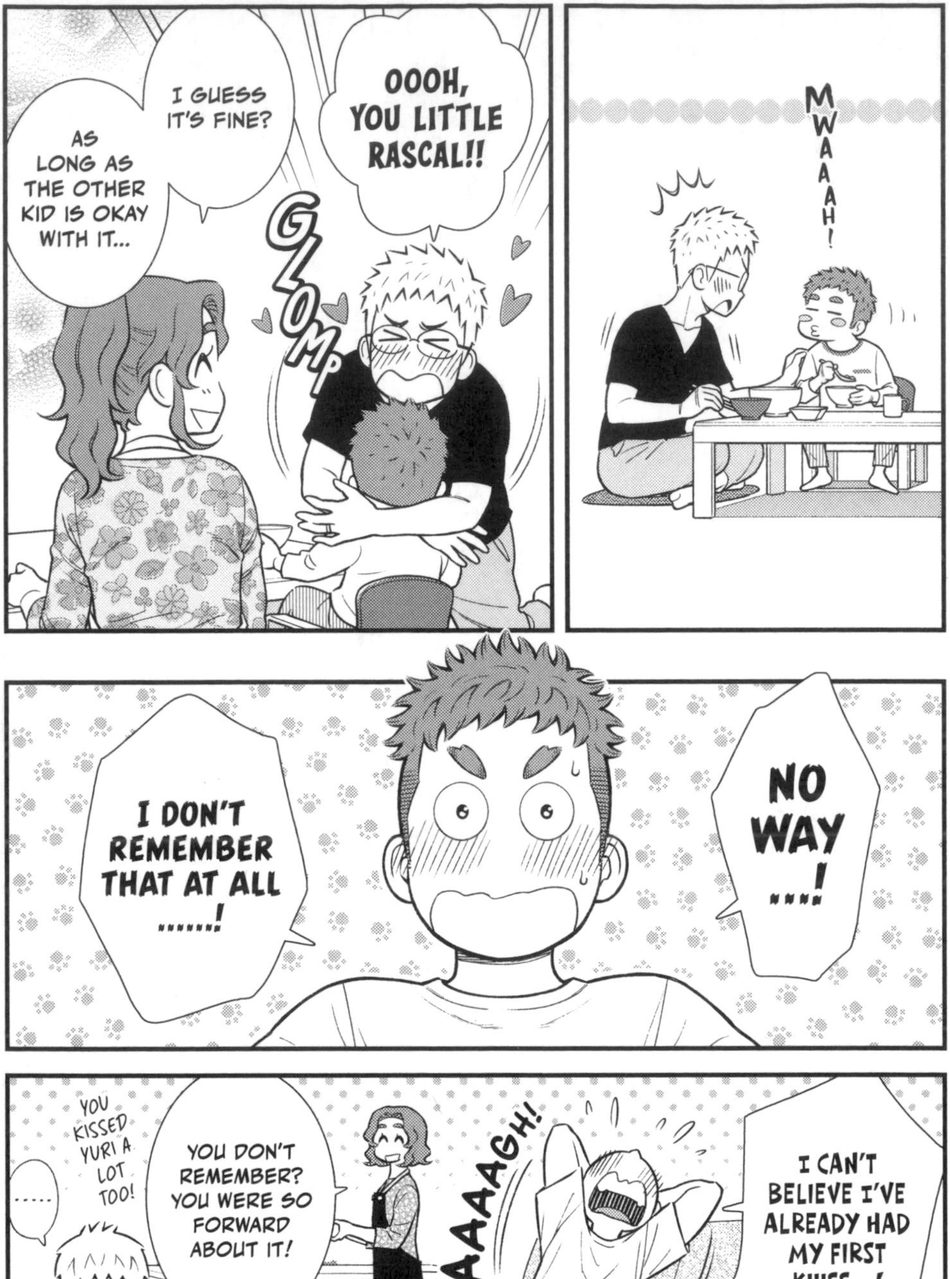
MWAAAAH!
OOOH, YOU LITTLE RASCAL!!
GLOMP
I GUESS IT'S FINE?
AS LONG AS THE OTHER KID IS OKAY WITH IT...
NO WAY ...!
I DON'T REMEMBER THAT AT ALL ......!
I CAN'T BELIEVE I'VE ALREADY HAD MY FIRST KIIISS...!
AAAAGH!
YOU DON'T REMEMBER? YOU WERE SO FORWARD ABOUT IT!
YOU KISSED YURI A LOT TOO!
.....

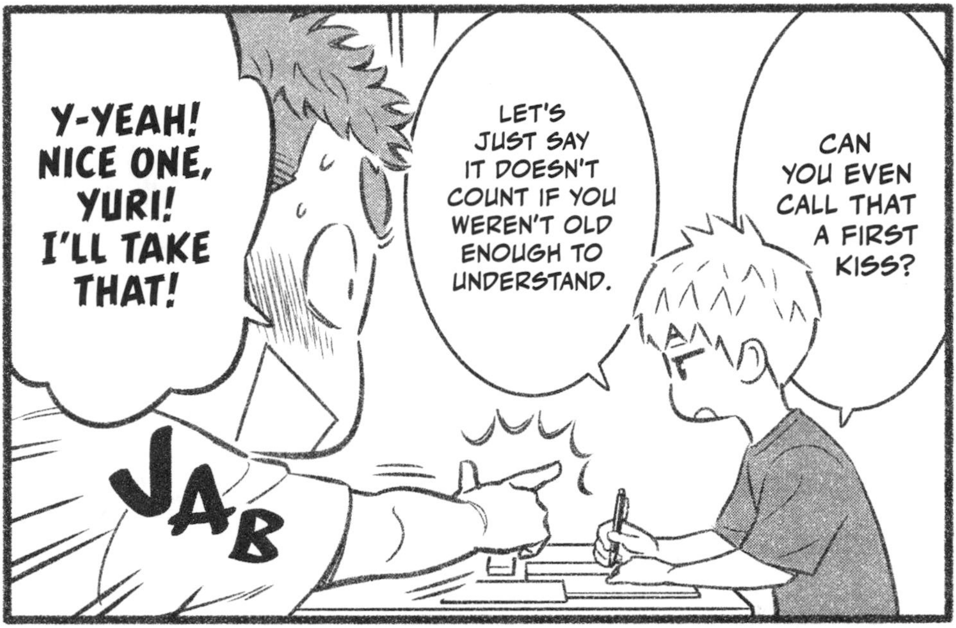
CAN YOU EVEN CALL THAT A FIRST KISS?
LET'S JUST SAY IT DOESN'T COUNT IF YOU WEREN'T OLD ENOUGH TO UNDERSTAND.
Y-YEAH! NICE ONE, YURI! I'LL TAKE THAT!
JAB

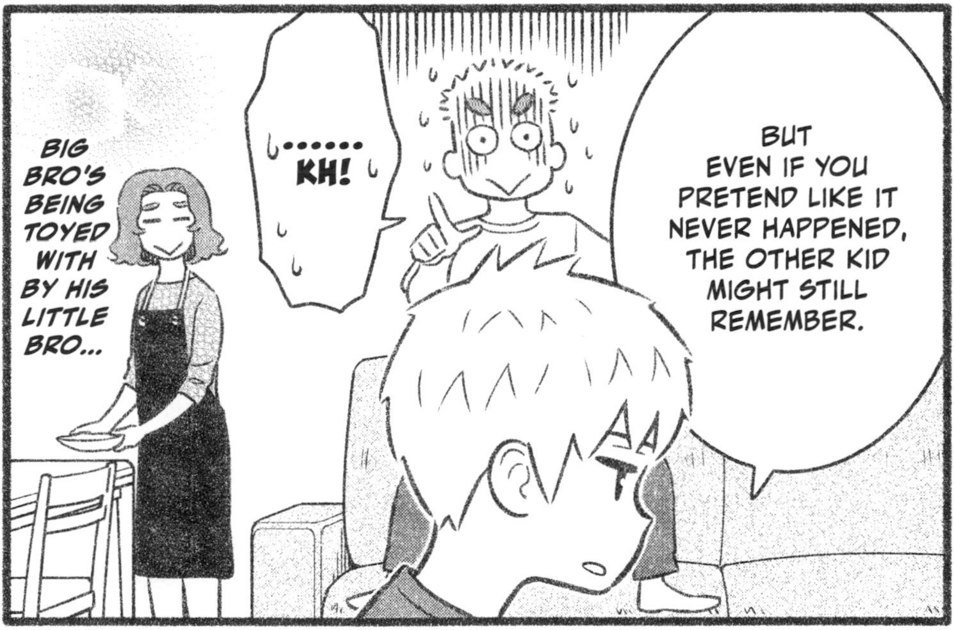
BUT EVEN IF YOU PRETEND LIKE IT NEVER HAPPENED, THE OTHER KID MIGHT STILL REMEMBER.
......KH!
BIG BRO'S BEING TOYED WITH BY HIS LITTLE BRO...

I Think
Our Son
Is Gay

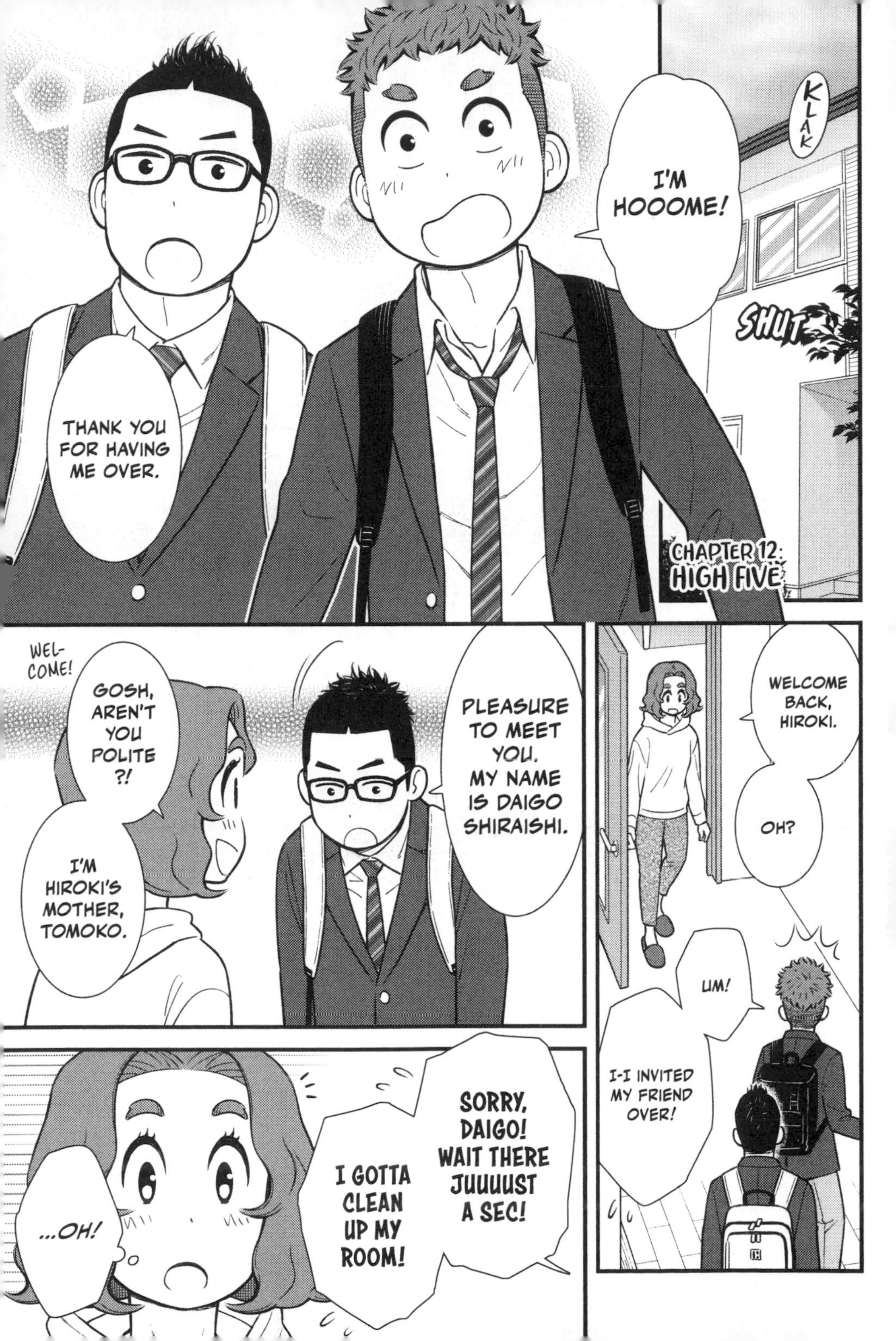
KLAK
I'M HOOOME!
SHUT
THANK YOU FOR HAVING ME OVER.
CHAPTER 12: HIGH FIVE
WELCOME BACK, HIROKI.
OH?
UM!
I-I INVITED MY FRIEND OVER!
PLEASURE TO MEET YOU. MY NAME IS DAIGO SHIRAISHI.
WEL-COME!
GOSH, AREN'T YOU POLITE?!
I'M HIROKI'S MOTHER, TOMOKO.
SORRY, DAIGO! WAIT THERE JUUUUST A SEC!
I GOTTA CLEAN UP MY ROOM!
...OH!

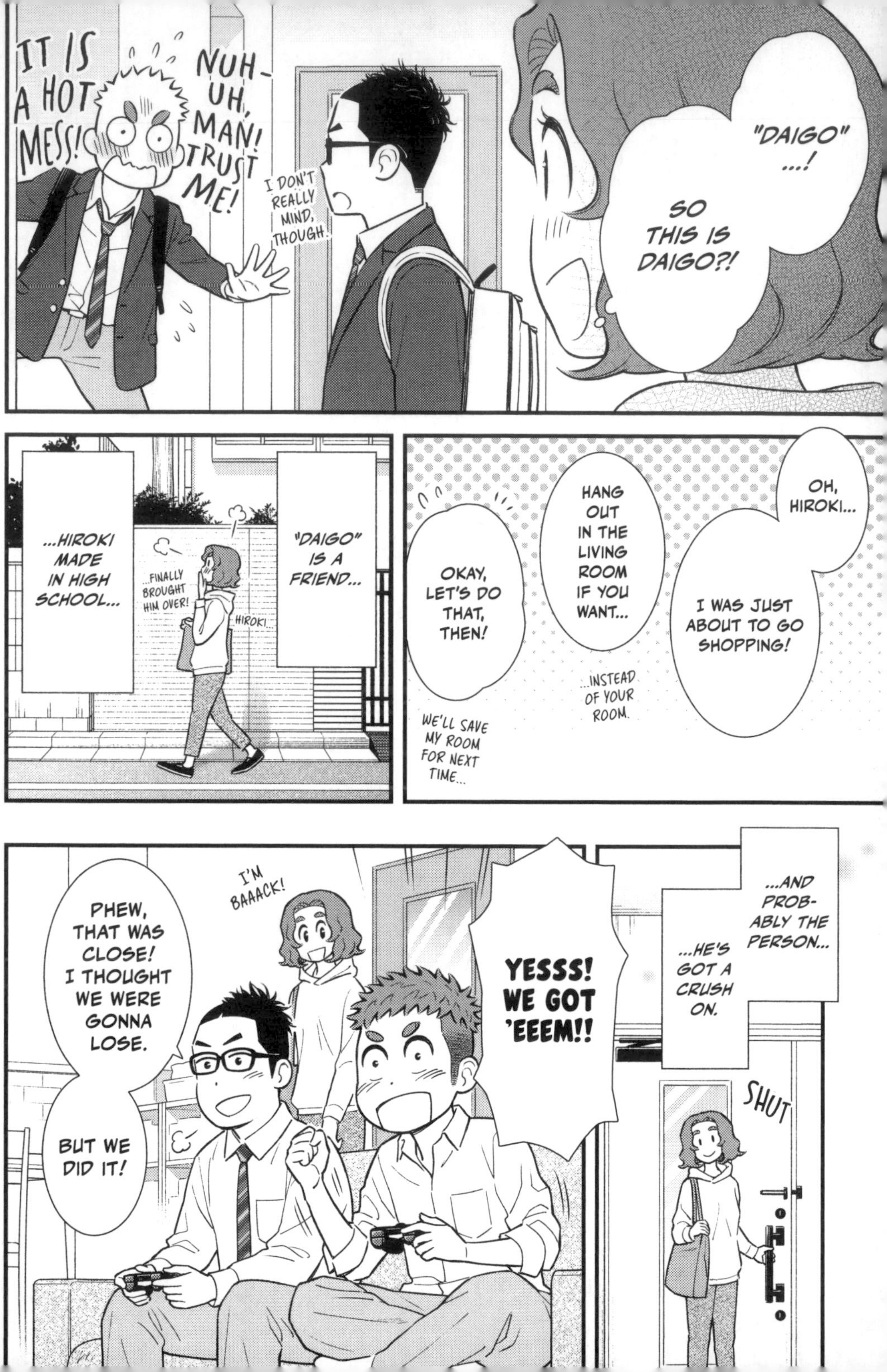
"DAIGO" ...!
SO THIS IS DAIGO?!
NUH-UH, MAN! TRUST ME!
IT IS A HOT MESS!
I DON'T REALLY MIND, THOUGH.
OH, HIROKI...
I WAS JUST ABOUT TO GO SHOPPING!
HANG OUT IN THE LIVING ROOM IF YOU WANT...
...INSTEAD OF YOUR ROOM.
OKAY, LET'S DO THAT, THEN!
WE'LL SAVE MY ROOM FOR NEXT TIME...
"DAIGO" IS A FRIEND...
...FINALLY BROUGHT HIM OVER!
HIROKI...
...HIROKI MADE IN HIGH SCHOOL...
...AND PROBABLY THE PERSON...
...HE'S GOT A CRUSH ON.
SHUT
YESSS! WE GOT 'EEEM!!
I'M BAAACK!
PHEW, THAT WAS CLOSE! I THOUGHT WE WERE GONNA LOSE.
BUT WE DID IT!

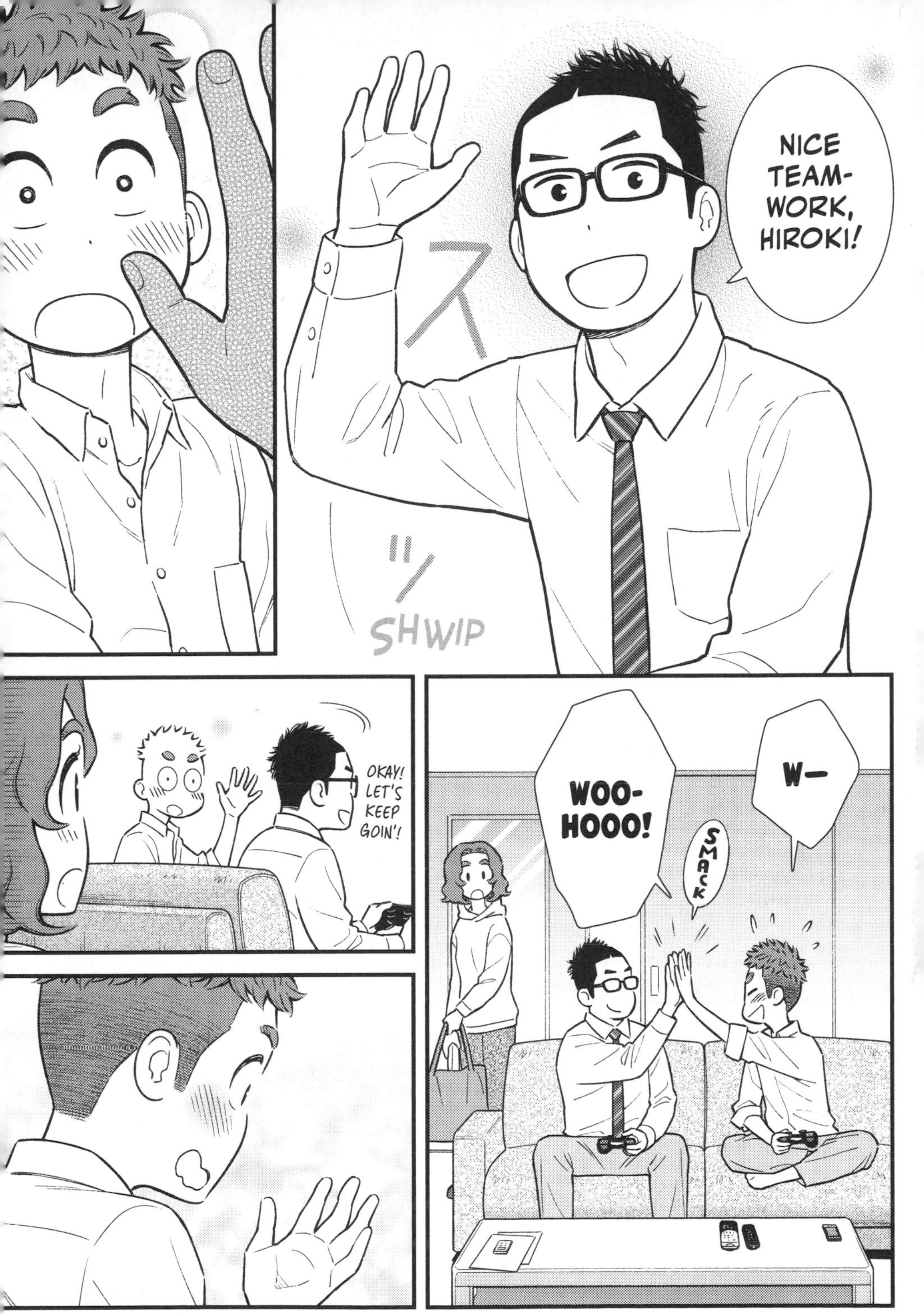
NICE TEAM-WORK, HIROKI!
ス
ッ
SHWIP
W—
SMACK
WOO-HOOO!
OKAY! LET'S KEEP GOIN'!

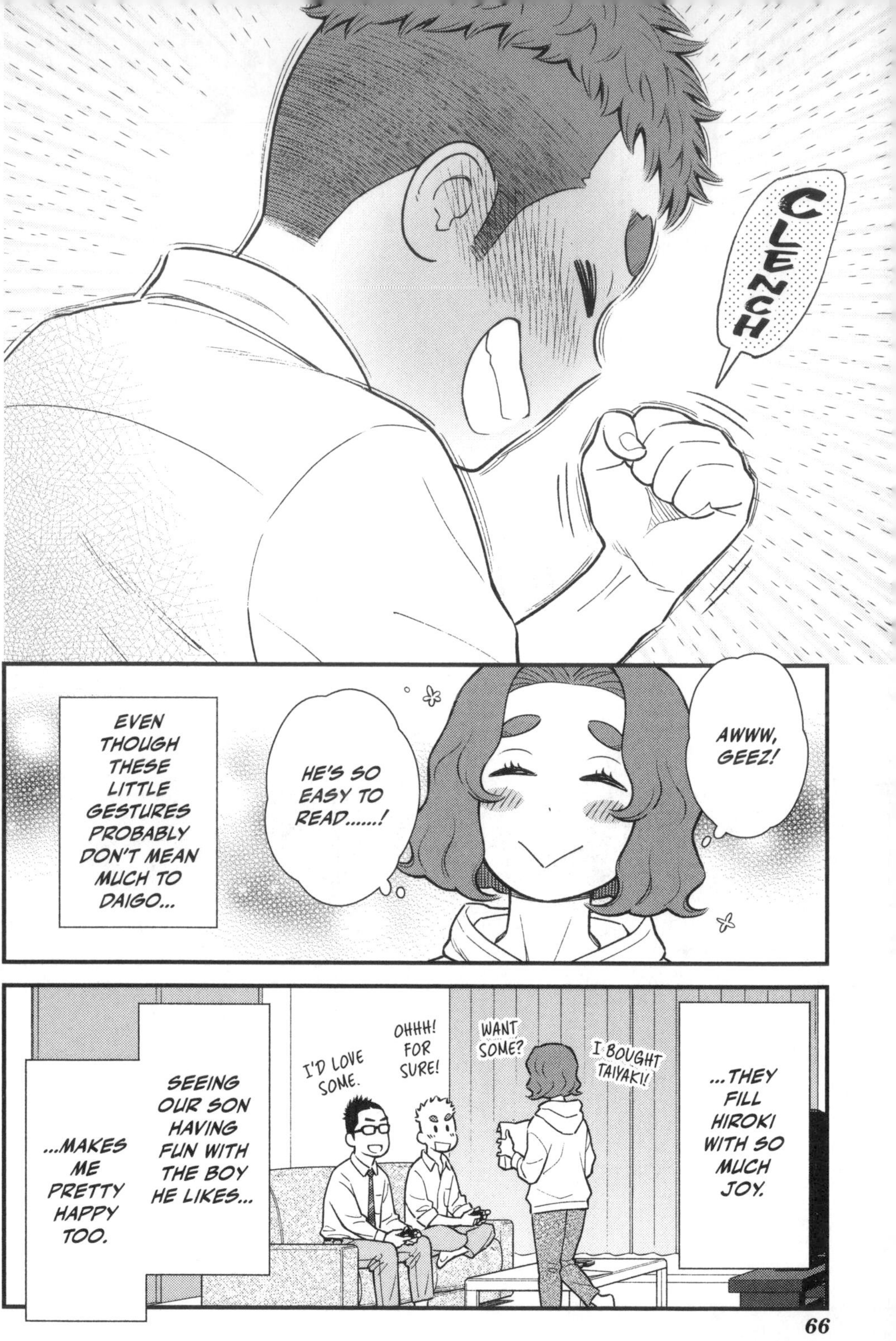
CLENCH
AWWW, GEEZ!
HE'S SO EASY TO READ......!
EVEN THOUGH THESE LITTLE GESTURES PROBABLY DON'T MEAN MUCH TO DAIGO...
...THEY FILL HIROKI WITH SO MUCH JOY.
I BOUGHT TAIYAKI!
WANT SOME?
OHHH! FOR SURE!
I'D LOVE SOME.
SEEING OUR SON HAVING FUN WITH THE BOY HE LIKES...
...MAKES ME PRETTY HAPPY TOO.

CHAPTER 13: A STRAIGHTFORWARD BOY

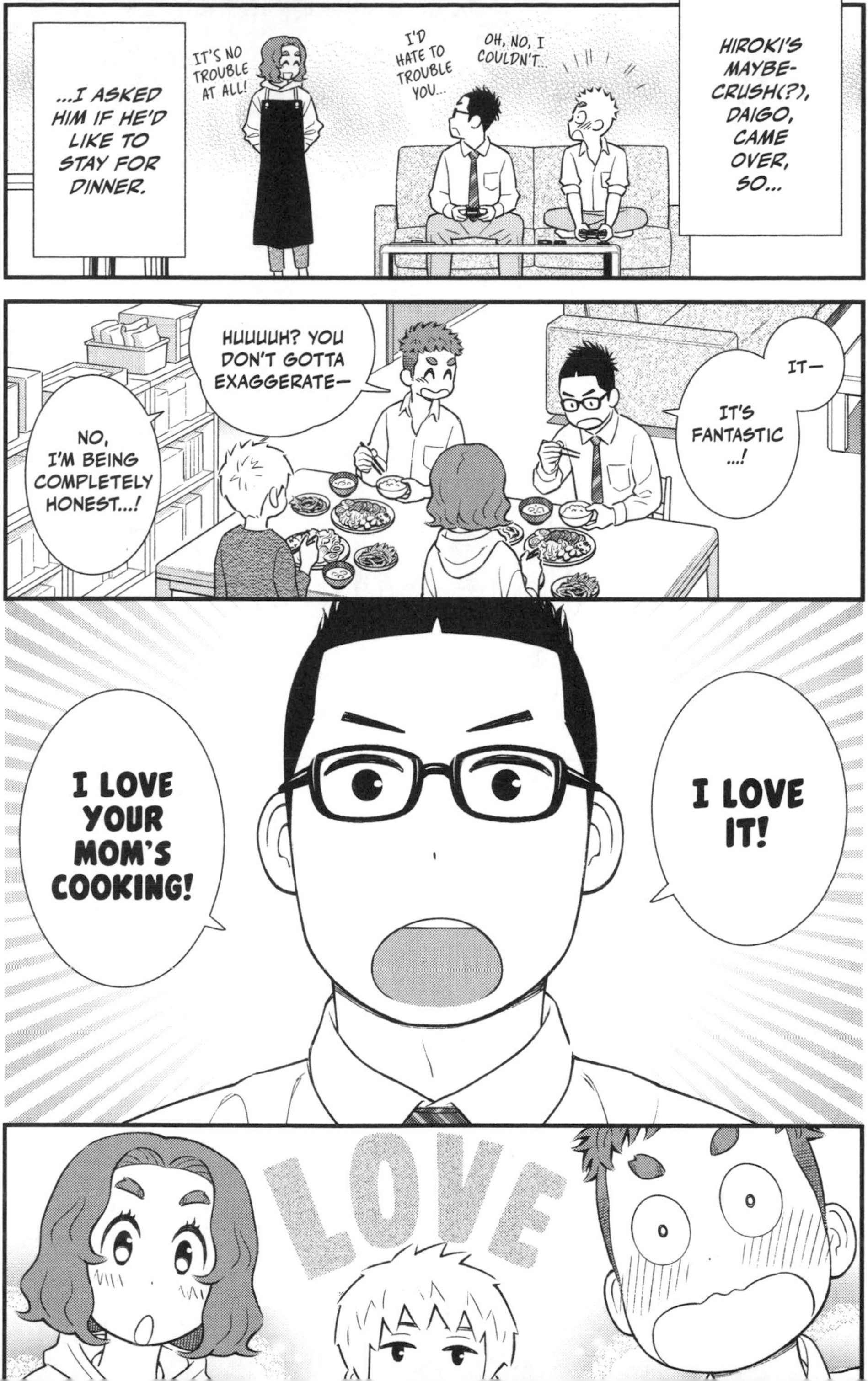
HIROKI'S MAYBE-CRUSH(?), DAIGO, CAME OVER, SO...
OH, NO, I COULDN'T...
I'D HATE TO TROUBLE YOU...
IT'S NO TROUBLE AT ALL!
...I ASKED HIM IF HE'D LIKE TO STAY FOR DINNER.
IT— IT'S FANTASTIC...!
HUUUUH? YOU DON'T GOTTA EXAGGERATE—
NO, I'M BEING COMPLETELY HONEST...!
I LOVE IT!
I LOVE YOUR MOM'S COOKING!
LOVE

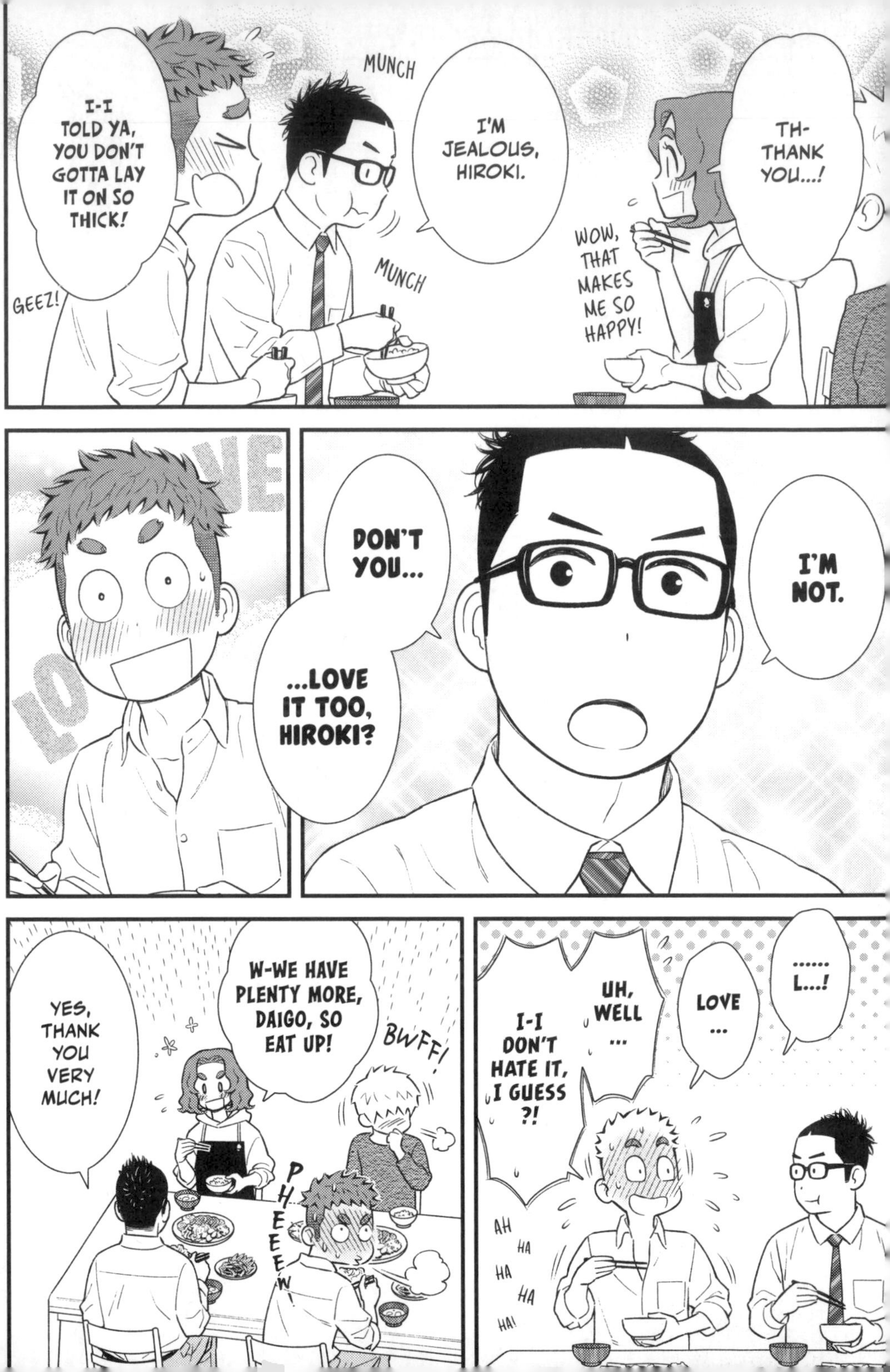
TH- THANK YOU...!
WOW, THAT MAKES ME SO HAPPY!
I'M JEALOUS, HIROKI.
MUNCH
MUNCH
I-I TOLD YA, YOU DON'T GOTTA LAY IT ON SO THICK!
GEEZ!
I'M NOT.
DON'T YOU...
...LOVE IT TOO, HIROKI?
......L...!
LOVE ...
UH, WELL ...
I-I DON'T HATE IT, I GUESS ?!
AH HA HA HA HA!
W-WE HAVE PLENTY MORE, DAIGO, SO EAT UP!
BWFF!
YES, THANK YOU VERY MUCH!
PHEEEEW!

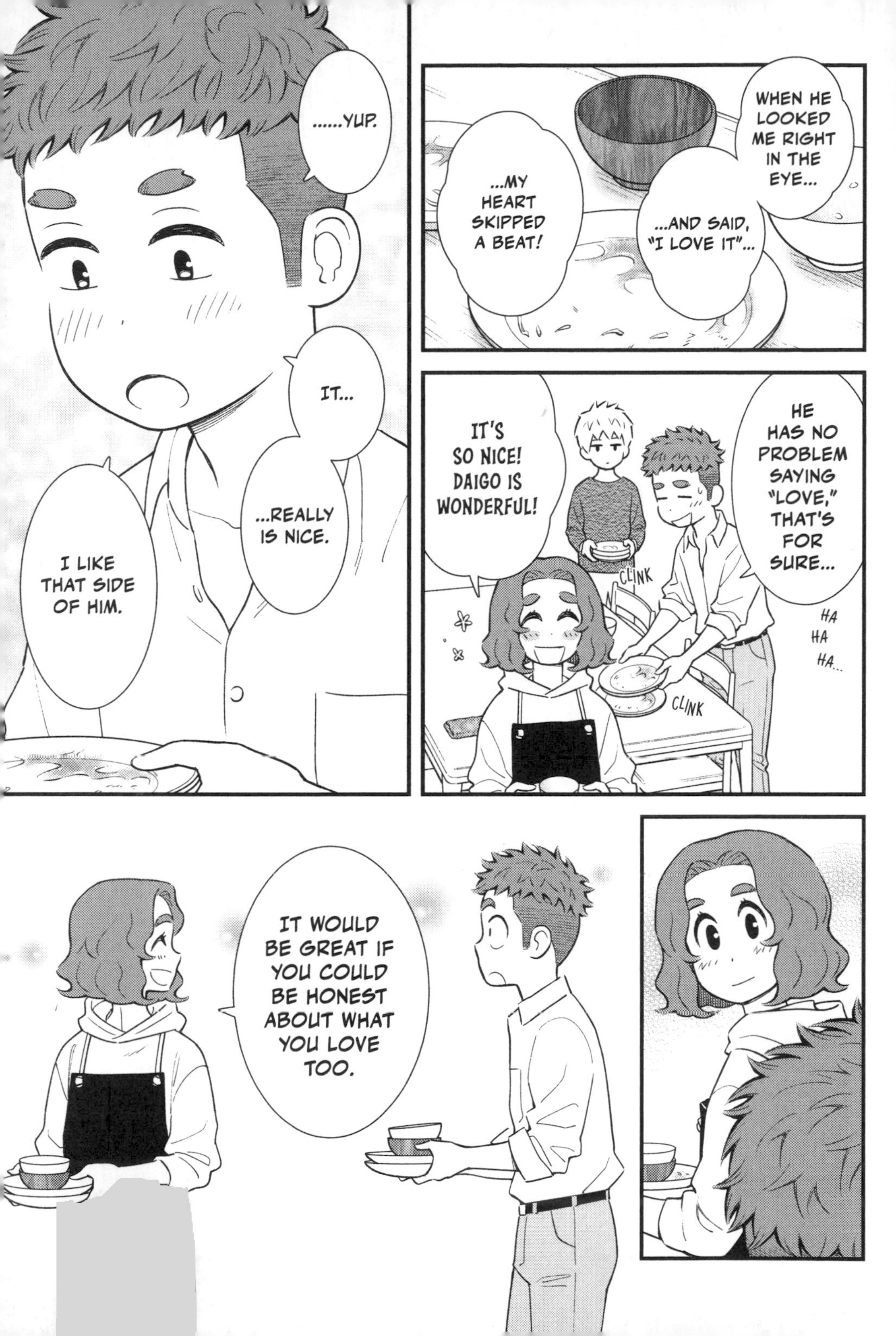
WHEN HE LOOKED ME RIGHT IN THE EYE...
...AND SAID, "I LOVE IT"...
...MY HEART SKIPPED A BEAT!
HE HAS NO PROBLEM SAYING "LOVE," THAT'S FOR SURE...
HA HA HA...
IT'S SO NICE! DAIGO IS WONDERFUL!
CLINK
CLINK
......YUP.
IT...
...REALLY IS NICE.
I LIKE THAT SIDE OF HIM.
IT WOULD BE GREAT IF YOU COULD BE HONEST ABOUT WHAT YOU LOVE TOO.

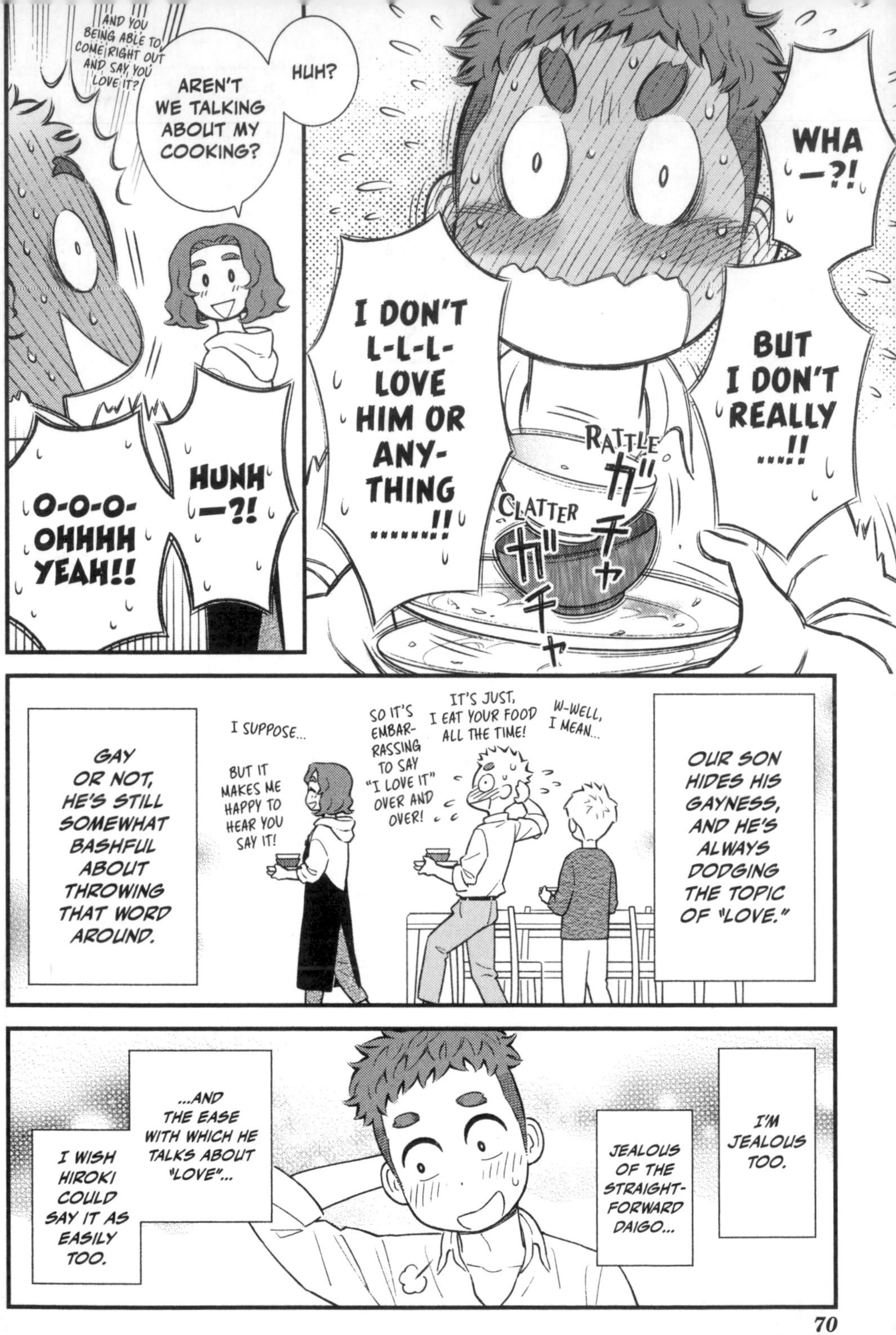
WHA—?!
BUT I DON'T REALLY.....!!
I DON'T L-L-L-LOVE HIM OR ANYTHING.......!!
RATTLE
CLATTER
AND YOU BEING ABLE TO COME RIGHT OUT AND SAY YOU LOVE IT?
HUH?
AREN'T WE TALKING ABOUT MY COOKING?
HUNH—?!
O-O-O-OHHHH YEAH!!
OUR SON HIDES HIS GAYNESS, AND HE'S ALWAYS DODGING THE TOPIC OF "LOVE."
W-WELL, I MEAN...
IT'S JUST, I EAT YOUR FOOD ALL THE TIME!
SO IT'S EMBARRASSING TO SAY "I LOVE IT" OVER AND OVER!
I SUPPOSE...
BUT IT MAKES ME HAPPY TO HEAR YOU SAY IT!
GAY OR NOT, HE'S STILL SOMEWHAT BASHFUL ABOUT THROWING THAT WORD AROUND.
I'M JEALOUS TOO.
JEALOUS OF THE STRAIGHT-FORWARD DAIGO...
...AND THE EASE WITH WHICH HE TALKS ABOUT "LOVE"...
I WISH HIROKI COULD SAY IT AS EASILY TOO.

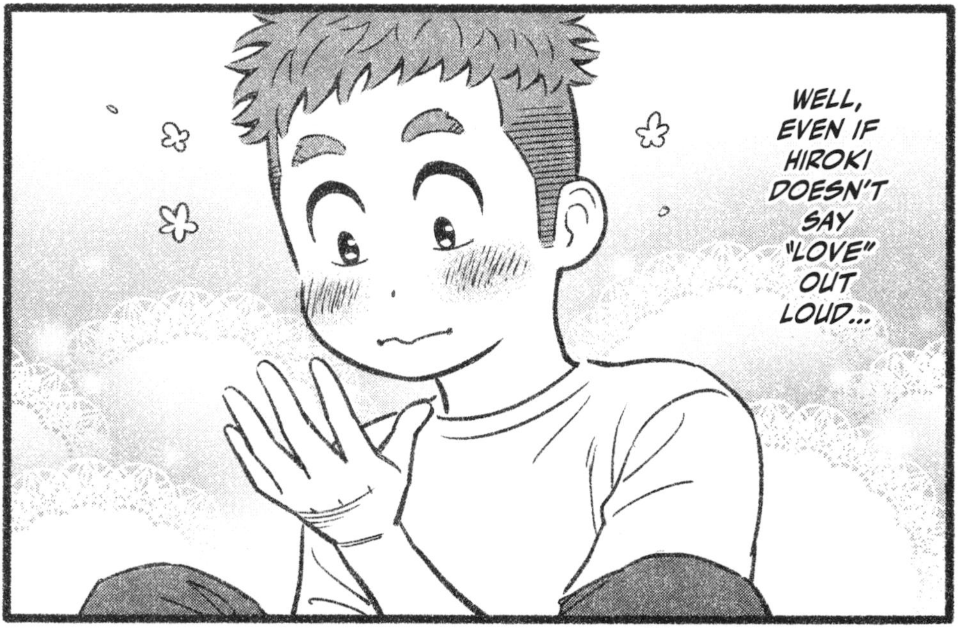
WELL, EVEN IF HIROKI DOESN'T SAY "LOVE" OUT LOUD...
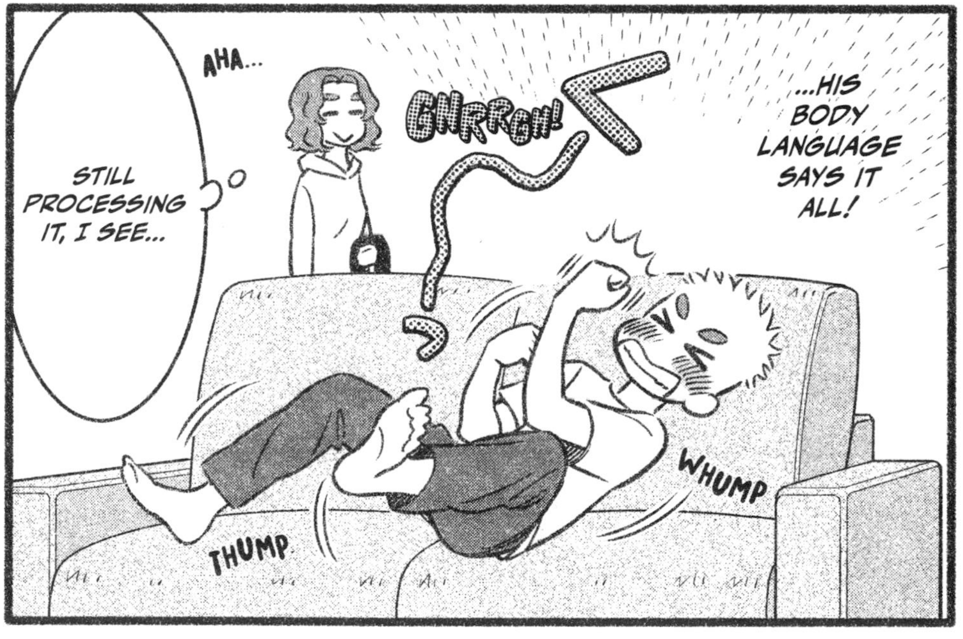
...HIS BODY LANGUAGE SAYS IT ALL!
GNRRGH!
AHA...
STILL PROCESSING IT, I SEE...
WHUMP
THUMP

I Think
Our Son
Is Gay

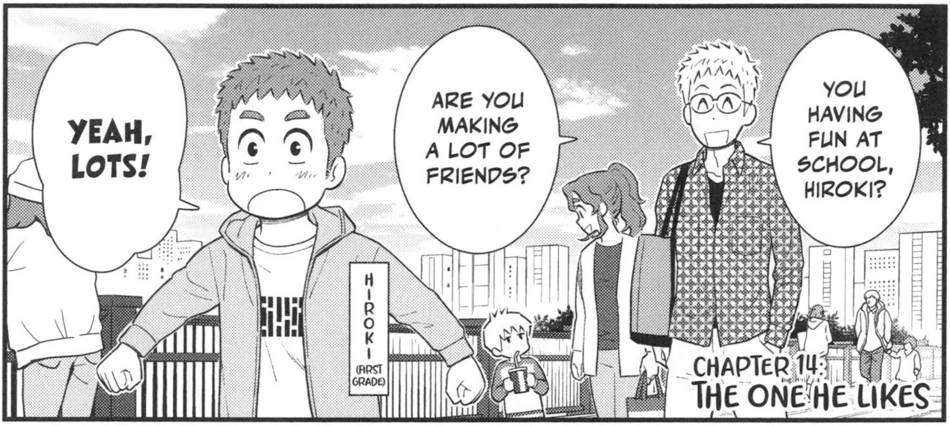
CHAPTER 14: THE ONE HE LIKES
YOU HAVING FUN AT SCHOOL, HIROKI?
ARE YOU MAKING A LOT OF FRIENDS?
HIROKI (FIRST GRADE)
YEAH, LOTS!

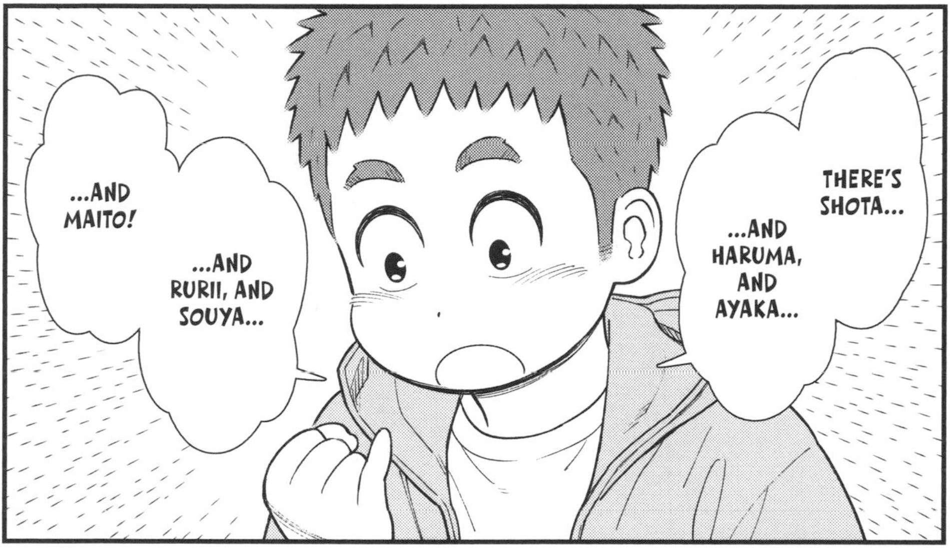
THERE'S SHOTA...
...AND HARUMA, AND AYAKA...
...AND RURII, AND SOUYA...
...AND MAITO!

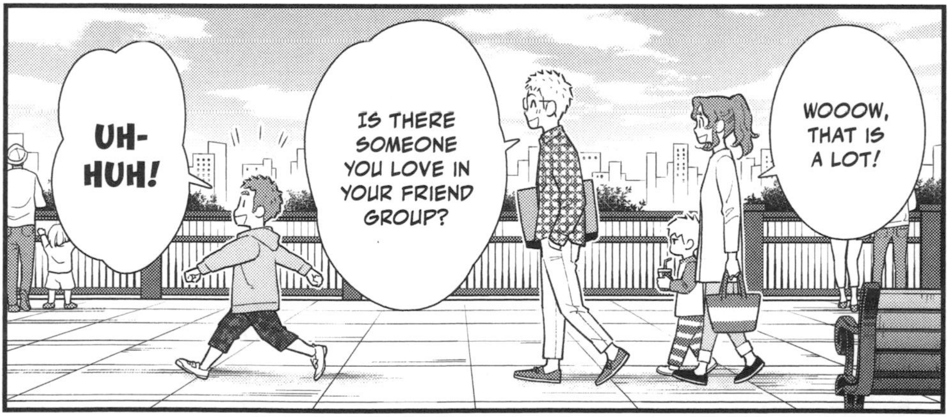
WOOOW, THAT IS A LOT!
IS THERE SOMEONE YOU LOVE IN YOUR FRIEND GROUP?
UH-HUH!

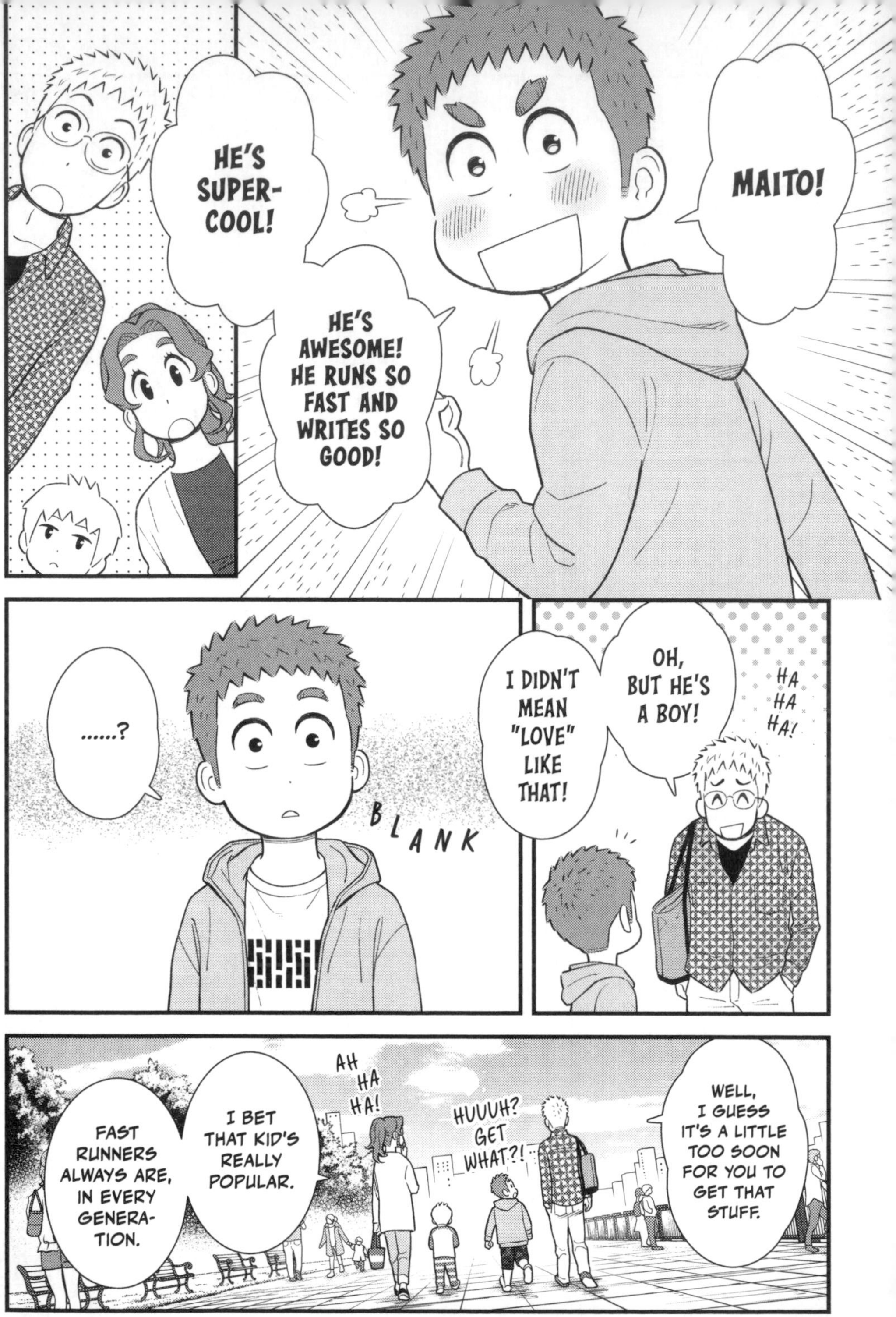
MAITO!
HE'S SUPER-COOL!
HE'S AWESOME! HE RUNS SO FAST AND WRITES SO GOOD!
OH, BUT HE'S A BOY!
HA HA HA!
I DIDN'T MEAN "LOVE" LIKE THAT!
......?
BLANK
WELL, I GUESS IT'S A LITTLE TOO SOON FOR YOU TO GET THAT STUFF.
HUUUH? GET WHAT?!
AH HA HA!
I BET THAT KID'S REALLY POPULAR.
FAST RUNNERS ALWAYS ARE, IN EVERY GENERATION.

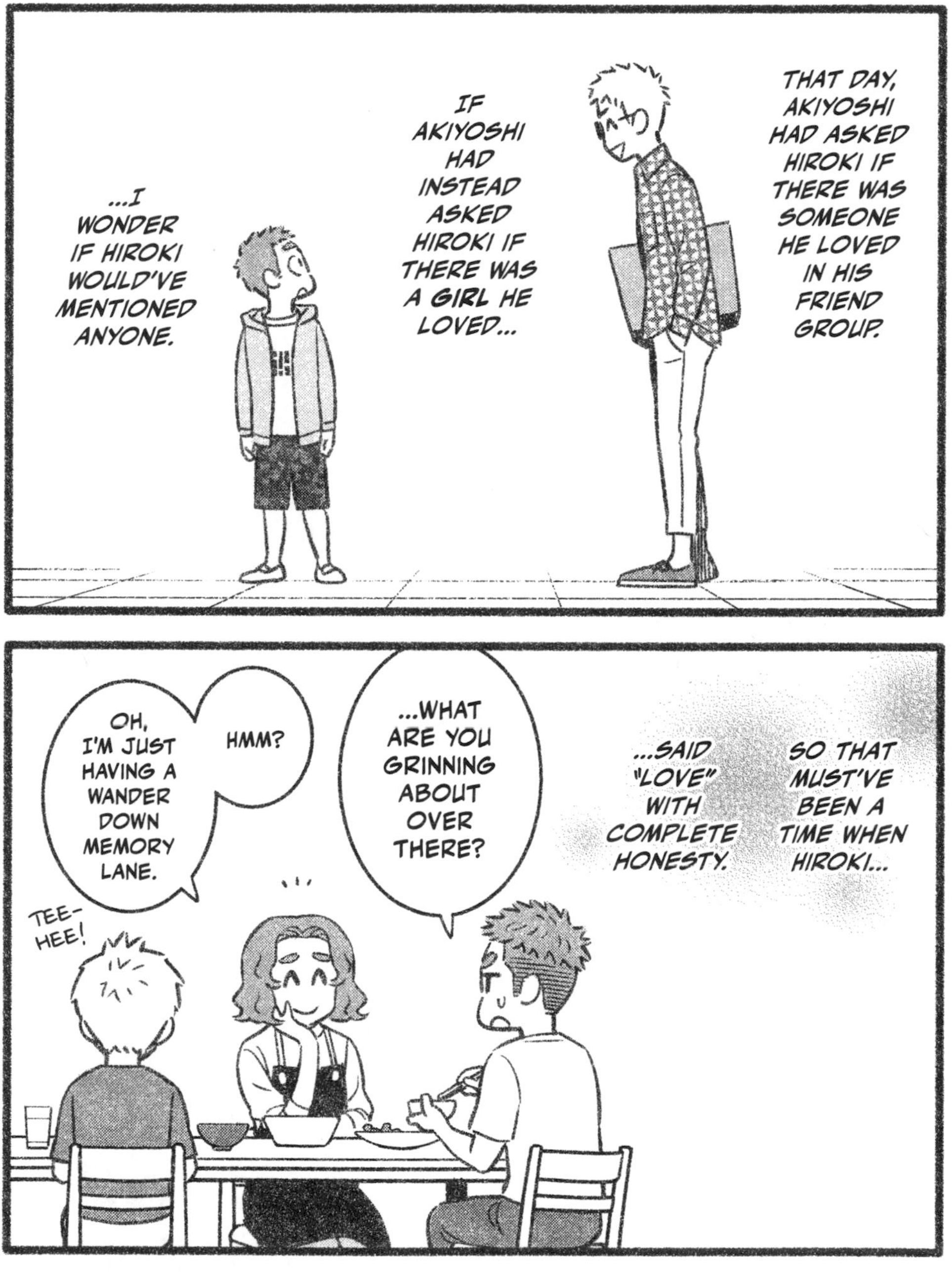
THAT DAY, AKIYOSHI HAD ASKED HIROKI IF THERE WAS SOMEONE HE LOVED IN HIS FRIEND GROUP.
IF AKIYOSHI HAD INSTEAD ASKED HIROKI IF THERE WAS A **GIRL** HE LOVED...
...I WONDER IF HIROKI WOULD'VE MENTIONED ANYONE.
SO THAT MUST'VE BEEN A TIME WHEN HIROKI...
...SAID "LOVE" WITH COMPLETE HONESTY.
...WHAT ARE YOU GRINNING ABOUT OVER THERE?
HMM?
OH, I'M JUST HAVING A WANDER DOWN MEMORY LANE.
TEE-HEE!

I Think
Our Son
Is Gay

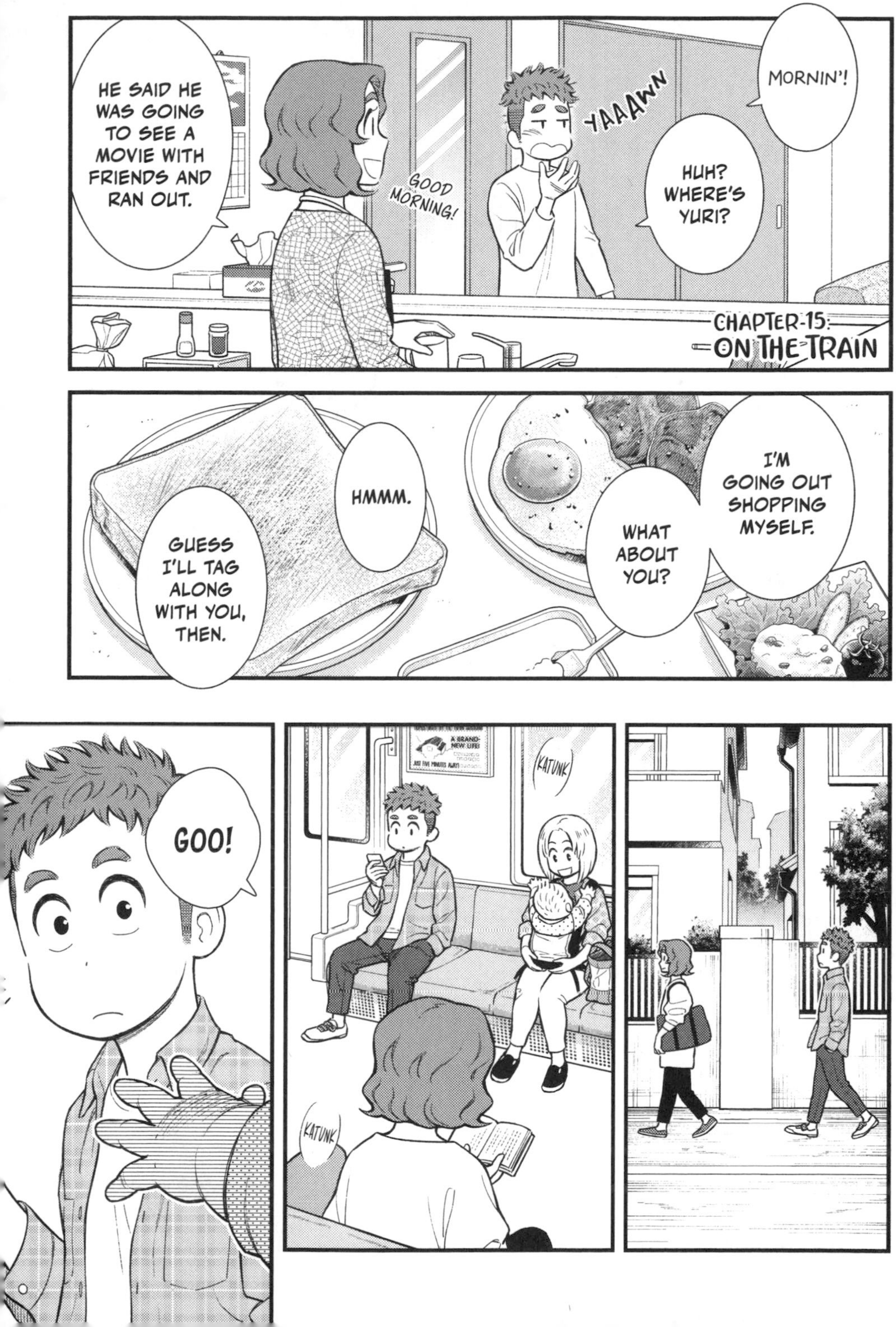
MORNIN'!
YAAAWN
HUH? WHERE'S YURI?
GOOD MORNING!
HE SAID HE WAS GOING TO SEE A MOVIE WITH FRIENDS AND RAN OUT.
CHAPTER 15: ON THE TRAIN
I'M GOING OUT SHOPPING MYSELF.
WHAT ABOUT YOU?
HMMM.
GUESS I'LL TAG ALONG WITH YOU, THEN.
A BRAND-NEW LIFE!
JUST FIVE MINUTES AWAY!
KATUNK
KATUNK
GOO!

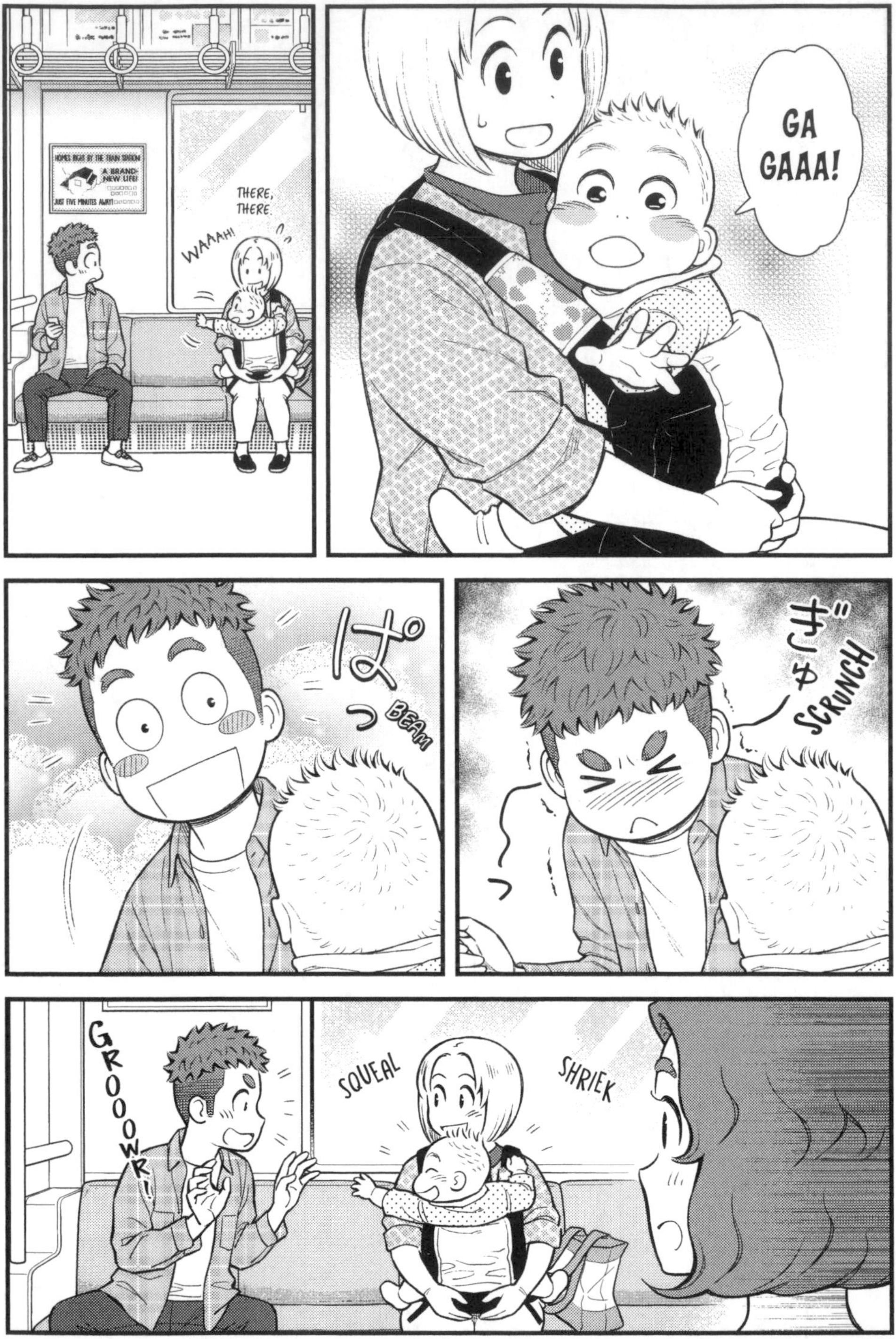
GA GAAA!
HOMES RIGHT BY THE TRAIN STATION!
A BRAND-NEW LIFE!
JUST FIVE MINUTES AWAY!
THERE, THERE.
WAAAH!
ぎゅ
SCRUNCH
ぱっ
BEAM
SHRIEK
SQUEAL
GROOOWR!

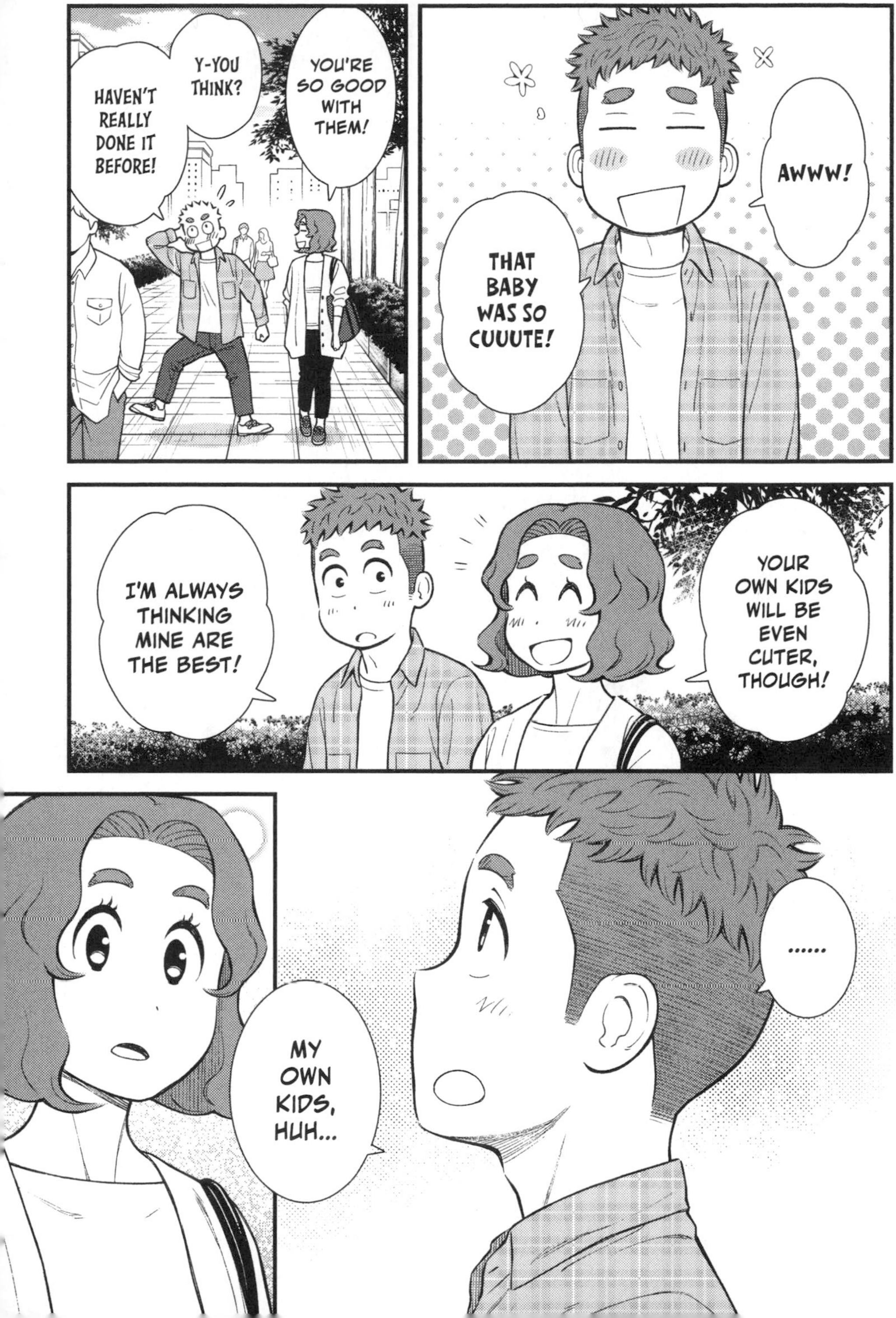
AWWW!
THAT BABY WAS SO CUUUTE!
YOU'RE SO GOOD WITH THEM!
Y-YOU THINK?
HAVEN'T REALLY DONE IT BEFORE!
YOUR OWN KIDS WILL BE EVEN CUTER, THOUGH!
I'M ALWAYS THINKING MINE ARE THE BEST!
......
MY OWN KIDS, HUH...

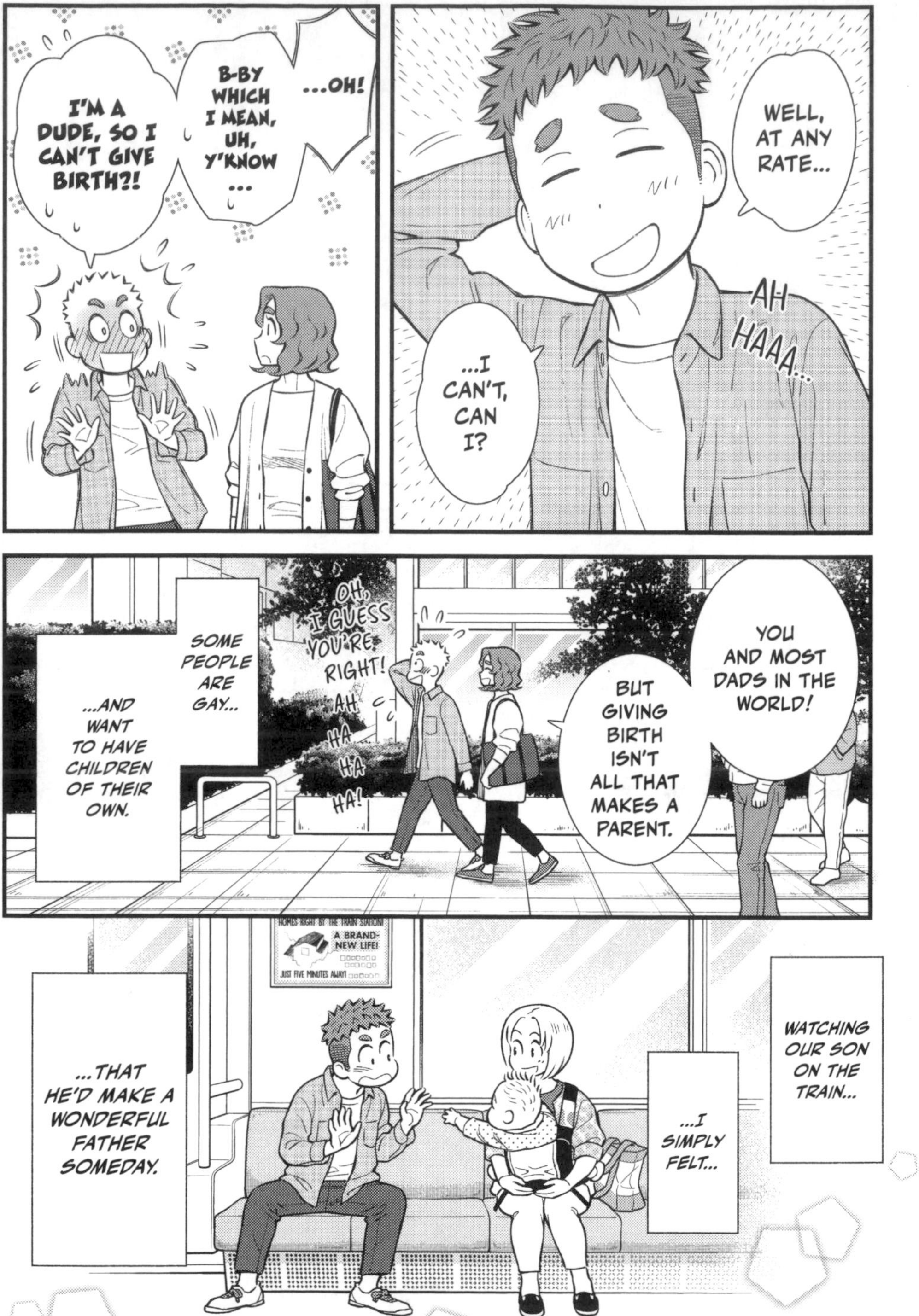
WELL, AT ANY RATE...
AH HAAA...
...I CAN'T, CAN I?
...OH!
B-BY WHICH I MEAN, UH, Y'KNOW...
I'M A DUDE, SO I CAN'T GIVE BIRTH?!
YOU AND MOST DADS IN THE WORLD!
BUT GIVING BIRTH ISN'T ALL THAT MAKES A PARENT.
OH, I GUESS YOU'RE RIGHT! AH HA HA HA!
SOME PEOPLE ARE GAY...
...AND WANT TO HAVE CHILDREN OF THEIR OWN.
HOMES RIGHT BY THE TRAIN STATION!
A BRAND-NEW LIFE!
JUST FIVE MINUTES AWAY!
WATCHING OUR SON ON THE TRAIN...
...I SIMPLY FELT...
...THAT HE'D MAKE A WONDERFUL FATHER SOMEDAY.

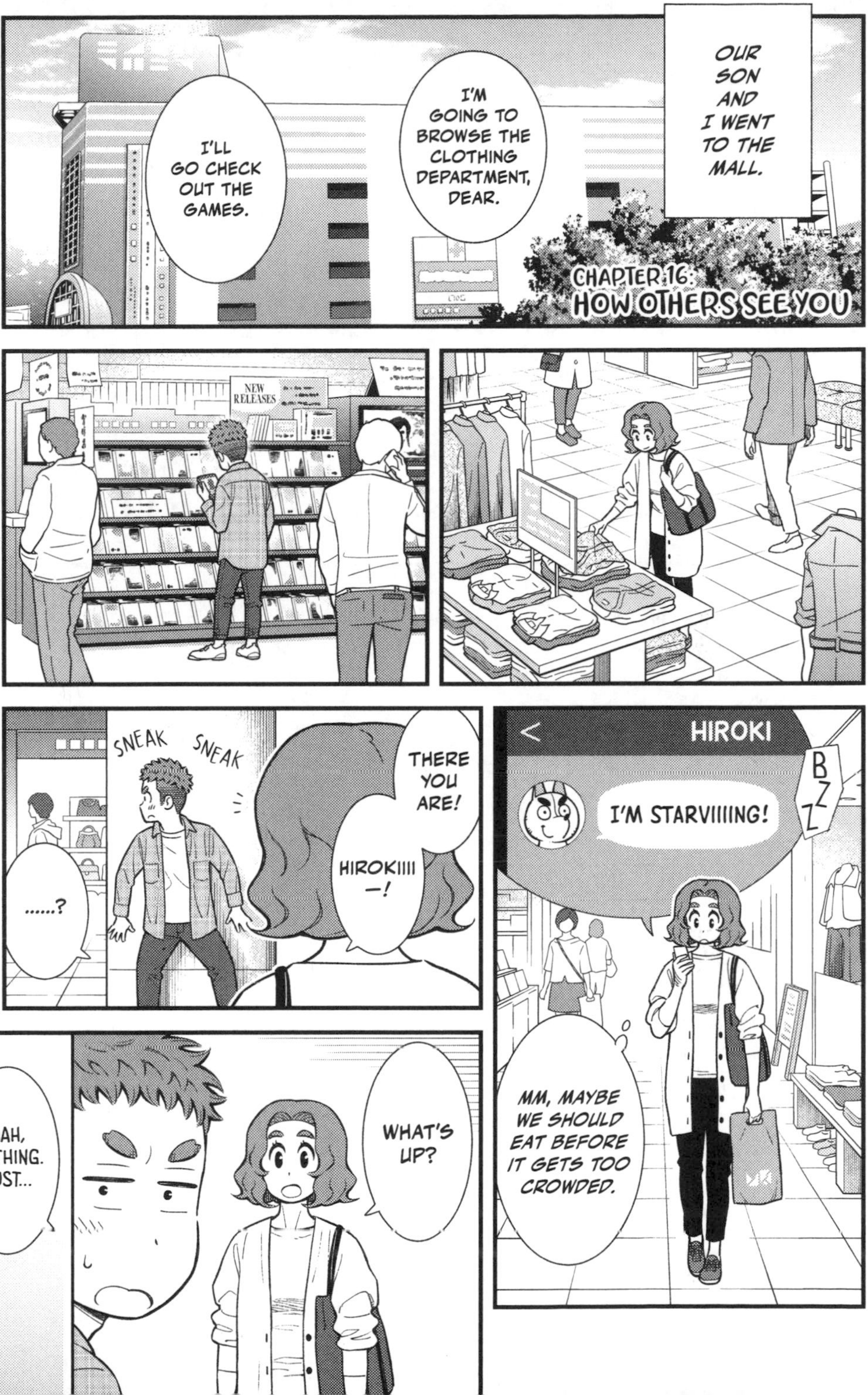
OUR SON AND I WENT TO THE MALL.
I'M GOING TO BROWSE THE CLOTHING DEPARTMENT, DEAR.
I'LL GO CHECK OUT THE GAMES.
CHAPTER 16: HOW OTHERS SEE YOU
NEW RELEASES
HIROKI
BZZ
I'M STARVIIIING!
MM, MAYBE WE SHOULD EAT BEFORE IT GETS TOO CROWDED.
THERE YOU ARE!
HIROKIIII—!
SNEAK SNEAK
......?
WHAT'S UP?
NAH, NOTHING. JUST...

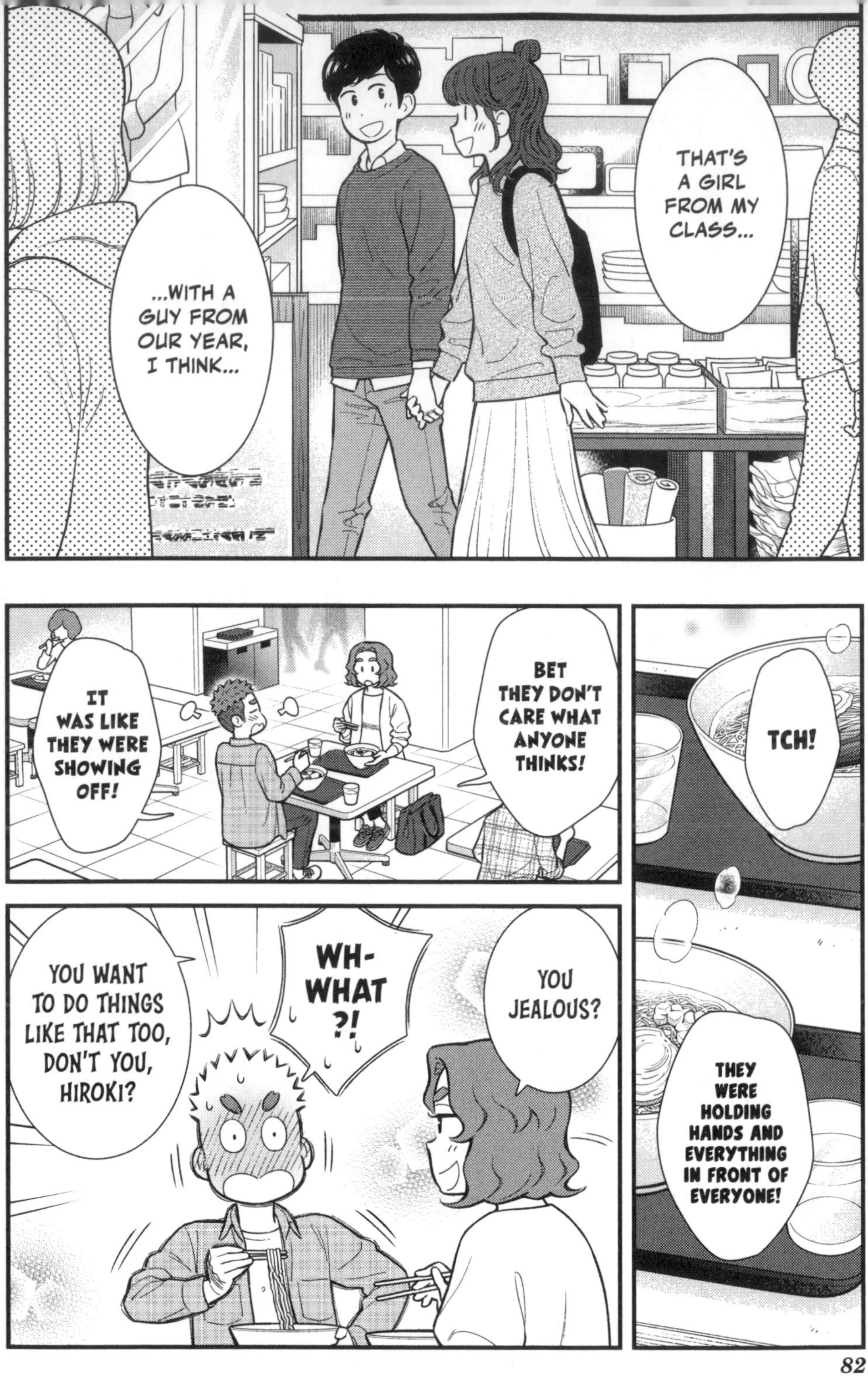
THAT'S A GIRL FROM MY CLASS...
...WITH A GUY FROM OUR YEAR, I THINK...
TCH!
THEY WERE HOLDING HANDS AND EVERYTHING IN FRONT OF EVERYONE!
BET THEY DON'T CARE WHAT ANYONE THINKS!
IT WAS LIKE THEY WERE SHOWING OFF!
YOU JEALOUS?
WH-WHAT?!
YOU WANT TO DO THINGS LIKE THAT TOO, DON'T YOU, HIROKI?

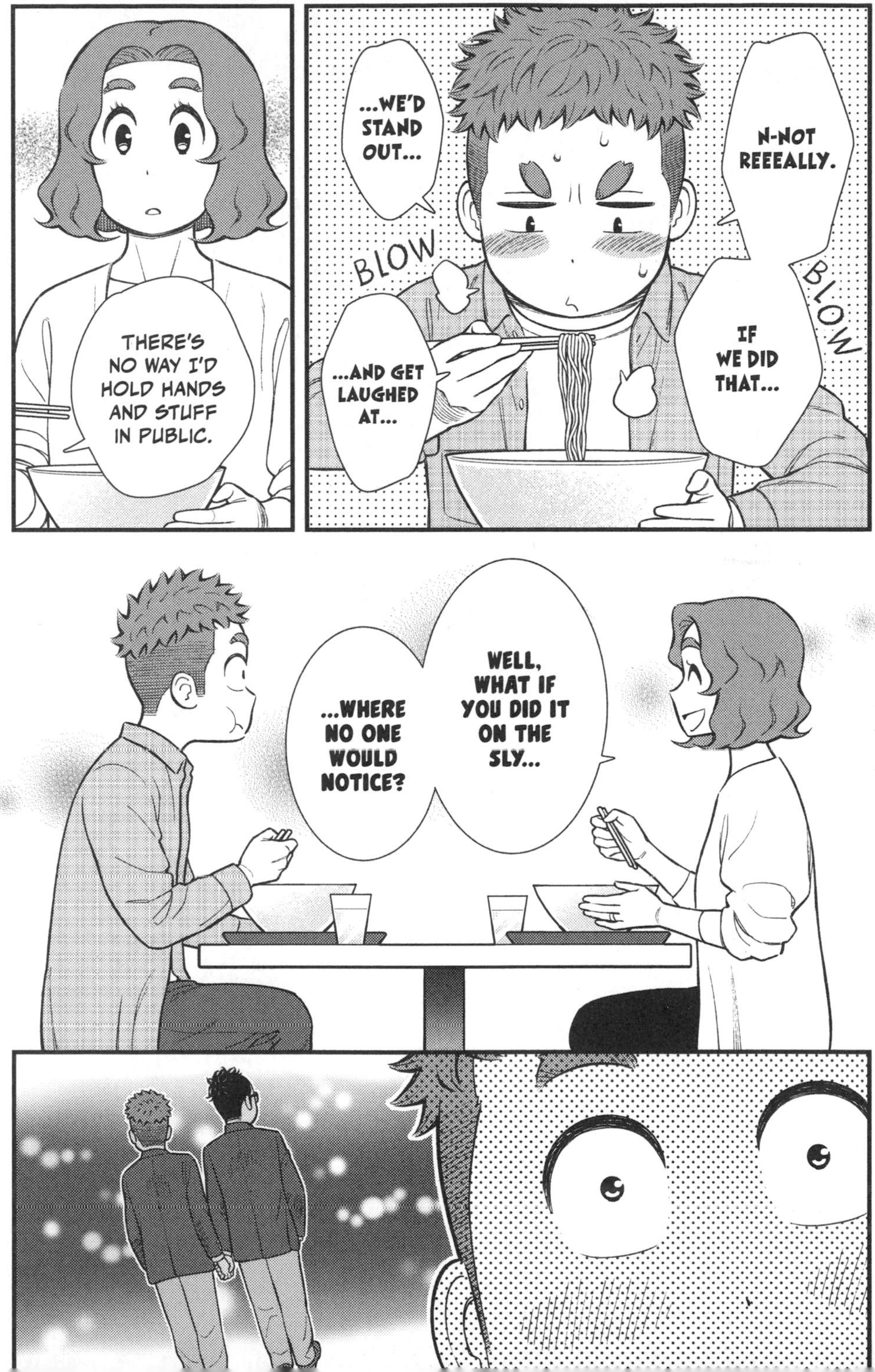
N-NOT REEEALLY.
BLOW
IF WE DID THAT...
...WE'D STAND OUT...
BLOW
...AND GET LAUGHED AT...
THERE'S NO WAY I'D HOLD HANDS AND STUFF IN PUBLIC.
WELL, WHAT IF YOU DID IT ON THE SLY...
...WHERE NO ONE WOULD NOTICE?

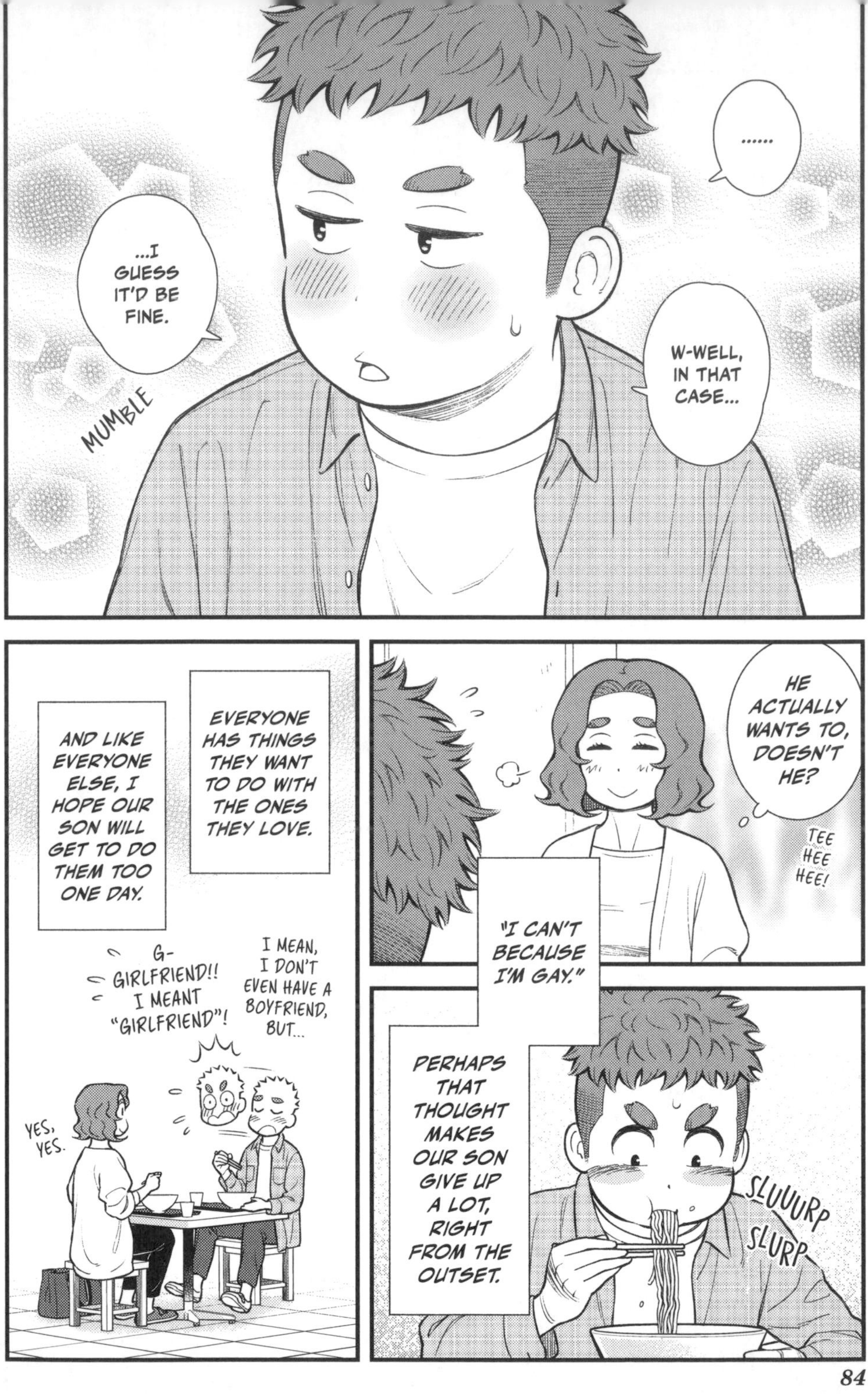
......
W-WELL, IN THAT CASE...
...I GUESS IT'D BE FINE.
MUMBLE
HE ACTUALLY WANTS TO, DOESN'T HE?
TEE HEE HEE!
"I CAN'T BECAUSE I'M GAY."
PERHAPS THAT THOUGHT MAKES OUR SON GIVE UP A LOT, RIGHT FROM THE OUTSET.
SLUUURP
SLURP
EVERYONE HAS THINGS THEY WANT TO DO WITH THE ONES THEY LOVE.
AND LIKE EVERYONE ELSE, I HOPE OUR SON WILL GET TO DO THEM TOO ONE DAY.
I MEAN, I DON'T EVEN HAVE A BOYFRIEND, BUT...
G-GIRLFRIEND!! I MEANT "GIRLFRIEND"!
YES, YES.

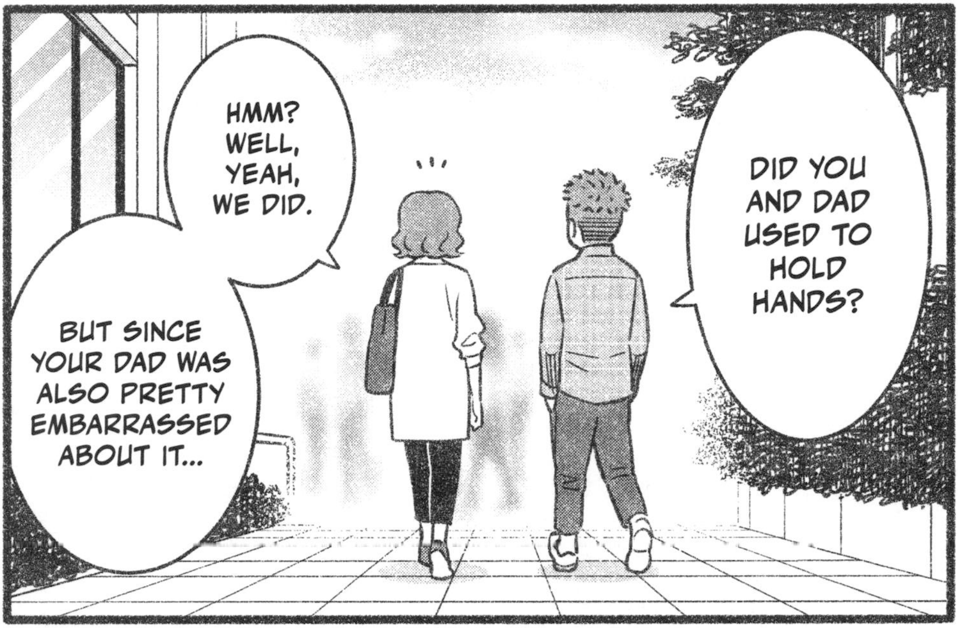
DID YOU AND DAD USED TO HOLD HANDS?
HMM? WELL, YEAH, WE DID.
BUT SINCE YOUR DAD WAS ALSO PRETTY EMBARRASSED ABOUT IT...

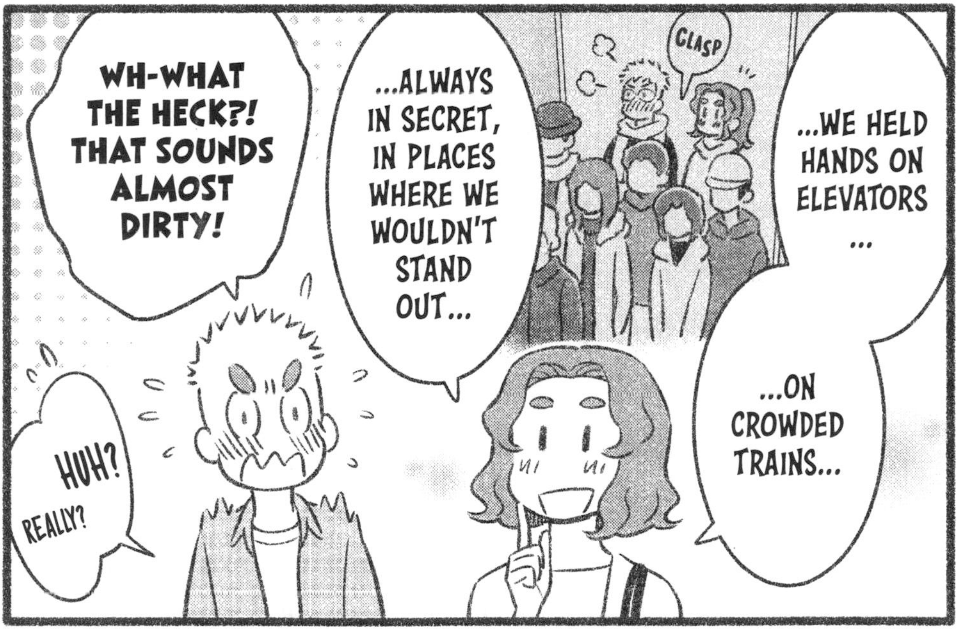
...WE HELD HANDS ON ELEVATORS ...
...ON CROWDED TRAINS...
CLASP
...ALWAYS IN SECRET, IN PLACES WHERE WE WOULDN'T STAND OUT...
WH-WHAT THE HECK?! THAT SOUNDS ALMOST DIRTY!
HUH?
REALLY?

I Think
Our Son
Is Gay

Chapter 17: Glasses

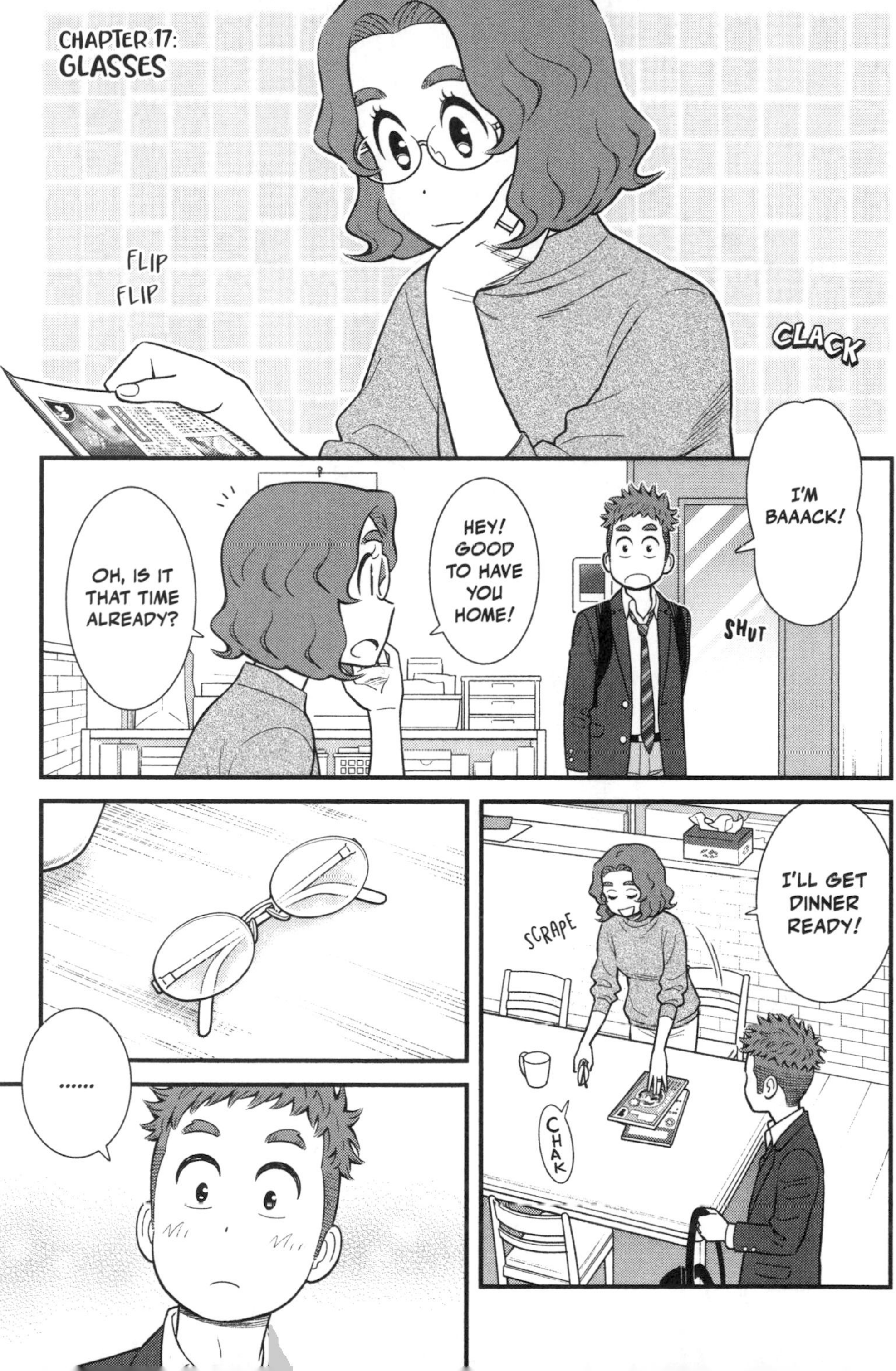
FLIP
FLIP
CLACK
I'M BAAACK!
SHUT
HEY! GOOD TO HAVE YOU HOME!
OH, IS IT THAT TIME ALREADY?
I'LL GET DINNER READY!
SCRAPE
CHAK
......

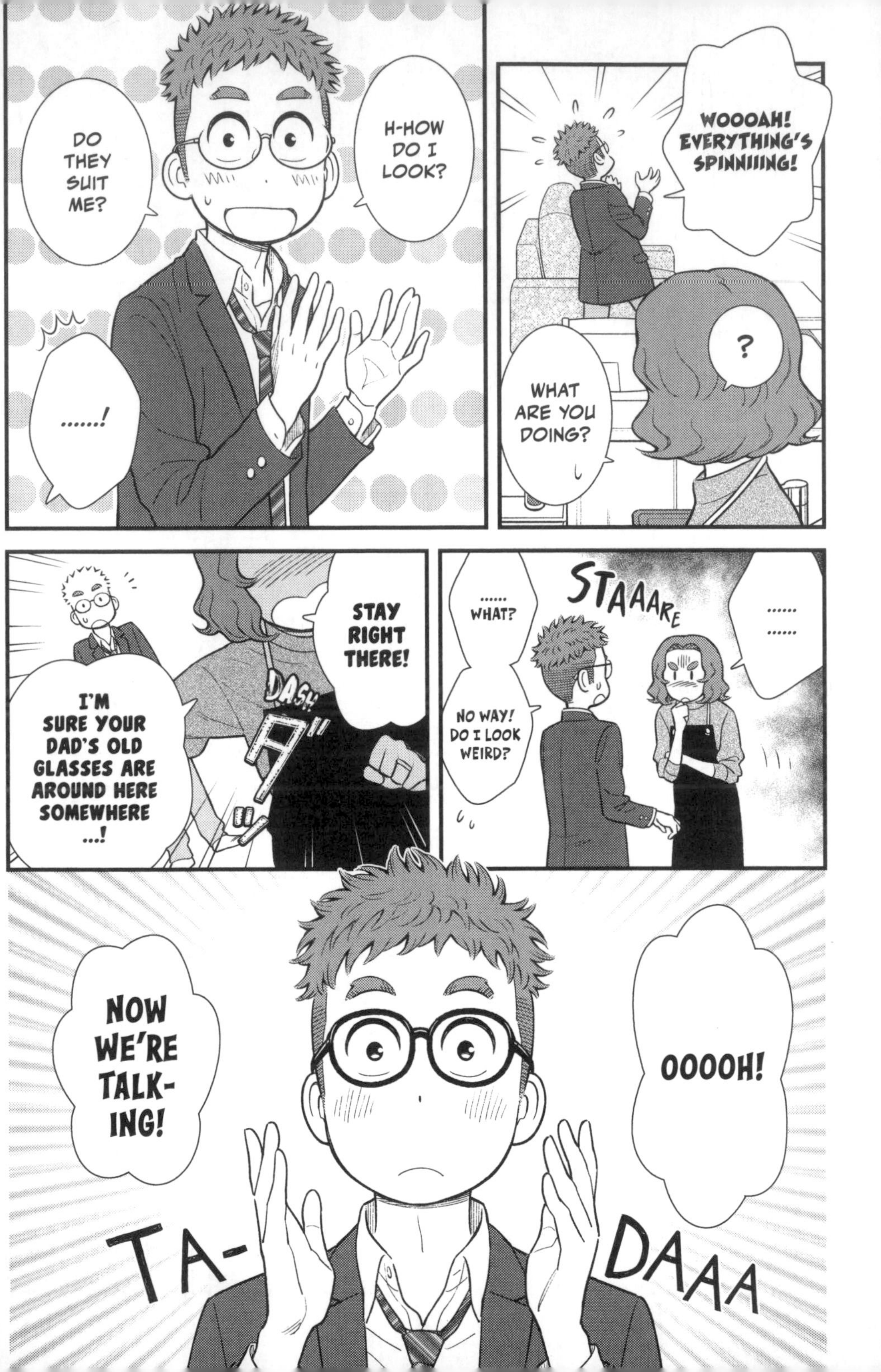
WOOOAH! EVERYTHING'S SPINNIIIING!
?
WHAT ARE YOU DOING?
H-HOW DO I LOOK?
DO THEY SUIT ME?
......!
STAAARE
....
...... WHAT?
NO WAY! DO I LOOK WEIRD?
STAY RIGHT THERE!
DASH
I'M SURE YOUR DAD'S OLD GLASSES ARE AROUND HERE SOMEWHERE ...!
OOOOH!
NOW WE'RE TALK-ING!
TA-DAAA

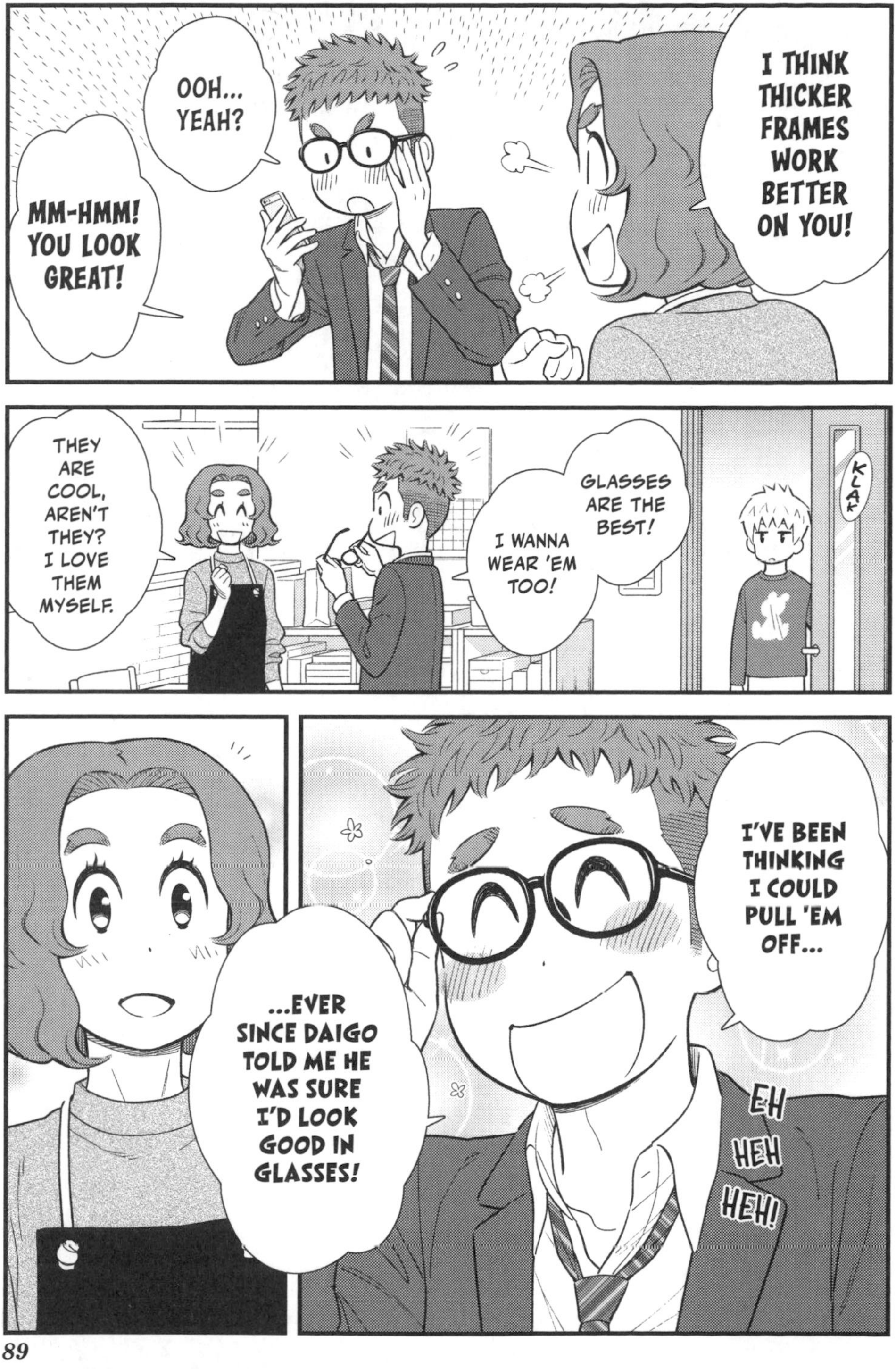
I THINK THICKER FRAMES WORK BETTER ON YOU!
OOH... YEAH?
MM-HMM! YOU LOOK GREAT!
KLAK
GLASSES ARE THE BEST!
I WANNA WEAR 'EM TOO!
THEY ARE COOL, AREN'T THEY? I LOVE THEM MYSELF.
I'VE BEEN THINKING I COULD PULL 'EM OFF...
EH HEH HEH!
...EVER SINCE DAIGO TOLD ME HE WAS SURE I'D LOOK GOOD IN GLASSES!

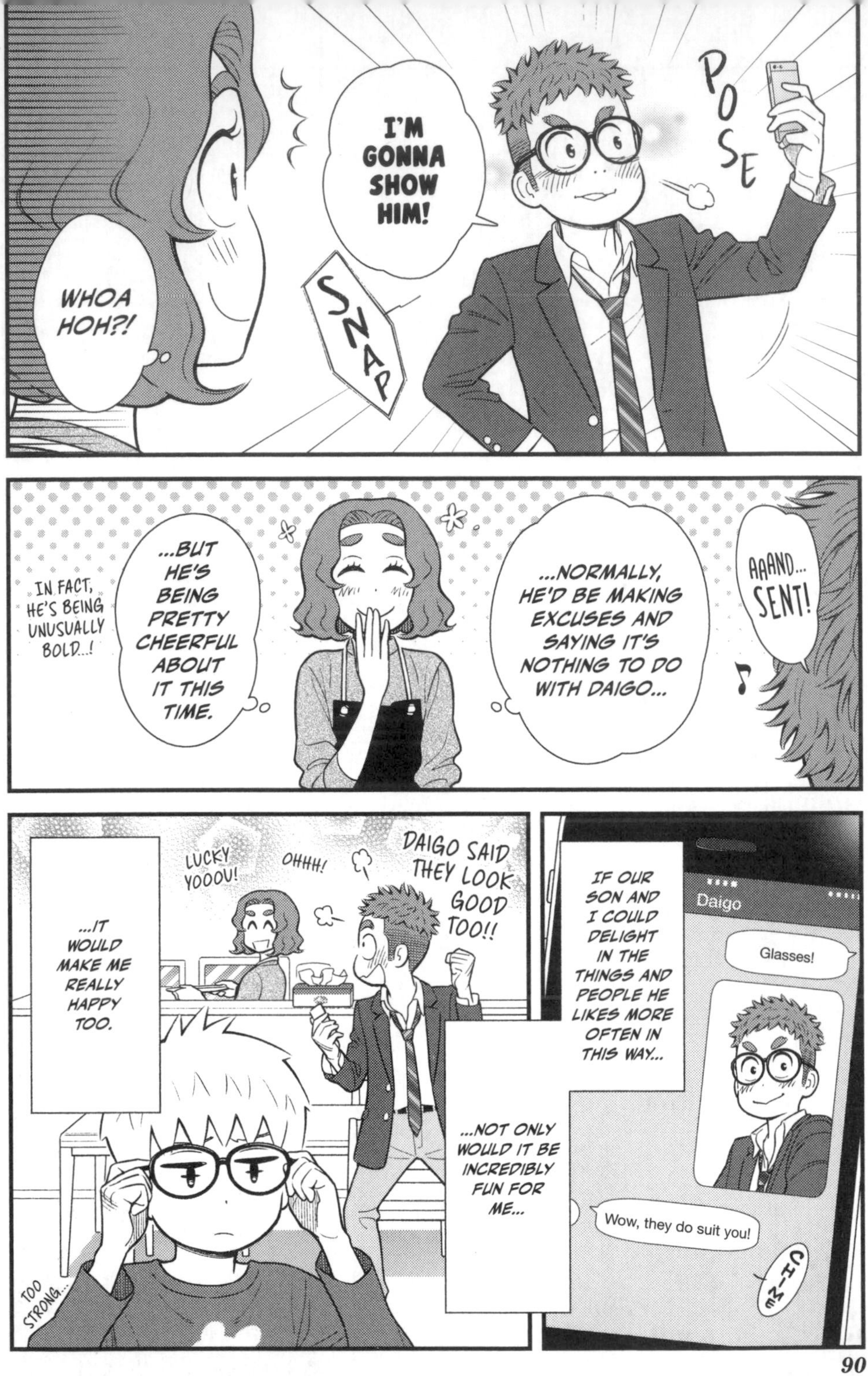
POSE
I'M GONNA SHOW HIM!
SNAP
WHOA HOH?!
AAAND... SENT!
♪
...NORMALLY, HE'D BE MAKING EXCUSES AND SAYING IT'S NOTHING TO DO WITH DAIGO...
...BUT HE'S BEING PRETTY CHEERFUL ABOUT IT THIS TIME.
IN FACT, HE'S BEING UNUSUALLY BOLD...!
Daigo
Glasses!
IF OUR SON AND I COULD DELIGHT IN THE THINGS AND PEOPLE HE LIKES MORE OFTEN IN THIS WAY...
Wow, they do suit you!
CHI-ME
...NOT ONLY WOULD IT BE INCREDIBLY FUN FOR ME...
DAIGO SAID THEY LOOK GOOD TOO!!
OHHH!
LUCKY YOOOU!
...IT WOULD MAKE ME REALLY HAPPY TOO.
TOO STRONG...

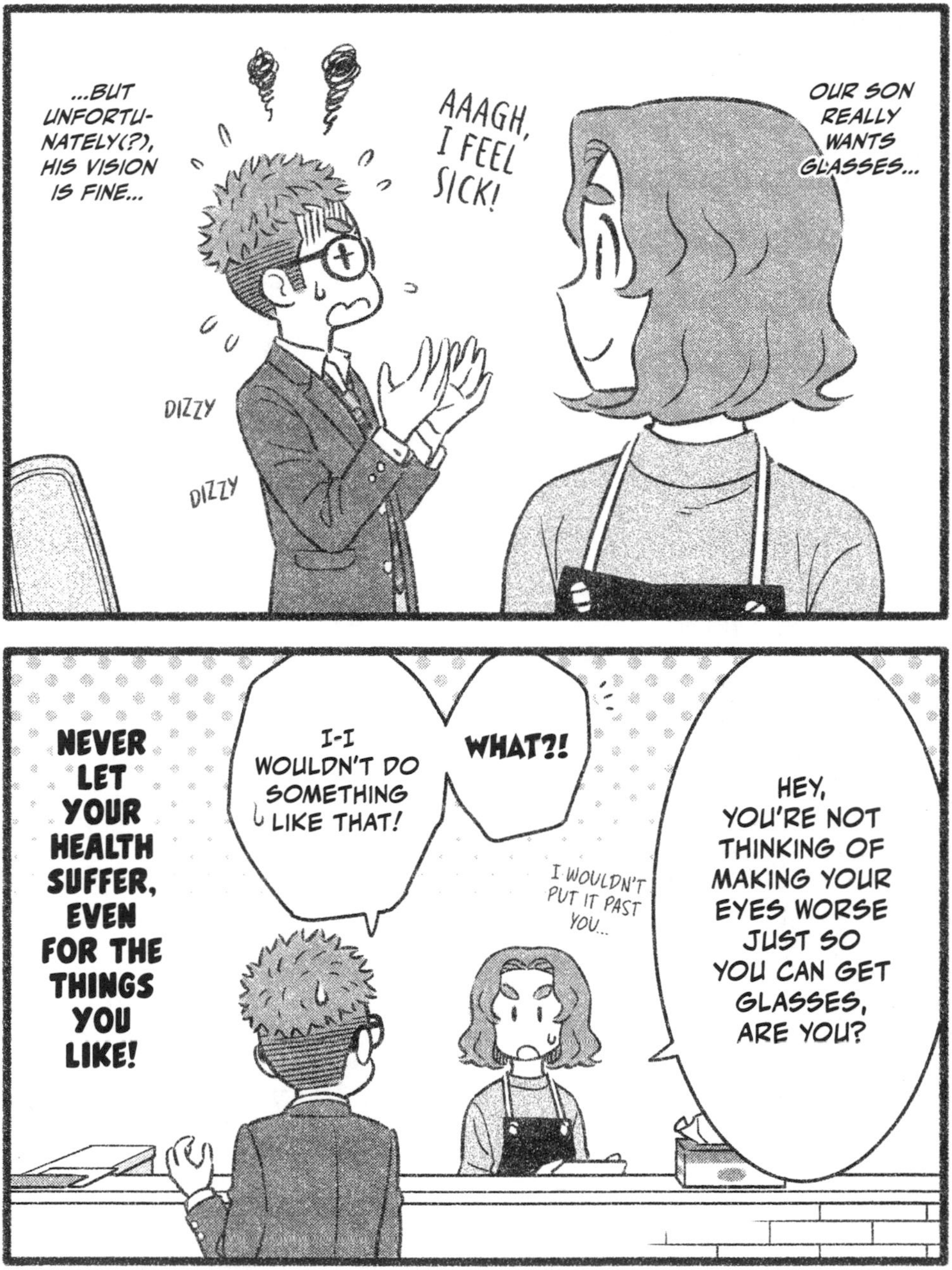
OUR SON REALLY WANTS GLASSES...
AAAGH, I FEEL SICK!
...BUT UNFORTU-NATELY(?), HIS VISION IS FINE...
DIZZY
DIZZY
HEY, YOU'RE NOT THINKING OF MAKING YOUR EYES WORSE JUST SO YOU CAN GET GLASSES, ARE YOU?
I WOULDN'T PUT IT PAST YOU...
WHAT?!
I-I WOULDN'T DO SOMETHING LIKE THAT!
NEVER LET YOUR HEALTH SUFFER, EVEN FOR THE THINGS YOU LIKE!

I Think Our Son Is Gay

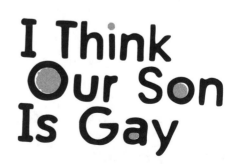

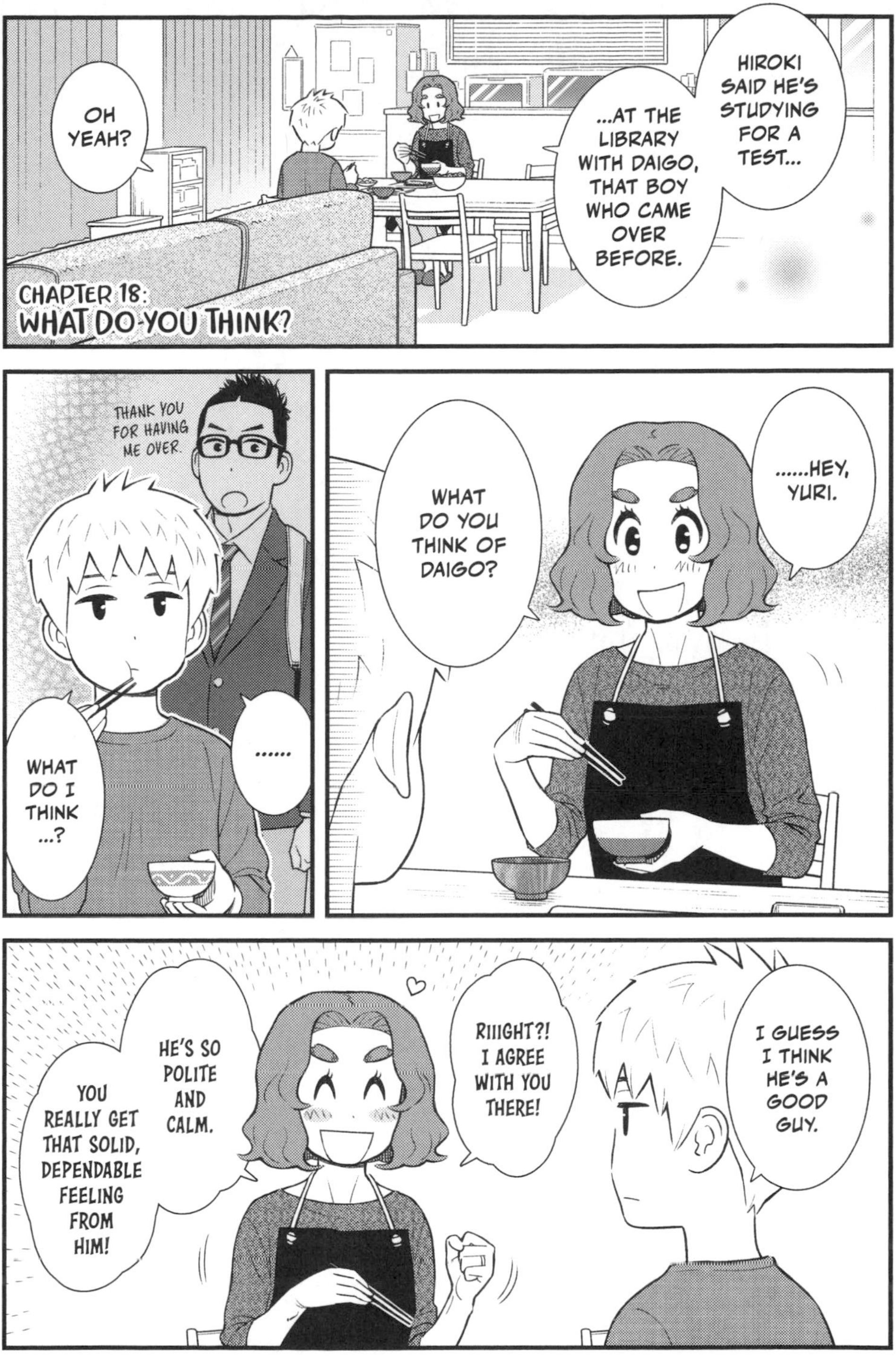
HIROKI SAID HE'S STUDYING FOR A TEST...
...AT THE LIBRARY WITH DAIGO, THAT BOY WHO CAME OVER BEFORE.
OH YEAH?
CHAPTER 18:
WHAT DO-YOU THINK?
......HEY, YURI.
WHAT DO YOU THINK OF DAIGO?
THANK YOU FOR HAVING ME OVER.
......
WHAT DO I THINK ...?
I GUESS I THINK HE'S A GOOD GUY.
RIIIGHT?! I AGREE WITH YOU THERE!
HE'S SO POLITE AND CALM.
YOU REALLY GET THAT SOLID, DEPENDABLE FEELING FROM HIM!

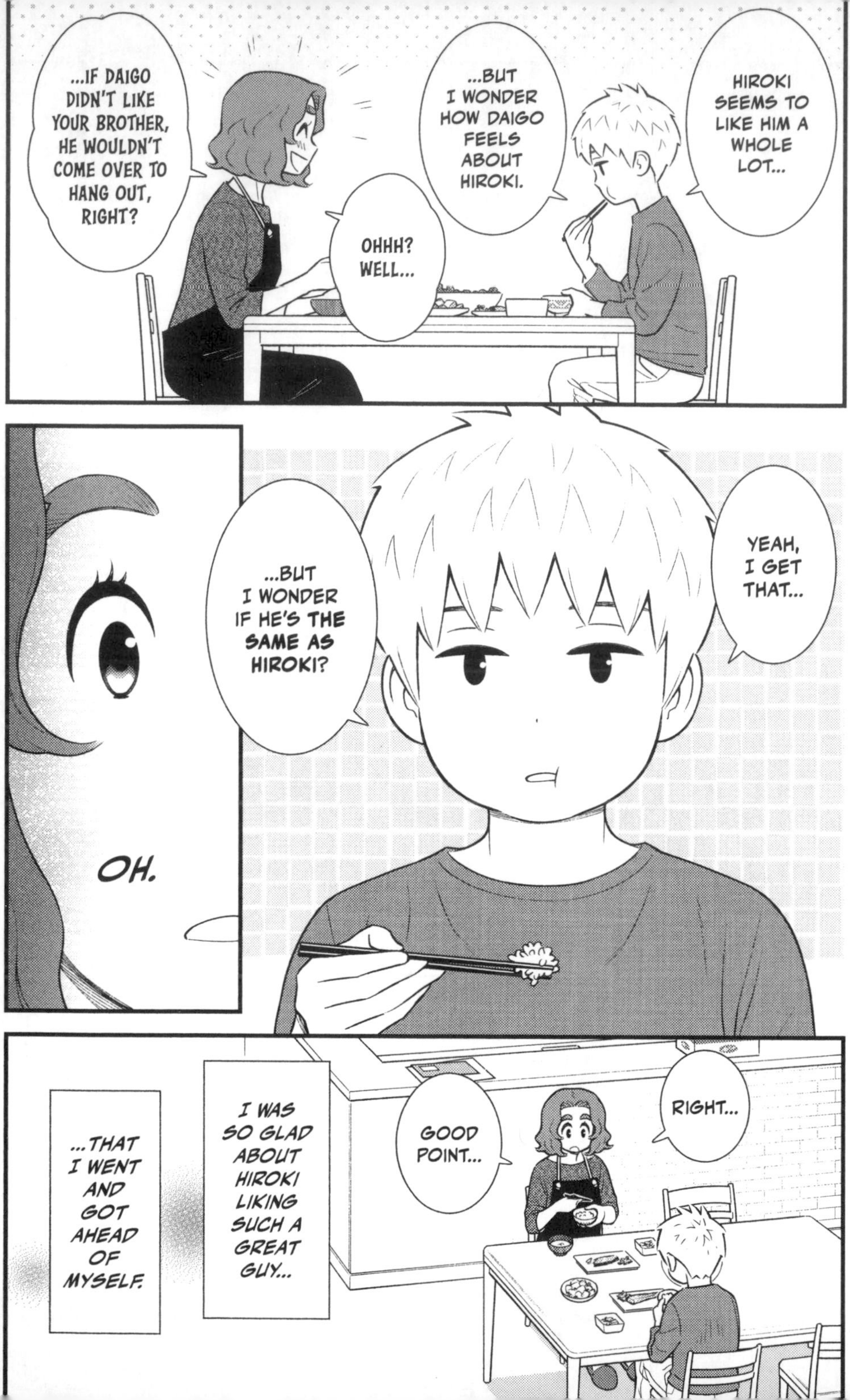
HIROKI SEEMS TO LIKE HIM A WHOLE LOT...
...BUT I WONDER HOW DAIGO FEELS ABOUT HIROKI.
OHHH? WELL...
...IF DAIGO DIDN'T LIKE YOUR BROTHER, HE WOULDN'T COME OVER TO HANG OUT, RIGHT?
YEAH, I GET THAT...
...BUT I WONDER IF HE'S THE SAME AS HIROKI?
OH.
RIGHT...
GOOD POINT...
I WAS SO GLAD ABOUT HIROKI LIKING SUCH A GREAT GUY...
...THAT I WENT AND GOT AHEAD OF MYSELF.

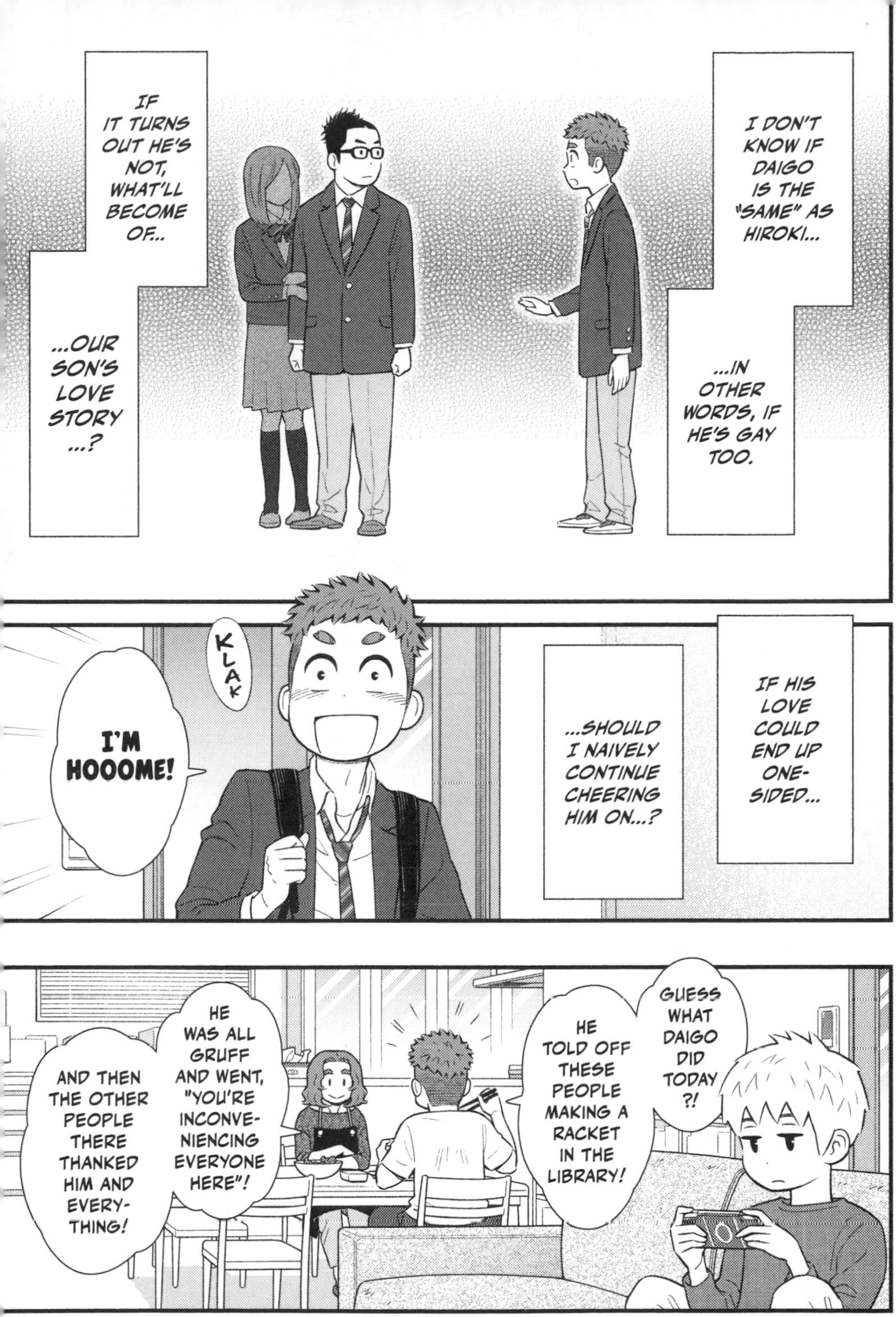
I DON'T KNOW IF DAIGO IS THE "SAME" AS HIROKI...
...IN OTHER WORDS, IF HE'S GAY TOO.
IF IT TURNS OUT HE'S NOT, WHAT'LL BECOME OF...
...OUR SON'S LOVE STORY ...?
IF HIS LOVE COULD END UP ONE-SIDED...
...SHOULD I NAIVELY CONTINUE CHEERING HIM ON...?
KLAK
I'M HOOOME!
GUESS WHAT DAIGO DID TODAY ?!
HE TOLD OFF THESE PEOPLE MAKING A RACKET IN THE LIBRARY!
HE WAS ALL GRUFF AND WENT, "YOU'RE INCONVE-NIENCING EVERYONE HERE"!
AND THEN THE OTHER PEOPLE THERE THANKED HIM AND EVERY-THING!

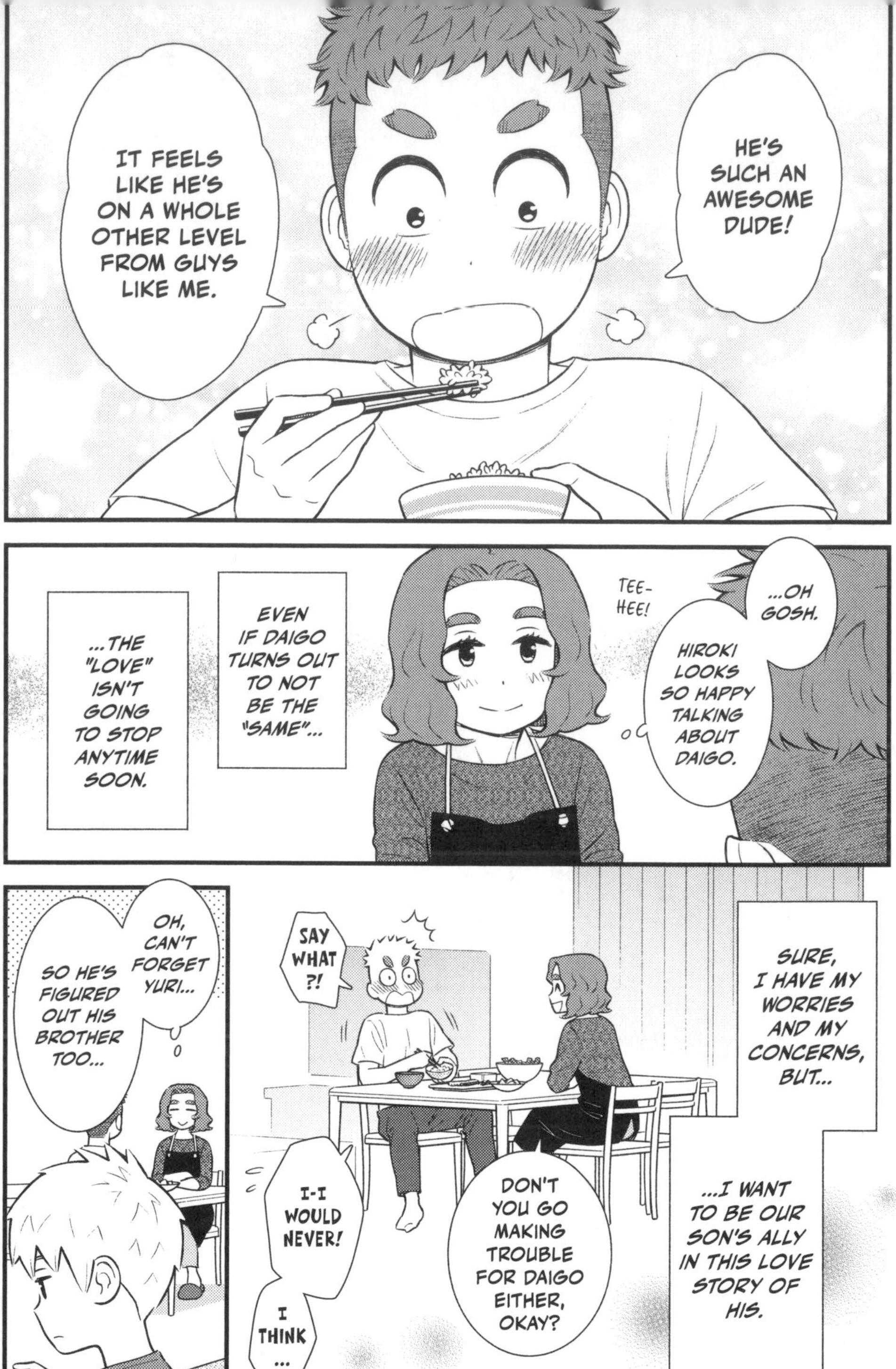
HE'S SUCH AN AWESOME DUDE!
IT FEELS LIKE HE'S ON A WHOLE OTHER LEVEL FROM GUYS LIKE ME.
...OH GOSH.
HIROKI LOOKS SO HAPPY TALKING ABOUT DAIGO.
TEE-HEE!
EVEN IF DAIGO TURNS OUT TO NOT BE THE "SAME"...
...THE "LOVE" ISN'T GOING TO STOP ANYTIME SOON.
SURE, I HAVE MY WORRIES AND MY CONCERNS, BUT...
...I WANT TO BE OUR SON'S ALLY IN THIS LOVE STORY OF HIS.
SAY WHAT?!
DON'T YOU GO MAKING TROUBLE FOR DAIGO EITHER, OKAY?
I-I WOULD NEVER!
I THINK...
OH, CAN'T FORGET YURI...
SO HE'S FIGURED OUT HIS BROTHER TOO...

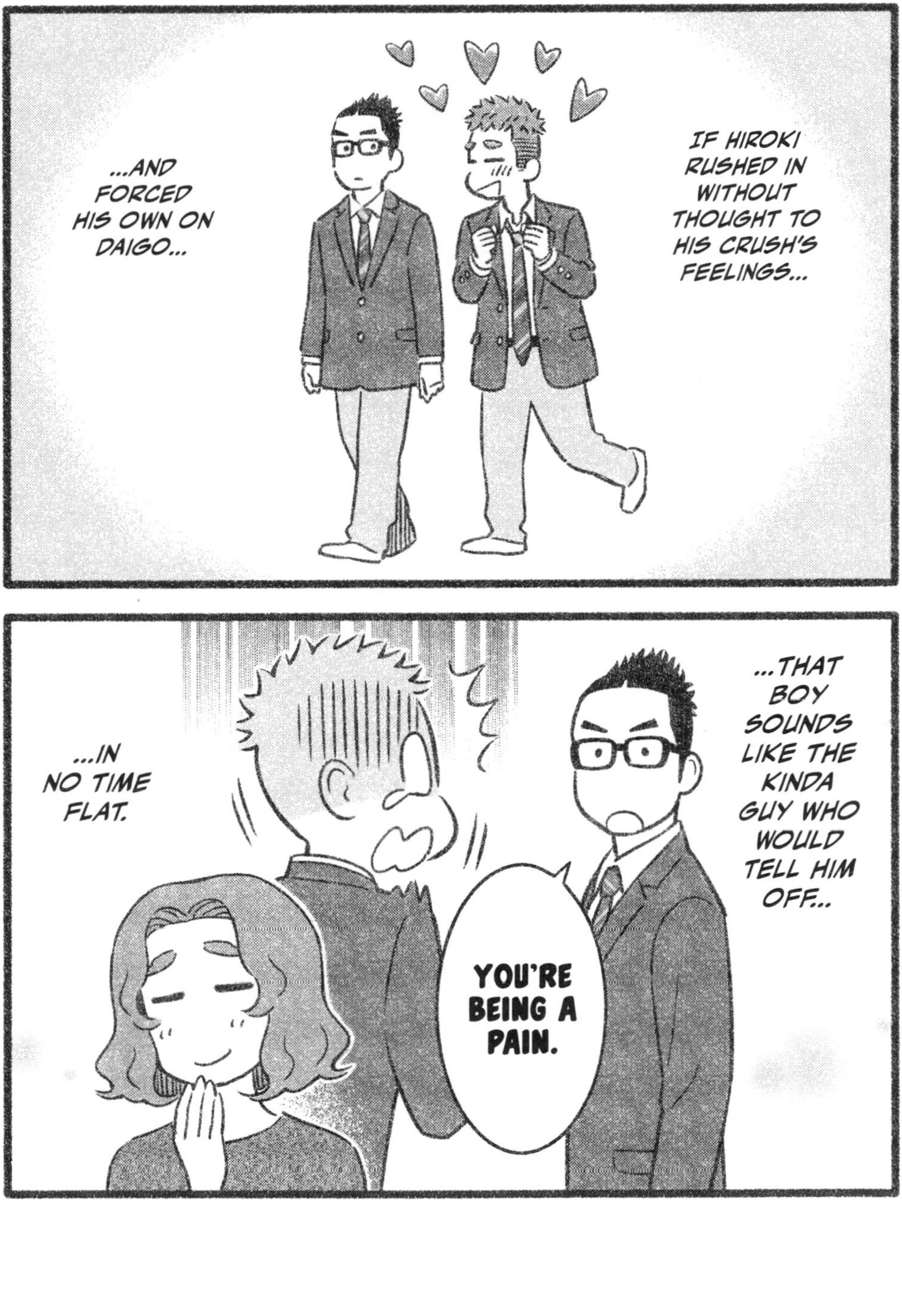
IF HIROKI RUSHED IN WITHOUT THOUGHT TO HIS CRUSH'S FEELINGS...
...AND FORCED HIS OWN ON DAIGO...
...THAT BOY SOUNDS LIKE THE KINDA GUY WHO WOULD TELL HIM OFF...
...IN NO TIME FLAT.
YOU'RE BEING A PAIN.

I Think
Our Son
Is Gay

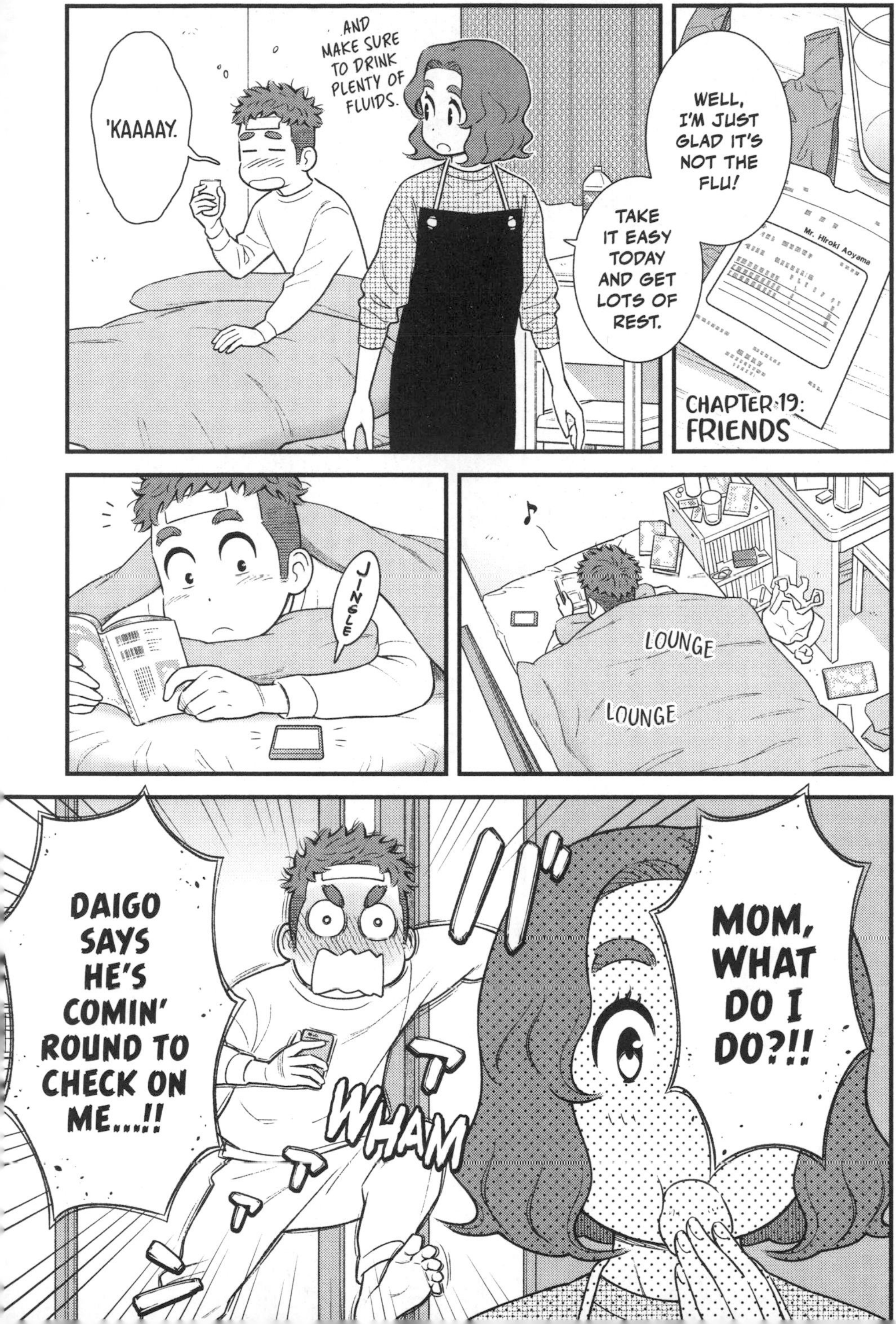
WELL, I'M JUST GLAD IT'S NOT THE FLU!
TAKE IT EASY TODAY AND GET LOTS OF REST.
Mr. Hiroki Aoyama
CHAPTER 19: FRIENDS
AND MAKE SURE TO DRINK PLENTY OF FLUIDS.
'KAAAAY.
LOUNGE
LOUNGE
JINGLE
MOM, WHAT DO I DO?!!
DAIGO SAYS HE'S COMIN' ROUND TO CHECK ON ME...!!
WHAM

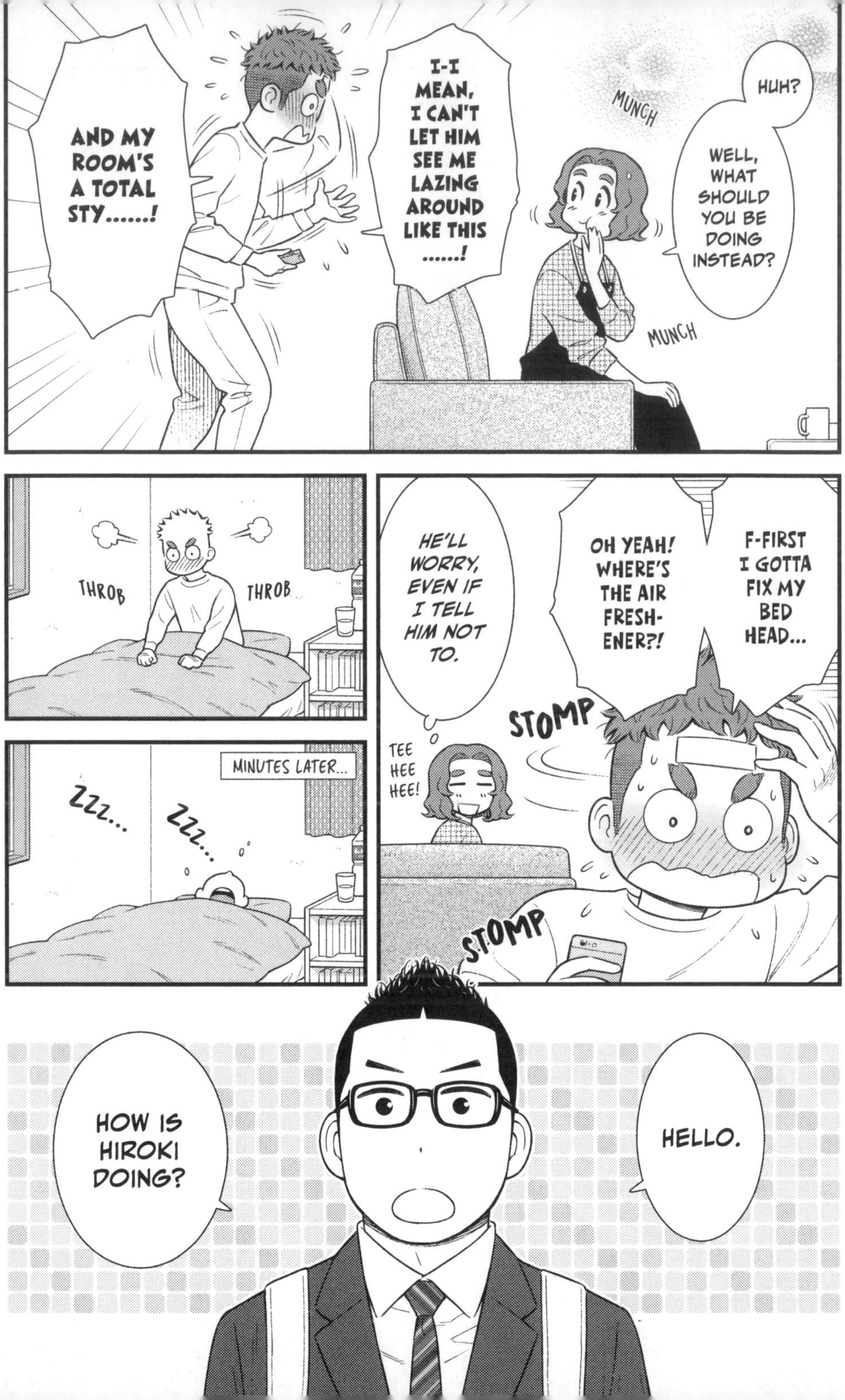
HUH?
MUNCH
WELL, WHAT SHOULD YOU BE DOING INSTEAD?
MUNCH
I-I MEAN, I CAN'T LET HIM SEE ME LAZING AROUND LIKE THIS ......!
AND MY ROOM'S A TOTAL STY......!
F-FIRST I GOTTA FIX MY BED HEAD...
OH YEAH! WHERE'S THE AIR FRESH-ENER?!
HE'LL WORRY, EVEN IF I TELL HIM NOT TO.
STOMP
TEE HEE HEE!
STOMP
THROB
THROB
MINUTES LATER...
ZZZ...
ZZZ...
HELLO.
HOW IS HIROKI DOING?

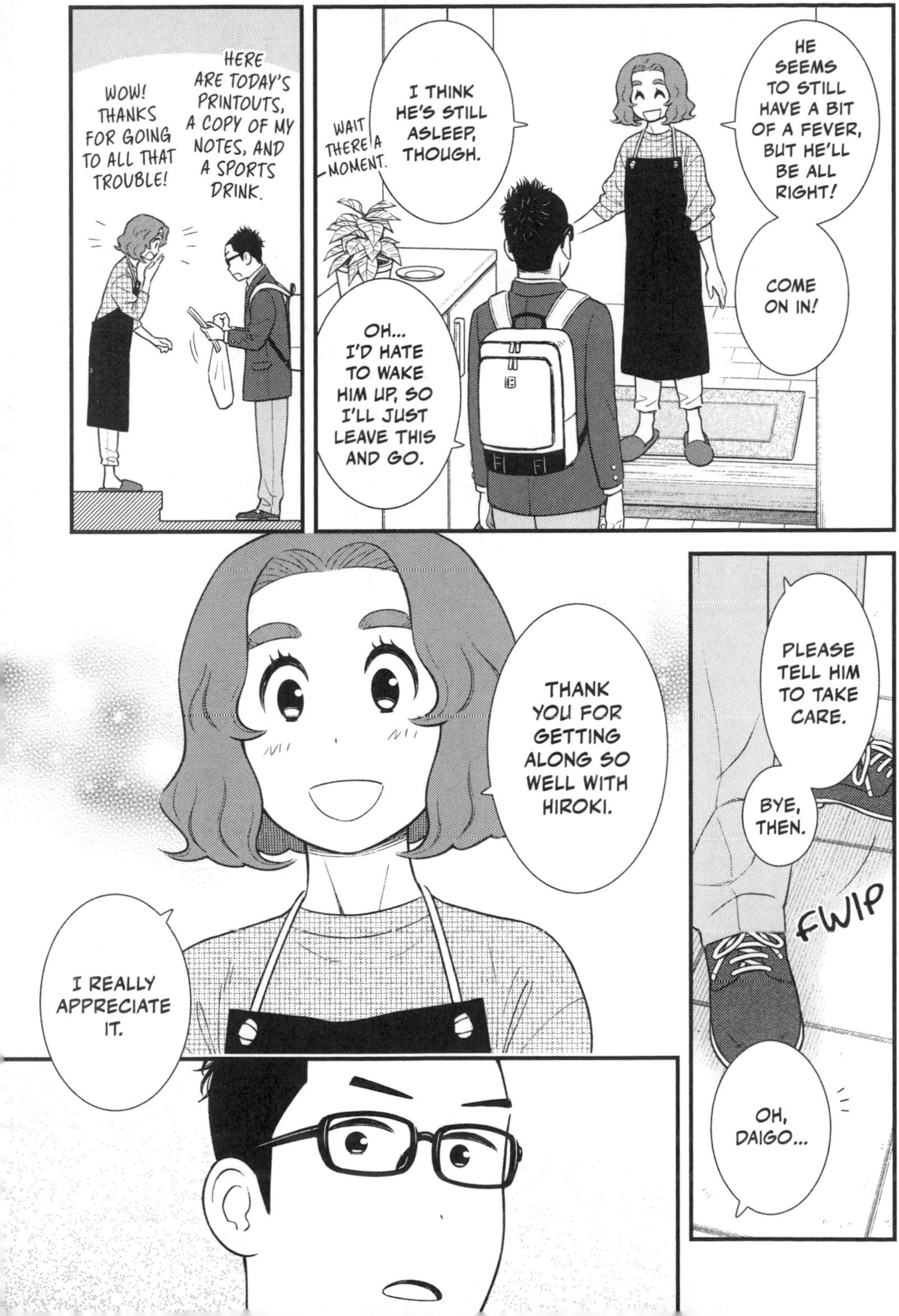
HE SEEMS TO STILL HAVE A BIT OF A FEVER, BUT HE'LL BE ALL RIGHT!
COME ON IN!
I THINK HE'S STILL ASLEEP, THOUGH.
WAIT THERE A MOMENT.
OH... I'D HATE TO WAKE HIM UP, SO I'LL JUST LEAVE THIS AND GO.
HERE ARE TODAY'S PRINTOUTS, A COPY OF MY NOTES, AND A SPORTS DRINK.
WOW! THANKS FOR GOING TO ALL THAT TROUBLE!
PLEASE TELL HIM TO TAKE CARE.
BYE, THEN.
FWIP
OH, DAIGO...
THANK YOU FOR GETTING ALONG SO WELL WITH HIROKI.
I REALLY APPRECIATE IT.

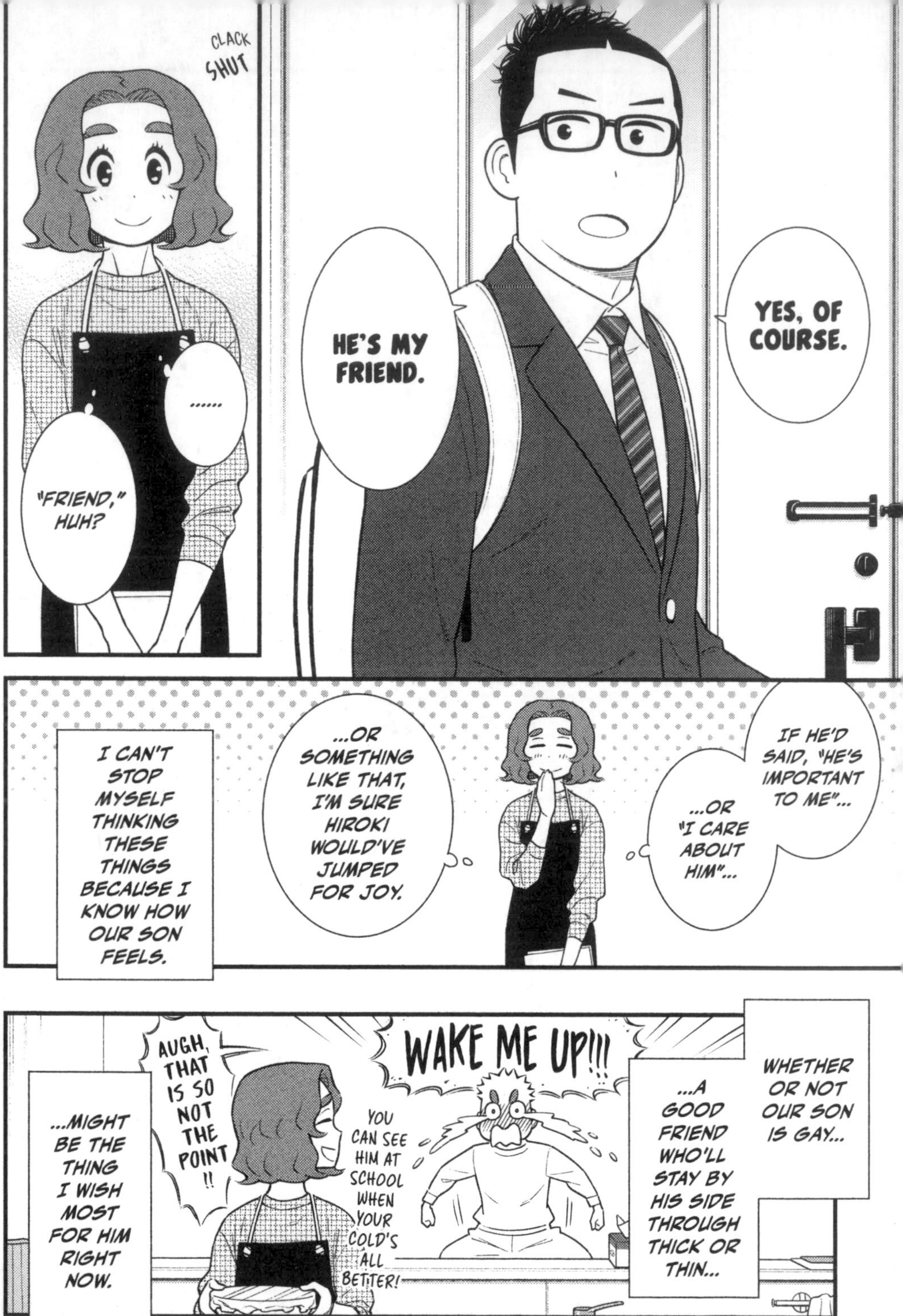

YES, OF COURSE.
HE'S MY FRIEND.
CLACK
SHUT
......
"FRIEND," HUH?
IF HE'D SAID, "HE'S IMPORTANT TO ME"...
...OR "I CARE ABOUT HIM"...
...OR SOMETHING LIKE THAT, I'M SURE HIROKI WOULD'VE JUMPED FOR JOY.
I CAN'T STOP MYSELF THINKING THESE THINGS BECAUSE I KNOW HOW OUR SON FEELS.
WHETHER OR NOT OUR SON IS GAY...
...A GOOD FRIEND WHO'LL STAY BY HIS SIDE THROUGH THICK OR THIN...
WAKE ME UP!!!
YOU CAN SEE HIM AT SCHOOL WHEN YOUR COLD'S ALL BETTER!
AUGH, THAT IS SO NOT THE POINT!!
...MIGHT BE THE THING I WISH MOST FOR HIM RIGHT NOW.

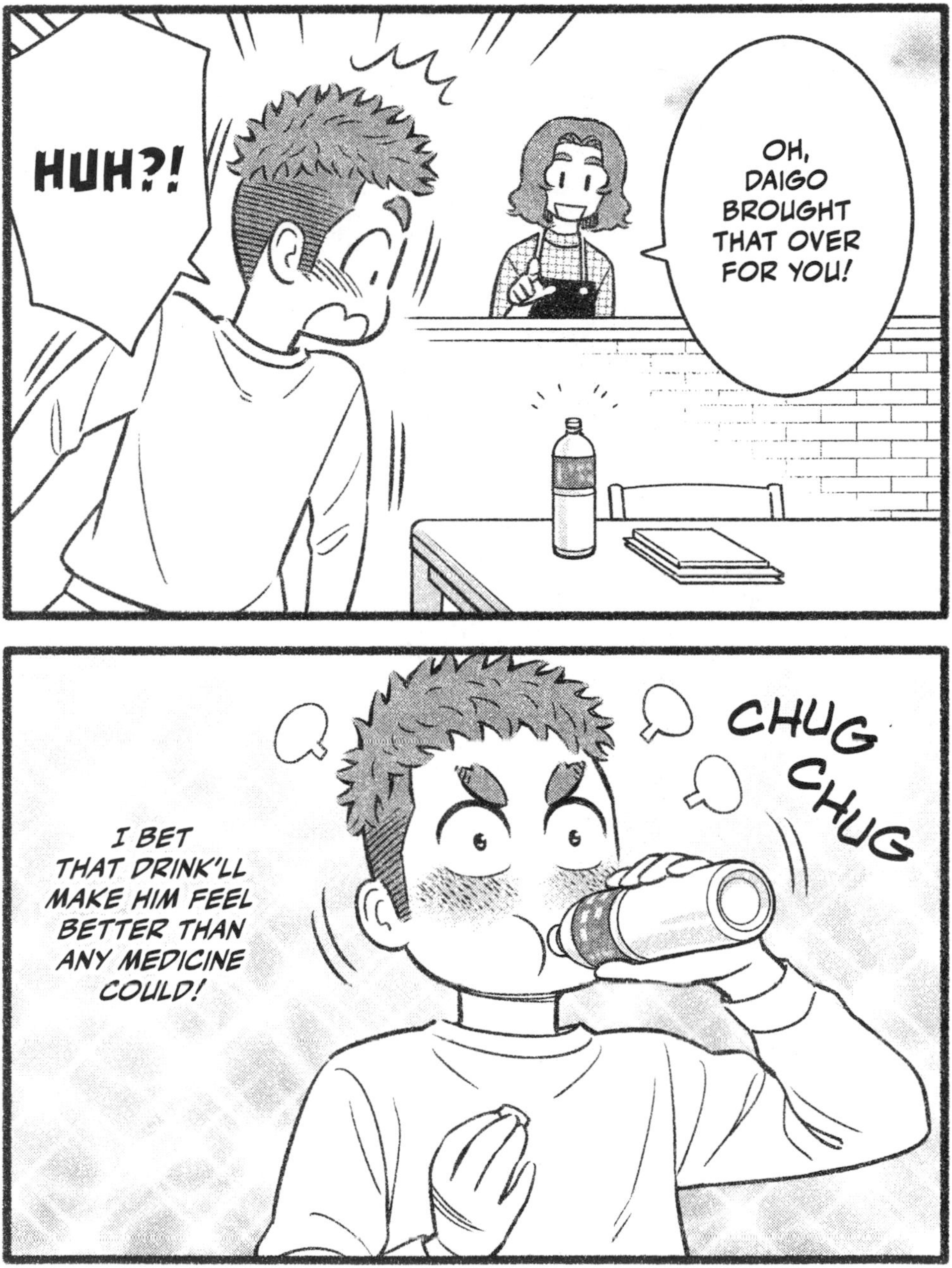
OH, DAIGO BROUGHT THAT OVER FOR YOU!
HUH?!
CHUG CHUG
I BET THAT DRINK'LL MAKE HIM FEEL BETTER THAN ANY MEDICINE COULD!

I Think Our Son Is Gay

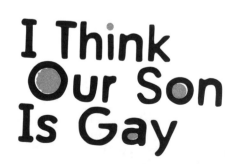

CHAPTER 20: PRESENT

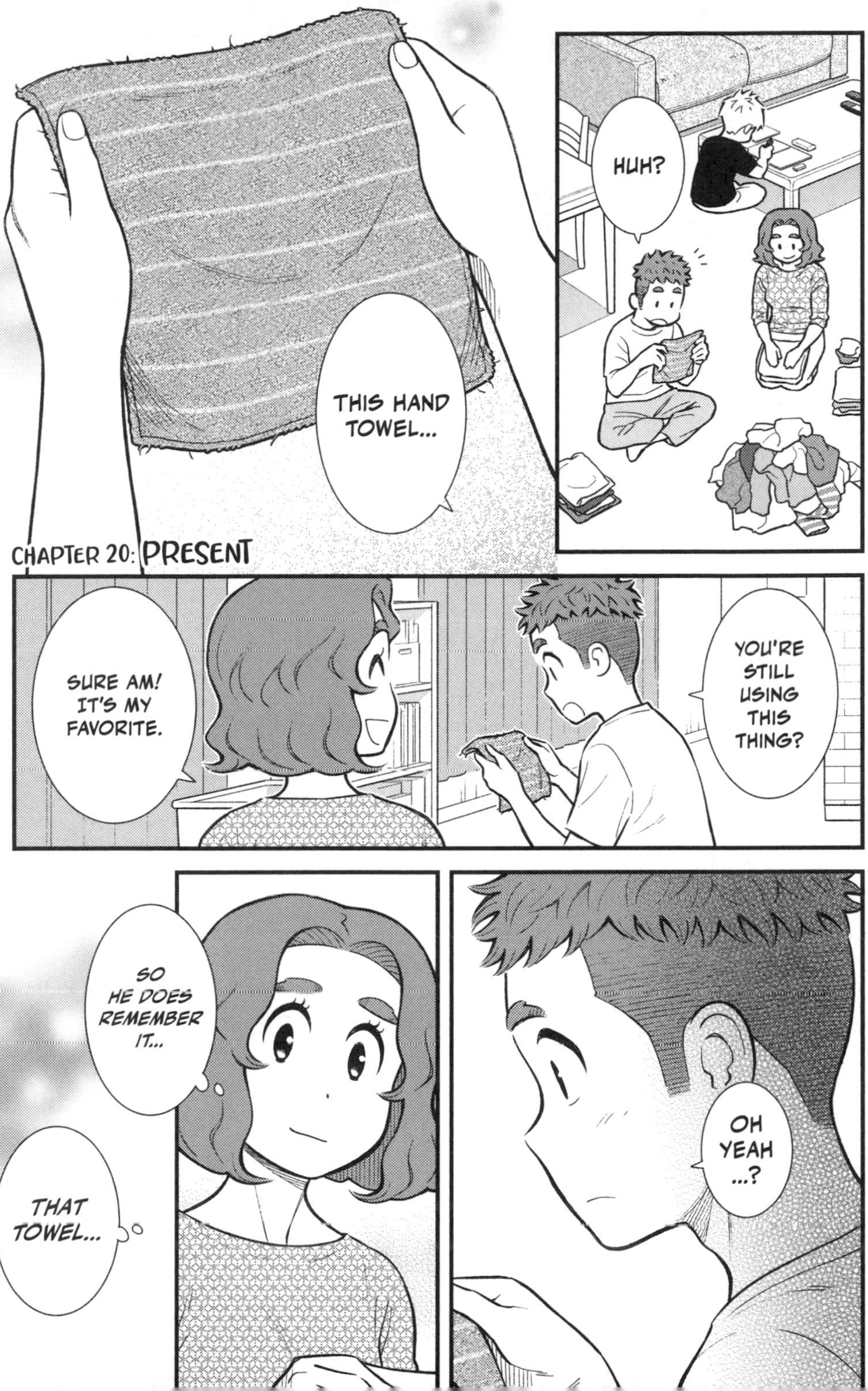
HUH?
THIS HAND TOWEL...
YOU'RE STILL USING THIS THING?
SURE AM! IT'S MY FAVORITE.
OH YEAH ...?
SO HE DOES REMEMBER IT...
THAT TOWEL...

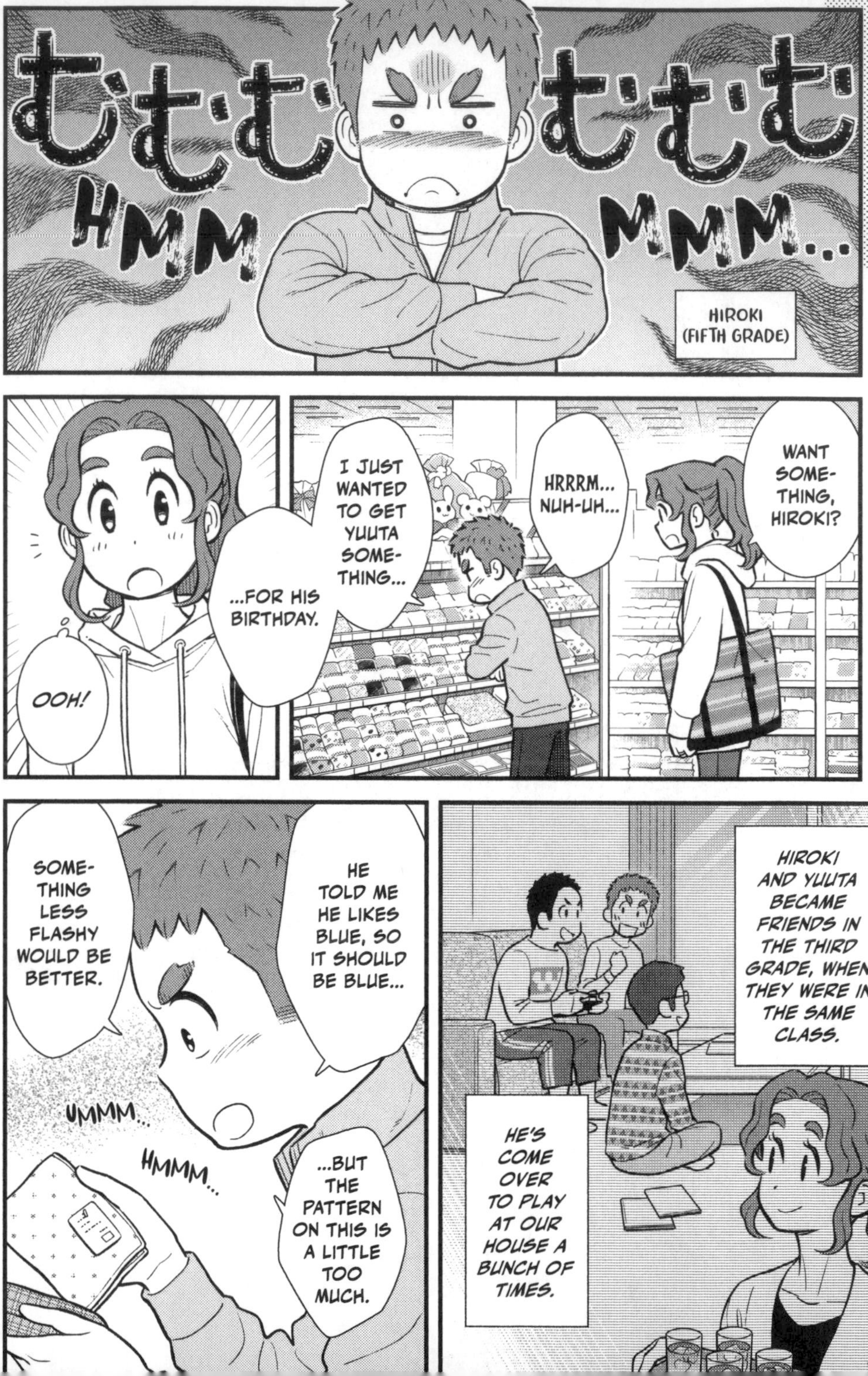
むむむ
むむむ
HMM MMM...
HIROKI (FIFTH GRADE)
WANT SOMETHING, HIROKI?
HRRRM... NUH-UH...
I JUST WANTED TO GET YUUTA SOMETHING...
...FOR HIS BIRTHDAY.
OOH!
HIROKI AND YUUTA BECAME FRIENDS IN THE THIRD GRADE, WHEN THEY WERE IN THE SAME CLASS.
HE'S COME OVER TO PLAY AT OUR HOUSE A BUNCH OF TIMES.
HE TOLD ME HE LIKES BLUE, SO IT SHOULD BE BLUE...
SOMETHING LESS FLASHY WOULD BE BETTER.
...BUT THE PATTERN ON THIS IS A LITTLE TOO MUCH.
UMMM...
HMMM...

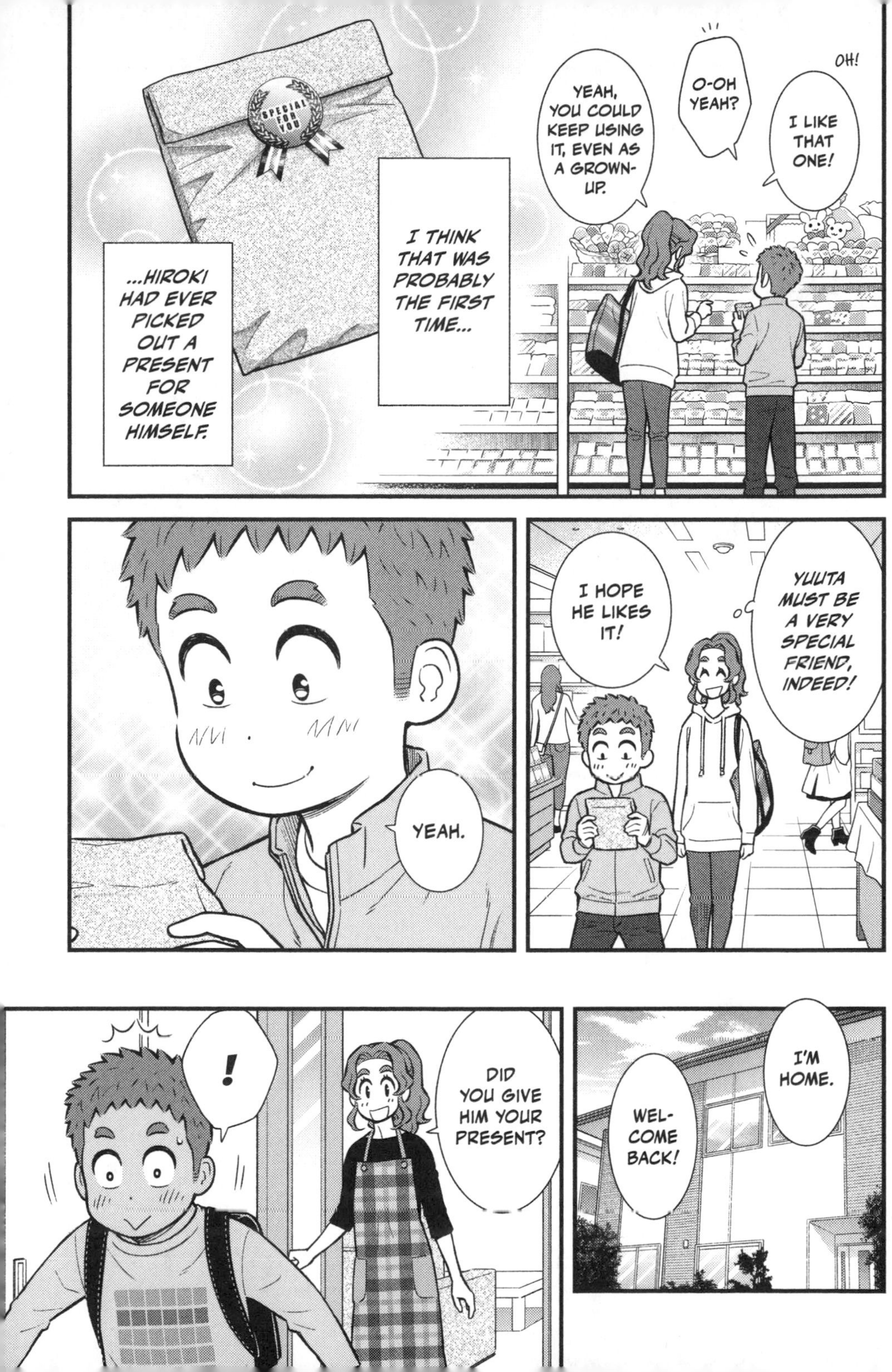
OH!
I LIKE THAT ONE!
O-OH YEAH?
YEAH, YOU COULD KEEP USING IT, EVEN AS A GROWN-UP.
I THINK THAT WAS PROBABLY THE FIRST TIME...
...HIROKI HAD EVER PICKED OUT A PRESENT FOR SOMEONE HIMSELF.
SPECIAL FOR YOU
YUUTA MUST BE A VERY SPECIAL FRIEND, INDEED!
I HOPE HE LIKES IT!
YEAH.
I'M HOME.
WEL-COME BACK!
DID YOU GIVE HIM YOUR PRESENT?
!

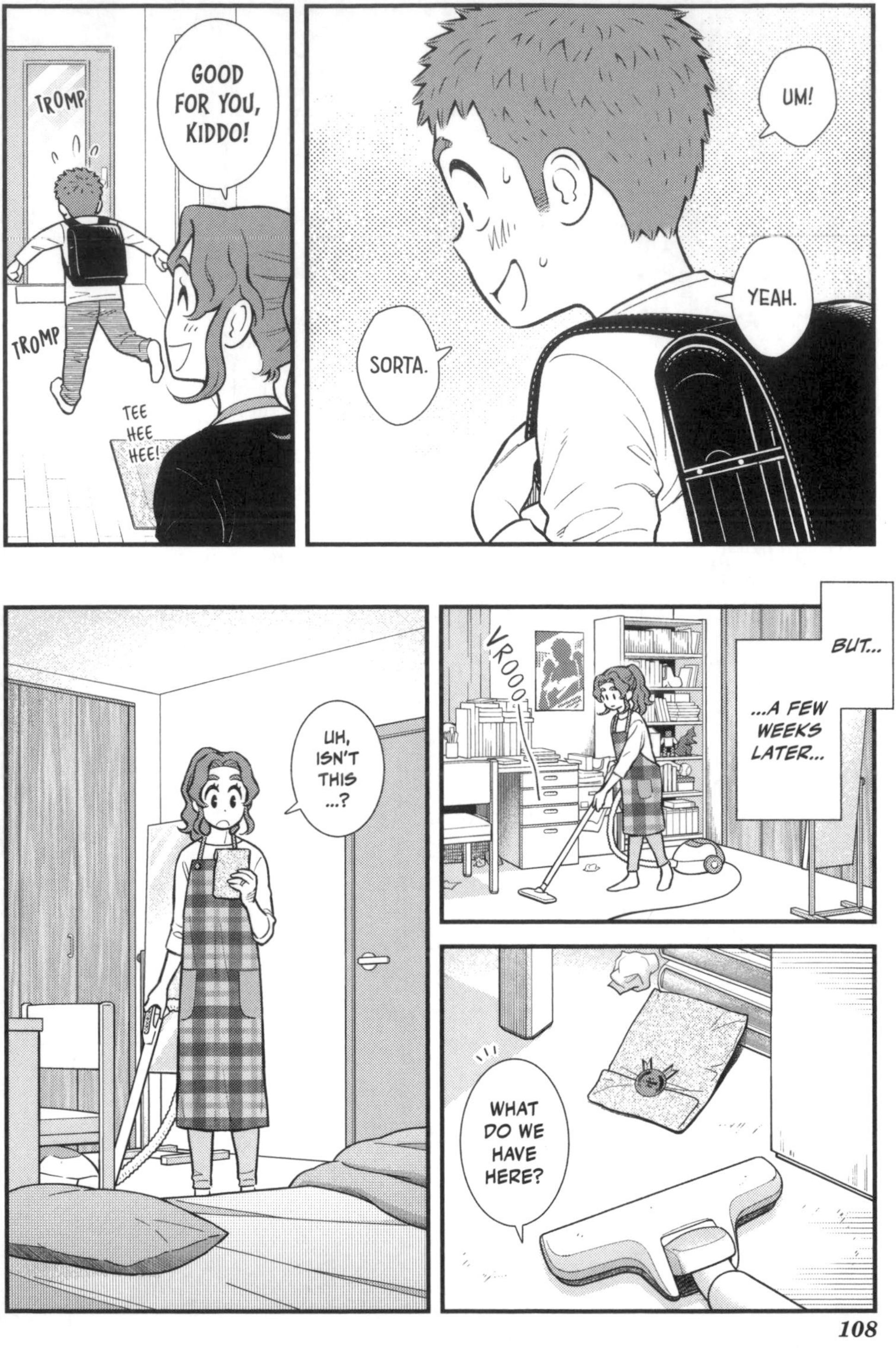
UM!
YEAH.
SORTA.
GOOD FOR YOU, KIDDO!
TROMP
TROMP
TEE HEE HEE!
BUT...
...A FEW WEEKS LATER...
VROOO
WHAT DO WE HAVE HERE?
UH, ISN'T THIS ...?

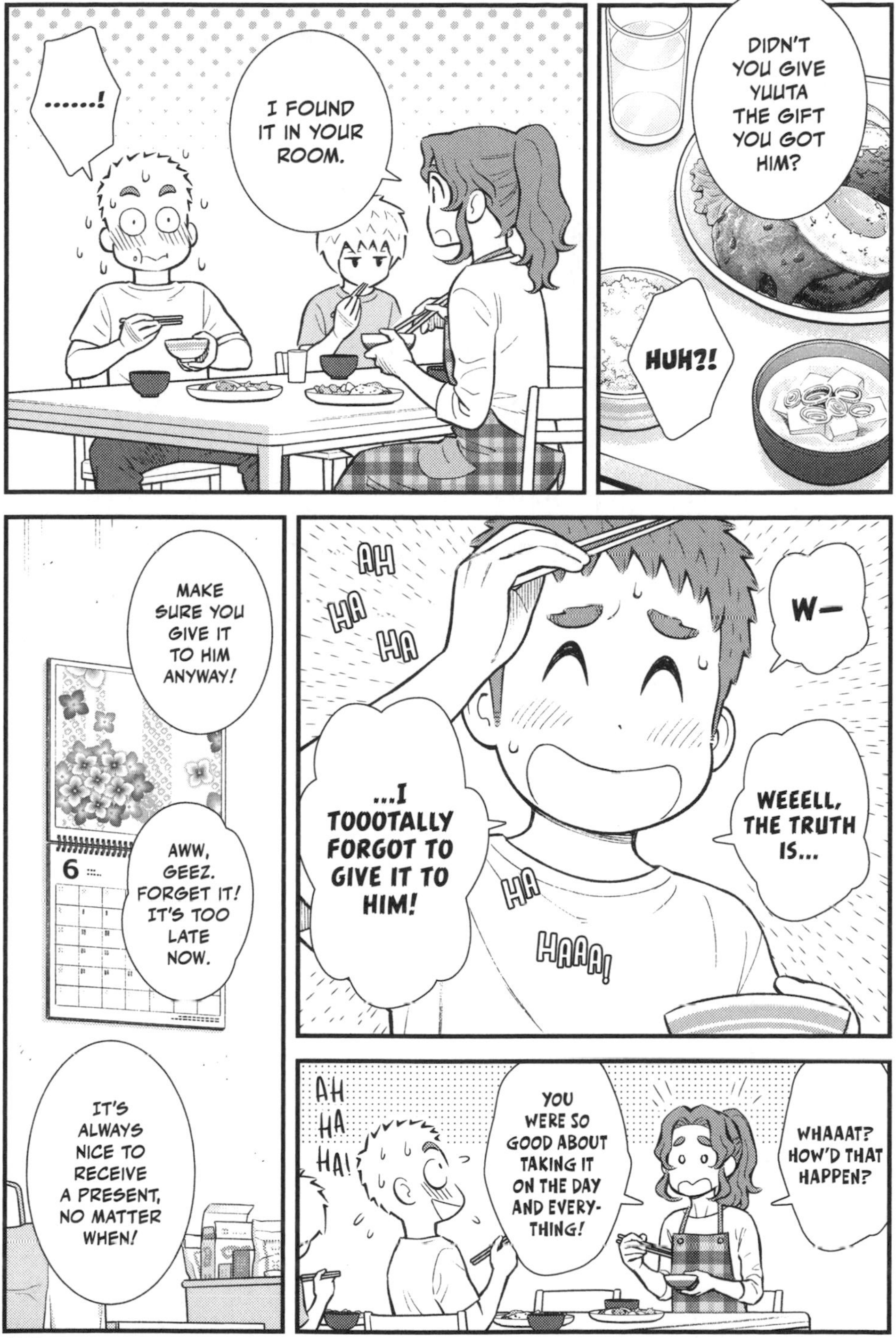
DIDN'T YOU GIVE YUUTA THE GIFT YOU GOT HIM?
HUH?!
I FOUND IT IN YOUR ROOM.
......!
W—
WEEELL, THE TRUTH IS...
AH HA HA
...I TOOOTALLY FORGOT TO GIVE IT TO HIM!
HA HAAA!
WHAAAT? HOW'D THAT HAPPEN?
YOU WERE SO GOOD ABOUT TAKING IT ON THE DAY AND EVERY-THING!
AH HA HA!
MAKE SURE YOU GIVE IT TO HIM ANYWAY!
6
AWW, GEEZ. FORGET IT! IT'S TOO LATE NOW.
IT'S ALWAYS NICE TO RECEIVE A PRESENT, NO MATTER WHEN!

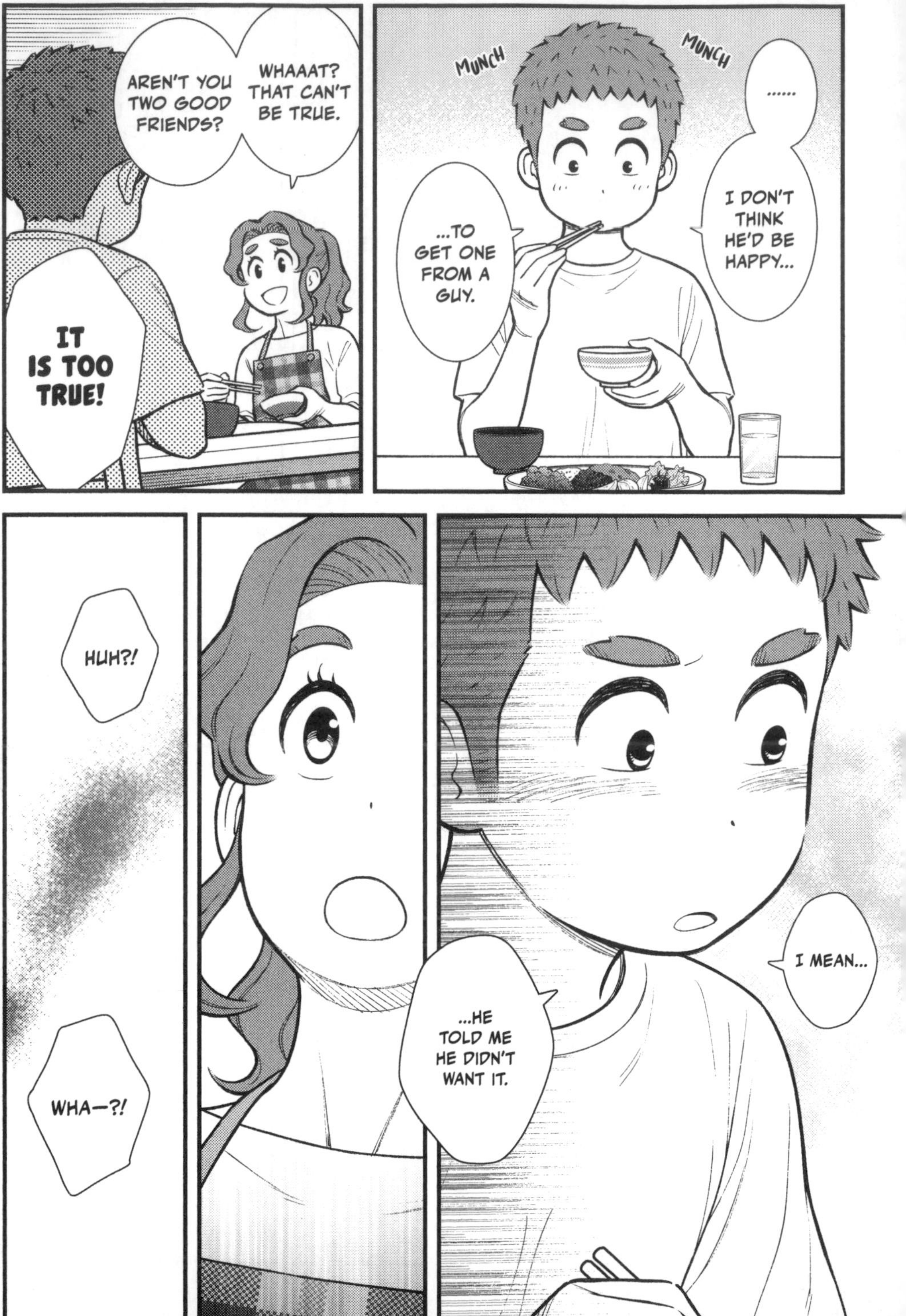
MUNCH
MUNCH
......
I DON'T THINK HE'D BE HAPPY...
...TO GET ONE FROM A GUY.
WHAAAT? THAT CAN'T BE TRUE.
AREN'T YOU TWO GOOD FRIENDS?
IT IS TOO TRUE!
I MEAN...
...HE TOLD ME HE DIDN'T WANT IT.
HUH?!
WHA—?!

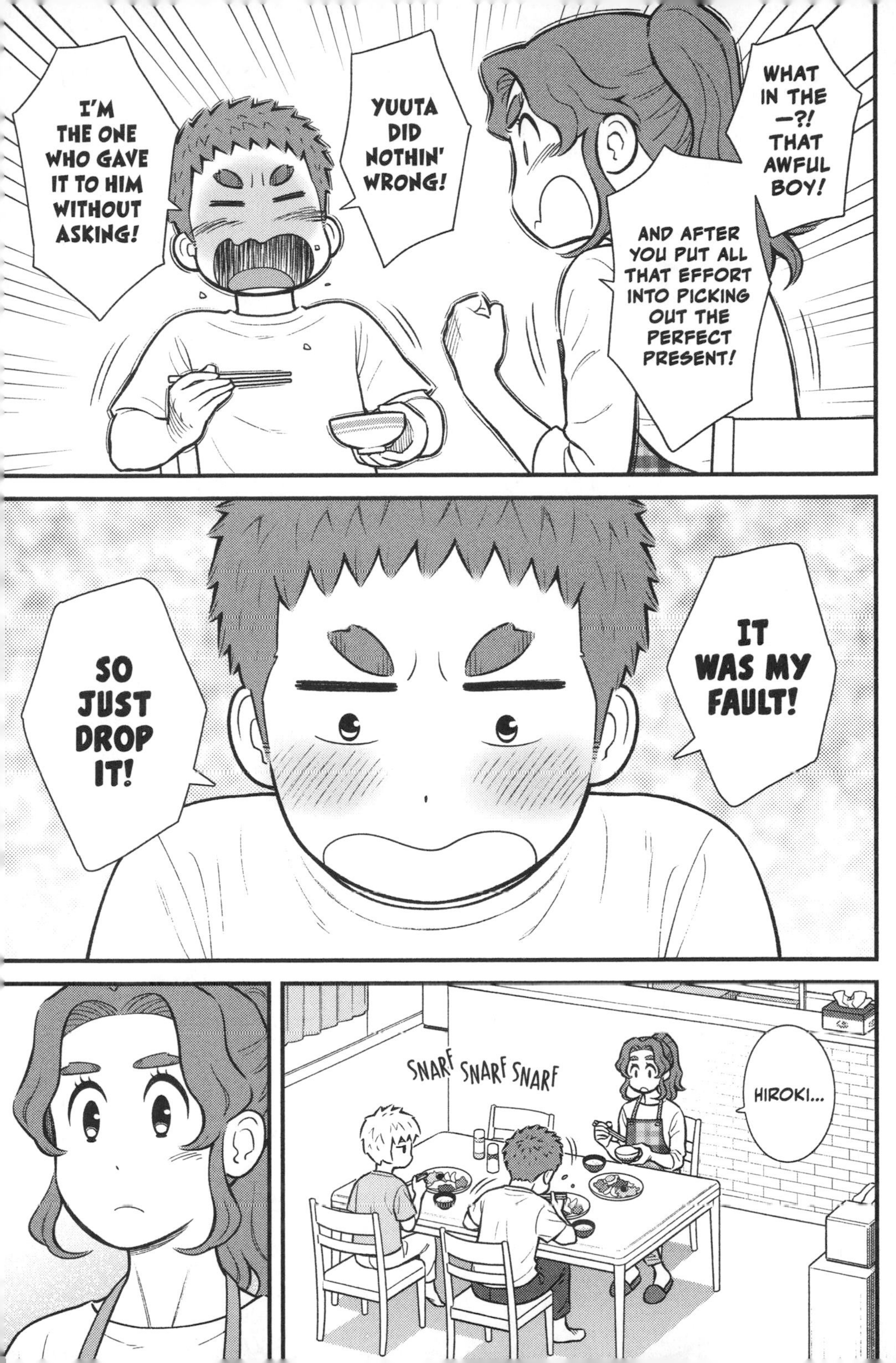
WHAT IN THE —?! THAT AWFUL BOY!
AND AFTER YOU PUT ALL THAT EFFORT INTO PICKING OUT THE PERFECT PRESENT!
YUUTA DID NOTHIN' WRONG!
I'M THE ONE WHO GAVE IT TO HIM WITHOUT ASKING!
IT WAS MY FAULT!
SO JUST DROP IT!
HIROKI...
SNARF SNARF SNARF

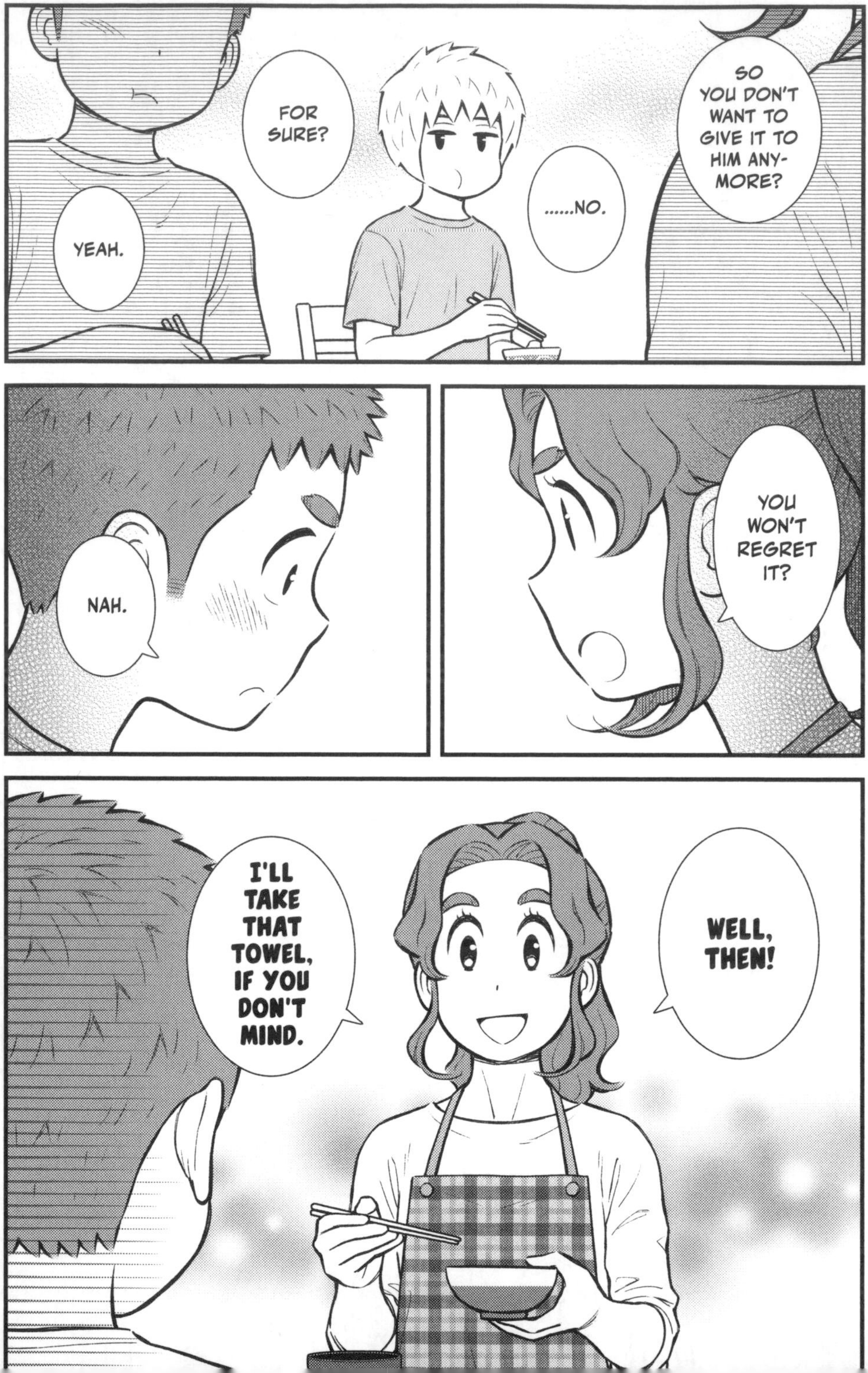
SO YOU DON'T WANT TO GIVE IT TO HIM ANY-MORE?
......NO.
FOR SURE?
YEAH.
YOU WON'T REGRET IT?
NAH.
WELL, THEN!
I'LL TAKE THAT TOWEL, IF YOU DON'T MIND.

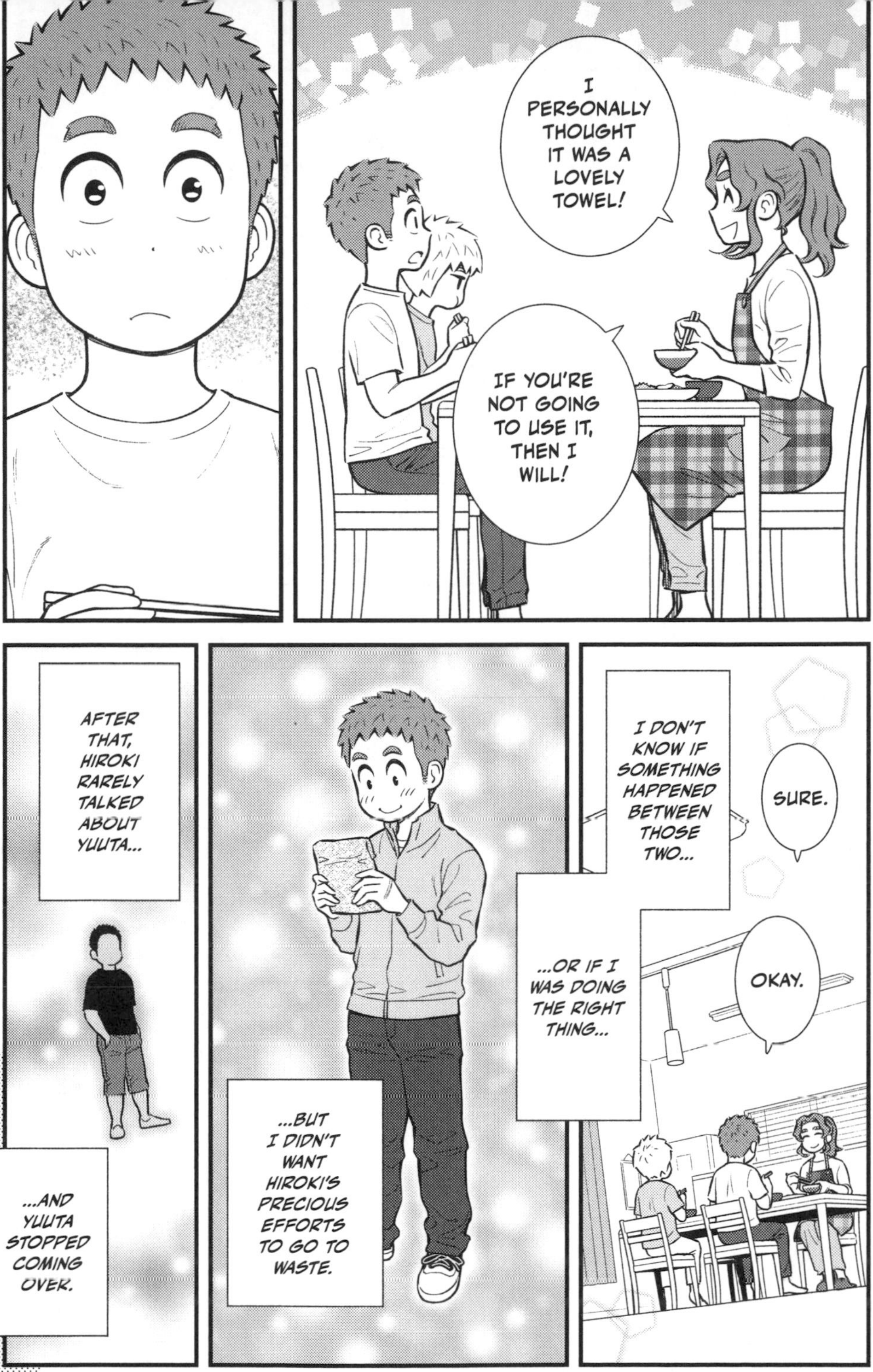
I PERSONALLY THOUGHT IT WAS A LOVELY TOWEL!
IF YOU'RE NOT GOING TO USE IT, THEN I WILL!
I DON'T KNOW IF SOMETHING HAPPENED BETWEEN THOSE TWO...
SURE.
...OR IF I WAS DOING THE RIGHT THING...
OKAY.
...BUT I DIDN'T WANT HIROKI'S PRECIOUS EFFORTS TO GO TO WASTE.
AFTER THAT, HIROKI RARELY TALKED ABOUT YUUTA...
...AND YUUTA STOPPED COMING OVER.

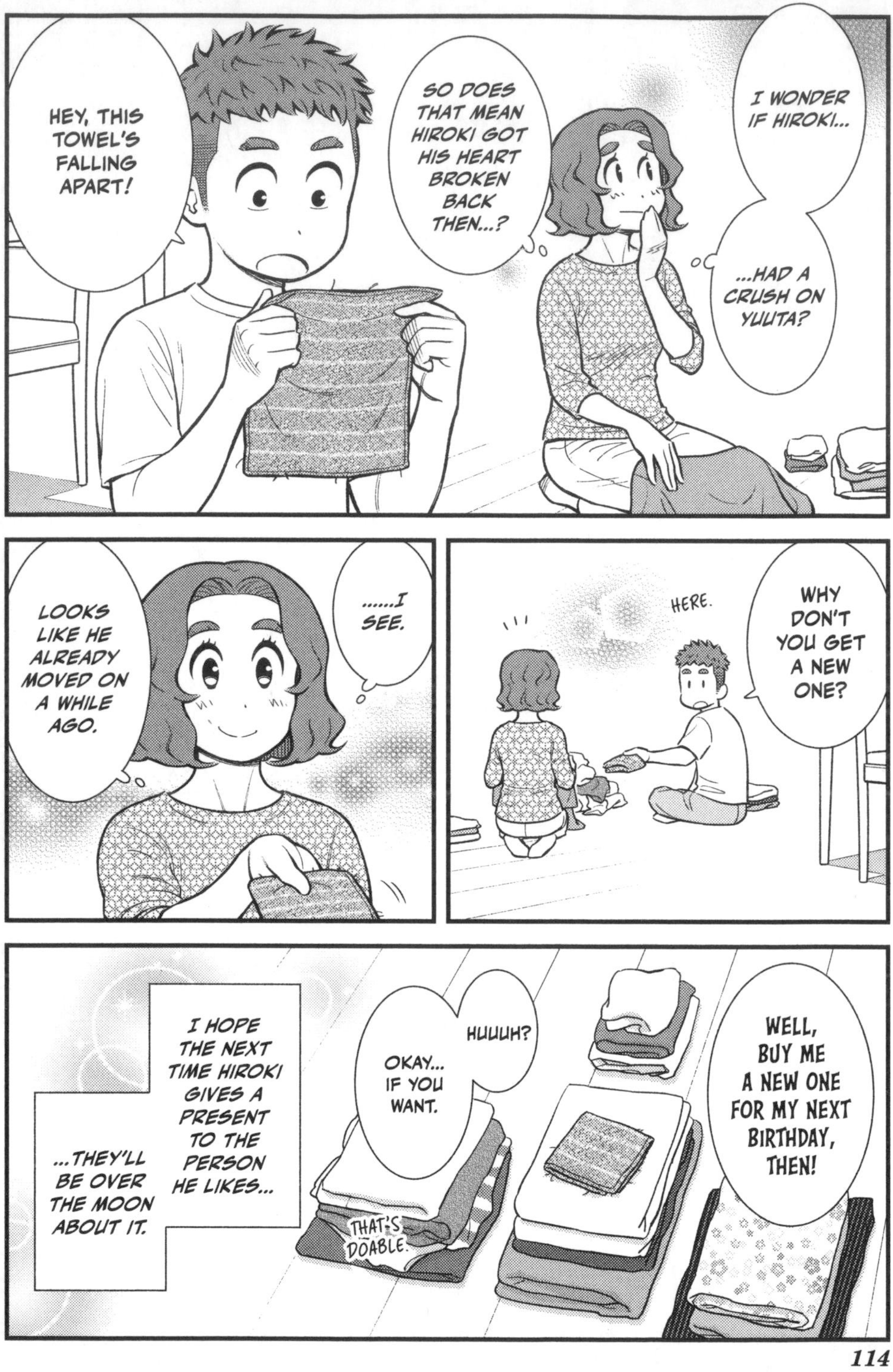
I WONDER IF HIROKI...
...HAD A CRUSH ON YUUTA?
SO DOES THAT MEAN HIROKI GOT HIS HEART BROKEN BACK THEN...?
HEY, THIS TOWEL'S FALLING APART!
WHY DON'T YOU GET A NEW ONE?
HERE.
......I SEE.
LOOKS LIKE HE ALREADY MOVED ON A WHILE AGO.
WELL, BUY ME A NEW ONE FOR MY NEXT BIRTHDAY, THEN!
HUUUH?
OKAY... IF YOU WANT.
THAT'S DOABLE.
I HOPE THE NEXT TIME HIROKI GIVES A PRESENT TO THE PERSON HE LIKES...
...THEY'LL BE OVER THE MOON ABOUT IT.

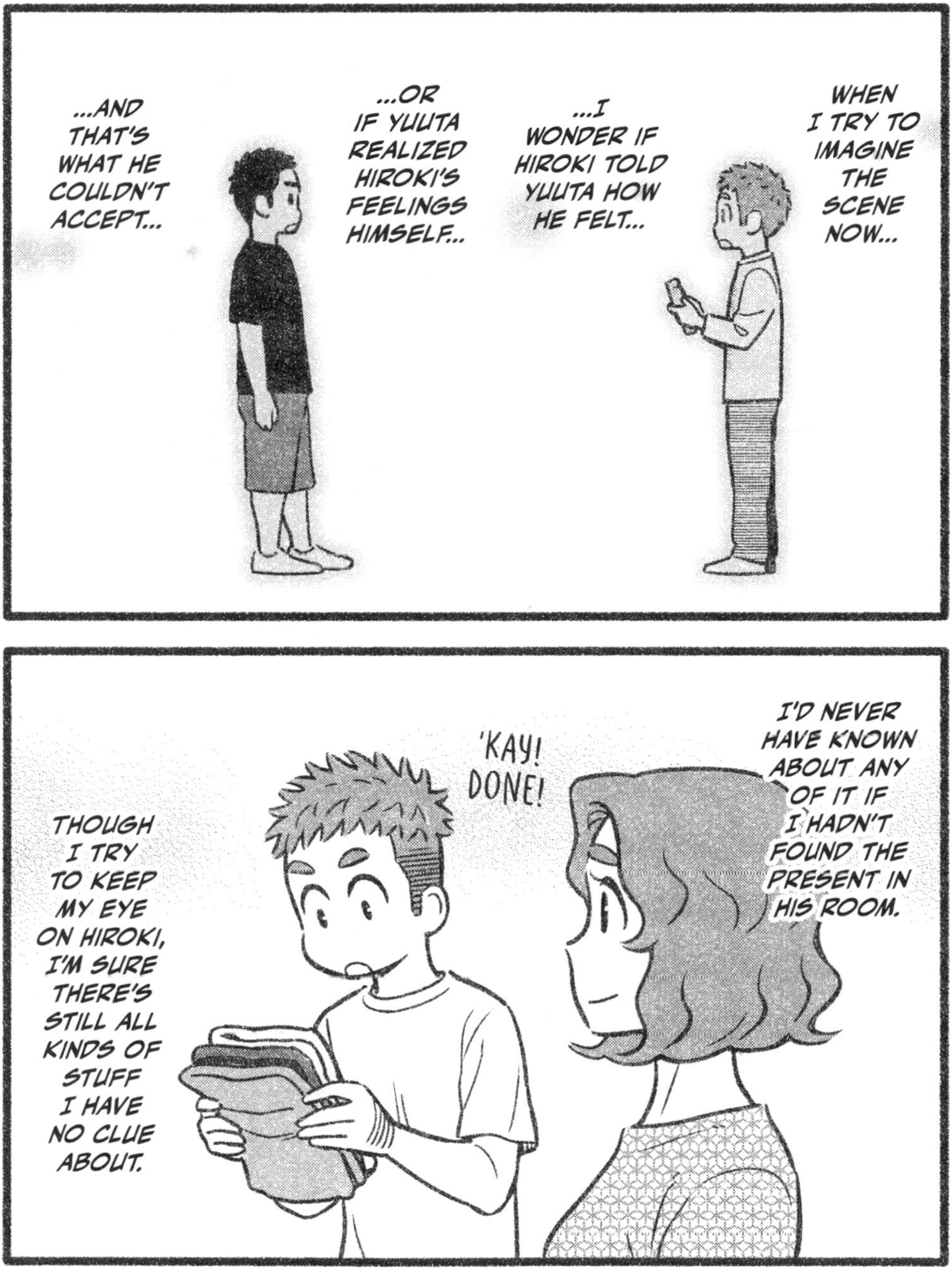
WHEN I TRY TO IMAGINE THE SCENE NOW...
...I WONDER IF HIROKI TOLD YUUTA HOW HE FELT...
...OR IF YUUTA REALIZED HIROKI'S FEELINGS HIMSELF...
...AND THAT'S WHAT HE COULDN'T ACCEPT...
I'D NEVER HAVE KNOWN ABOUT ANY OF IT IF I HADN'T FOUND THE PRESENT IN HIS ROOM.
'KAY! DONE!
THOUGH I TRY TO KEEP MY EYE ON HIROKI, I'M SURE THERE'S STILL ALL KINDS OF STUFF I HAVE NO CLUE ABOUT.

I Think
Our Son
Is Gay

CHAPTER 21: I THINK OUR SON IS...

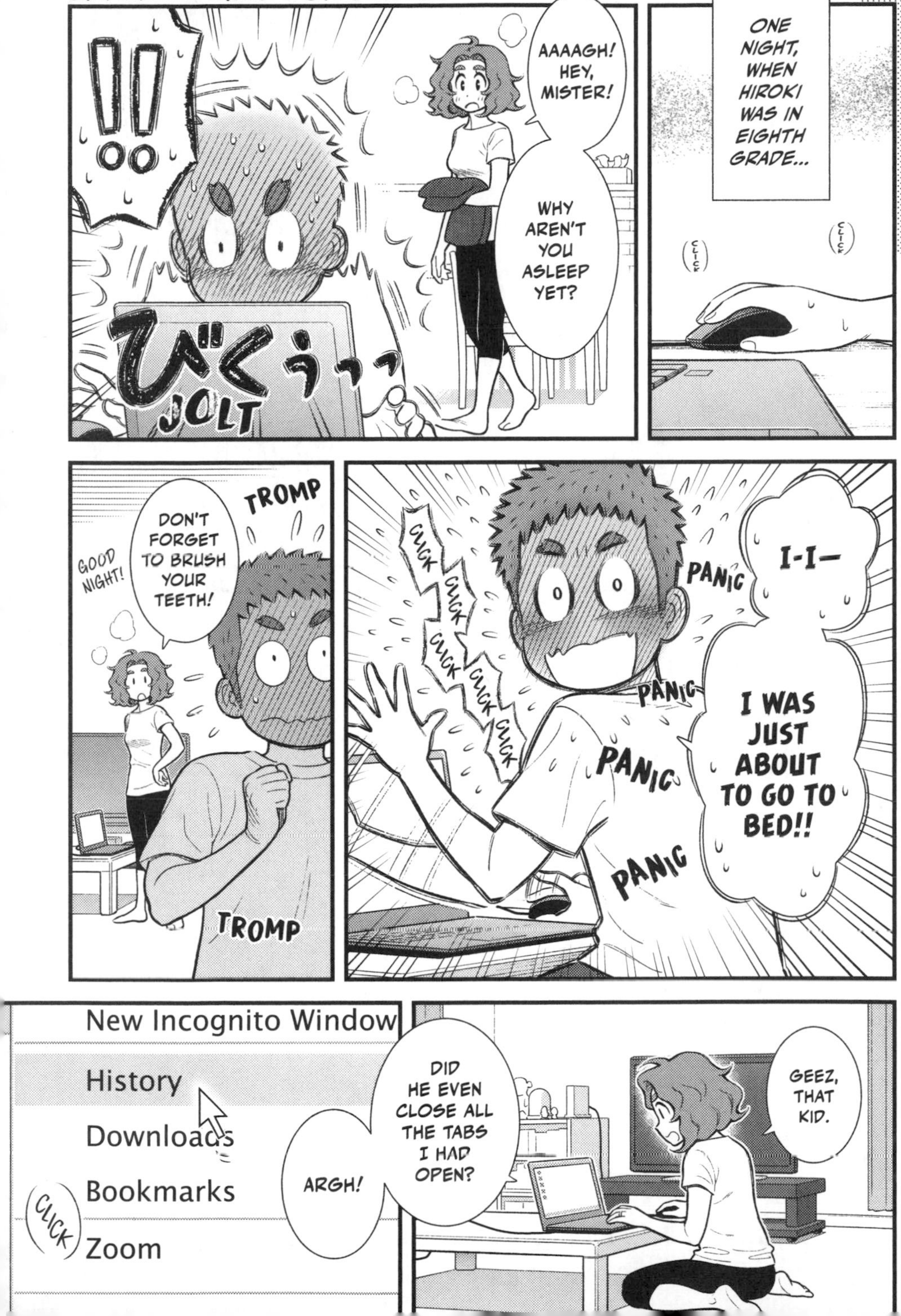
ONE NIGHT, WHEN HIROKI WAS IN EIGHTH GRADE...
CLICK
CLICK
AAAAGH! HEY, MISTER!
WHY AREN'T YOU ASLEEP YET?
!!
びくぅっっ
JOLT
I-I—
I WAS JUST ABOUT TO GO TO BED!!
PANIC
PANIC
PANIC
PANIC
CLICK
CLICK
CLICK
CLICK
CLICK
CLICK
TROMP
DON'T FORGET TO BRUSH YOUR TEETH!
GOOD NIGHT!
TROMP
GEEZ, THAT KID.
DID HE EVEN CLOSE ALL THE TABS I HAD OPEN?
ARGH!
New Incognito Window
History
Downloads
Bookmarks
Zoom
CLICK

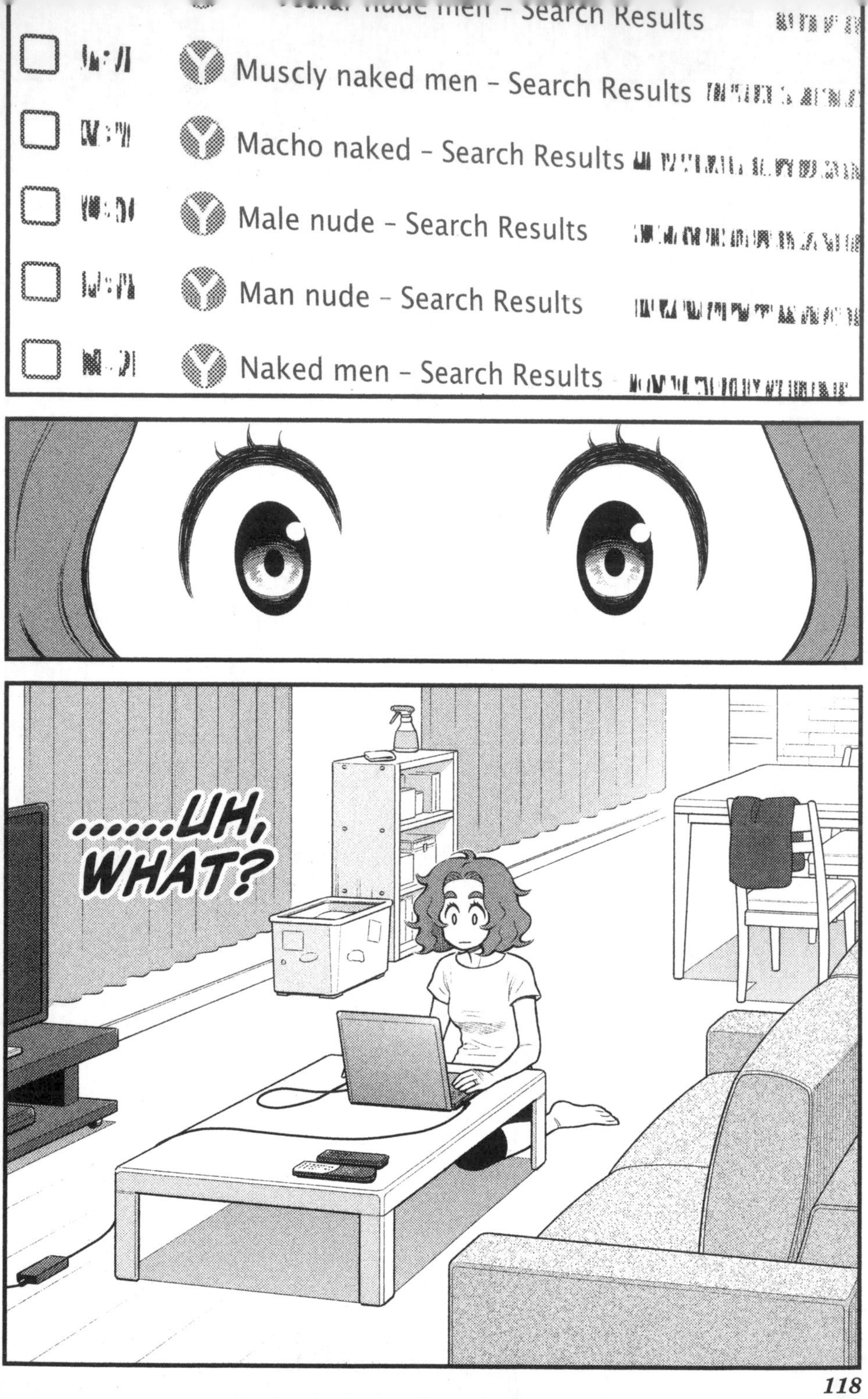
Muscly naked men - Search Results
Macho naked - Search Results
Male nude - Search Results
Man nude - Search Results
Naked men - Search Results
......UH, WHAT?

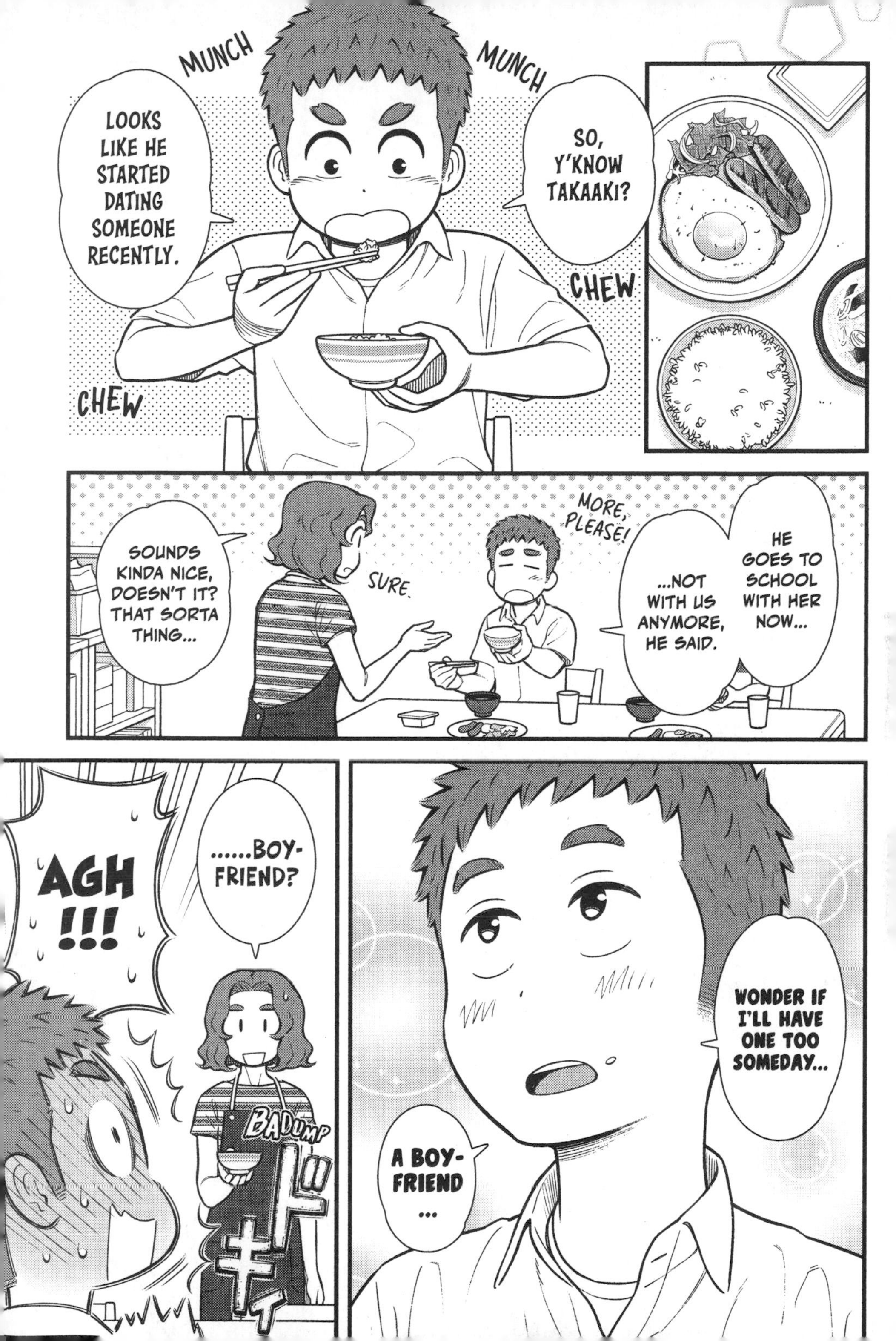
MUNCH
SO, Y'KNOW TAKAAKI?
MUNCH
LOOKS LIKE HE STARTED DATING SOMEONE RECENTLY.
CHEW
CHEW
HE GOES TO SCHOOL WITH HER NOW...
...NOT WITH US ANYMORE, HE SAID.
MORE, PLEASE!
SURE.
SOUNDS KINDA NICE, DOESN'T IT? THAT SORTA THING...
WONDER IF I'LL HAVE ONE TOO SOMEDAY...
A BOY-FRIEND ...
......BOY-FRIEND?
AGH !!!
BADUMP

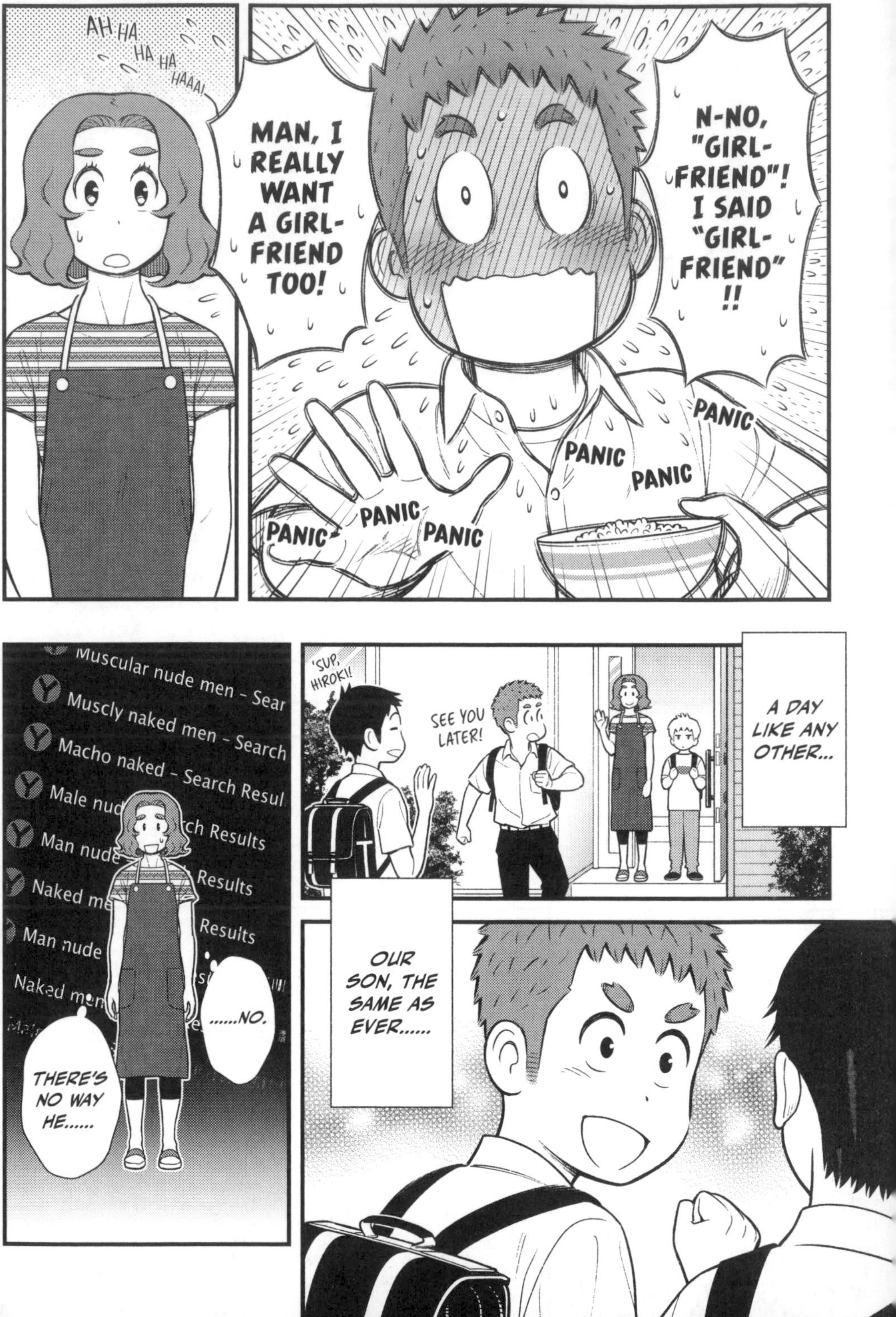
N-NO, "GIRL-FRIEND"! I SAID "GIRL-FRIEND"!!
MAN, I REALLY WANT A GIRL-FRIEND TOO!
PANIC
PANIC
PANIC
PANIC
PANIC
PANIC
AH HA HA HA HAAA!
A DAY LIKE ANY OTHER...
SEE YOU LATER!
'SUP, HIROKI!
OUR SON, THE SAME AS EVER......
Muscular nude men – Sear
Muscly naked men – Search
Macho naked – Search Resul
Male nud ch Results
Man nude Results
Naked me Results
Man nude
Naked men
......NO.
THERE'S NO WAY HE......

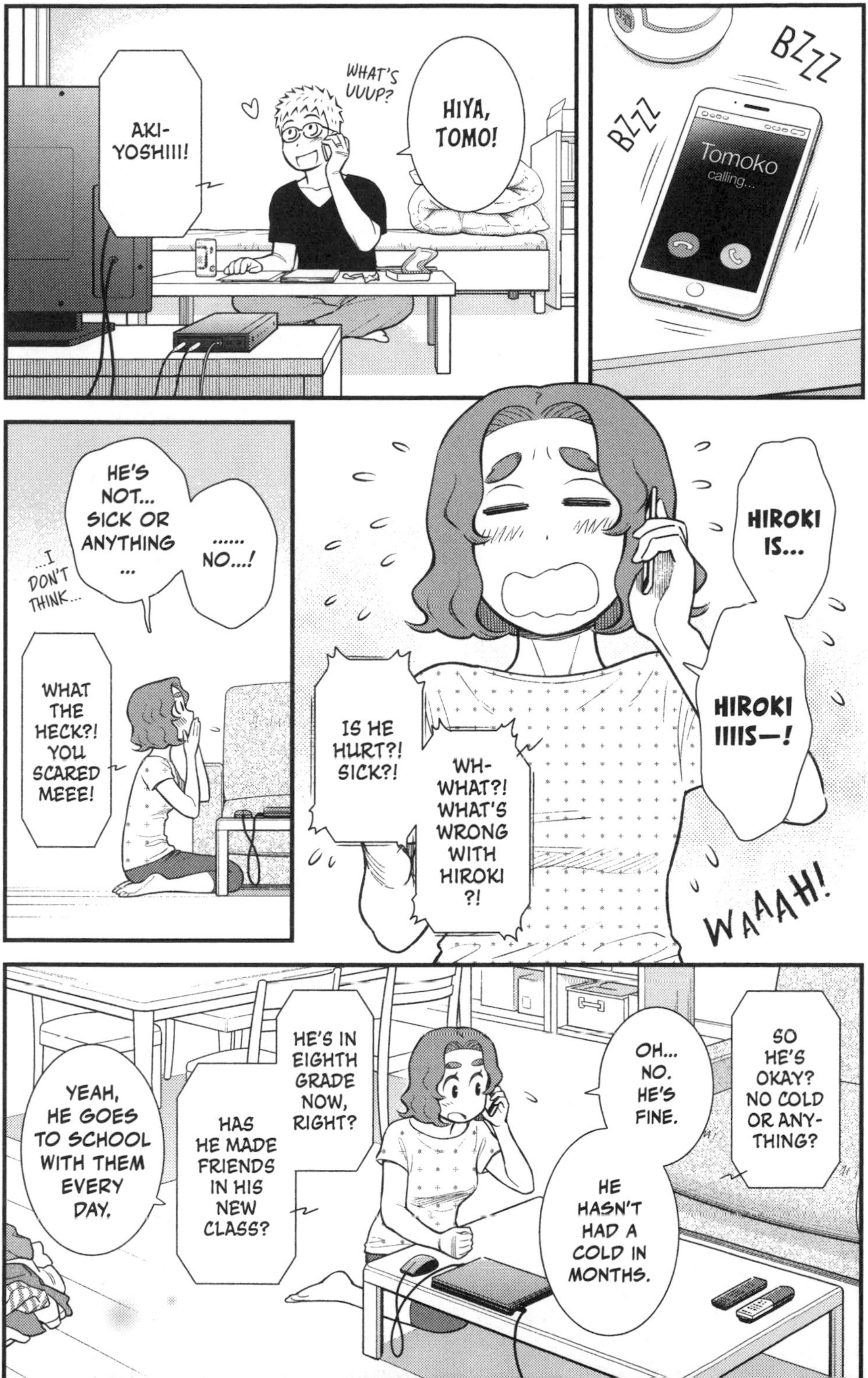
BZZZ
BZZZ
Tomoko
calling...
HIYA, TOMO!
WHAT'S UUUP?
AKI-YOSHIIII!
HIROKI IS...
HIROKI IIIIS—!
WH-WHAT?! WHAT'S WRONG WITH HIROKI?!
IS HE HURT?! SICK?!
WAAAH!
...... NO...!
HE'S NOT... SICK OR ANYTHING ...
...I DON'T THINK...
WHAT THE HECK?! YOU SCARED MEEE!
SO HE'S OKAY? NO COLD OR ANY-THING?
OH... NO. HE'S FINE.
HE HASN'T HAD A COLD IN MONTHS.
HE'S IN EIGHTH GRADE NOW, RIGHT?
HAS HE MADE FRIENDS IN HIS NEW CLASS?
YEAH, HE GOES TO SCHOOL WITH THEM EVERY DAY.

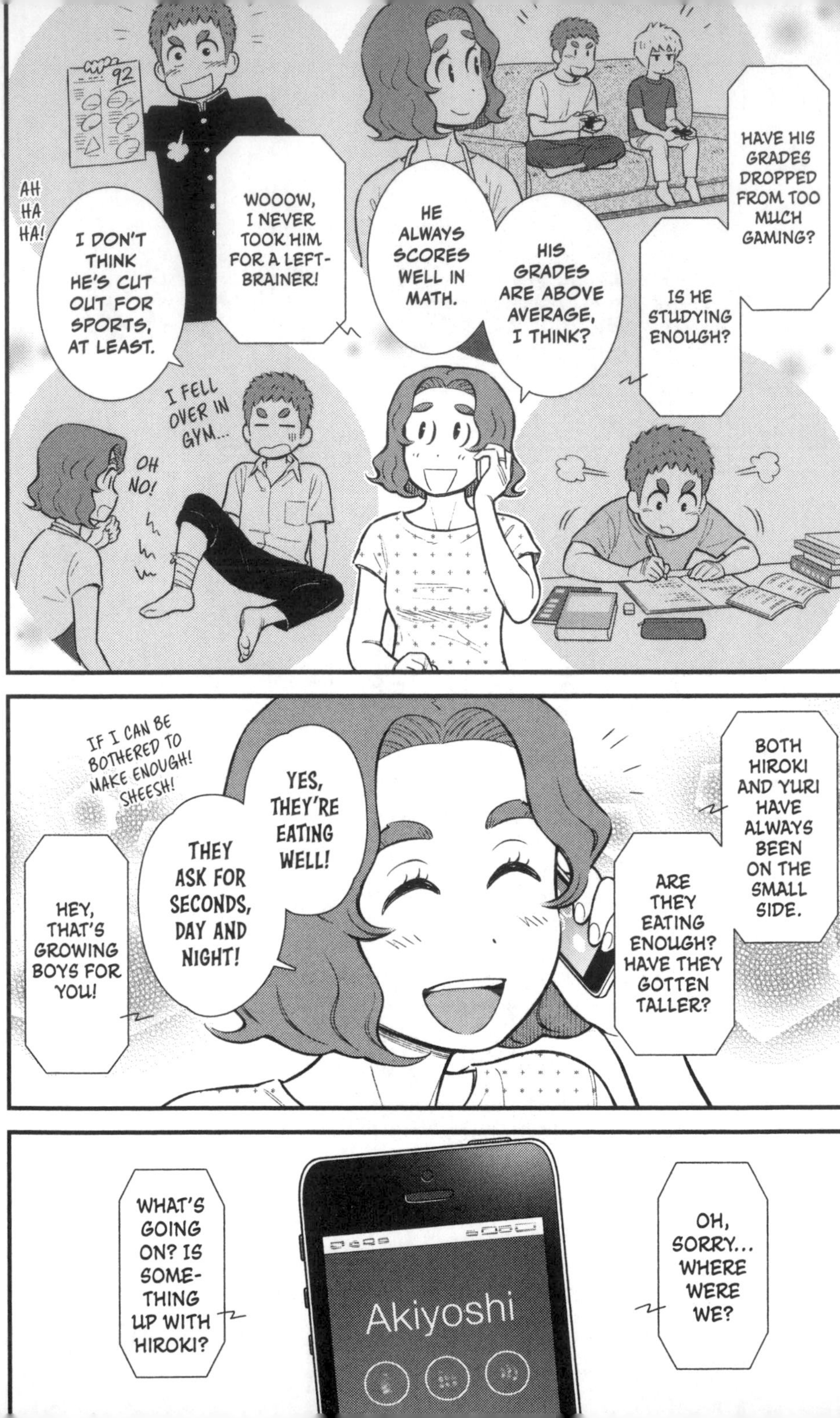
HAVE HIS GRADES DROPPED FROM TOO MUCH GAMING?
IS HE STUDYING ENOUGH?
HIS GRADES ARE ABOVE AVERAGE, I THINK?
HE ALWAYS SCORES WELL IN MATH.
WOOOW, I NEVER TOOK HIM FOR A LEFT-BRAINER!
AH HA HA!
I DON'T THINK HE'S CUT OUT FOR SPORTS, AT LEAST.
I FELL OVER IN GYM...
OH NO!
BOTH HIROKI AND YURI HAVE ALWAYS BEEN ON THE SMALL SIDE.
ARE THEY EATING ENOUGH? HAVE THEY GOTTEN TALLER?
YES, THEY'RE EATING WELL!
THEY ASK FOR SECONDS, DAY AND NIGHT!
IF I CAN BE BOTHERED TO MAKE ENOUGH! SHEESH!
HEY, THAT'S GROWING BOYS FOR YOU!
OH, SORRY... WHERE WERE WE?
Akiyoshi
WHAT'S GOING ON? IS SOMETHING UP WITH HIROKI?

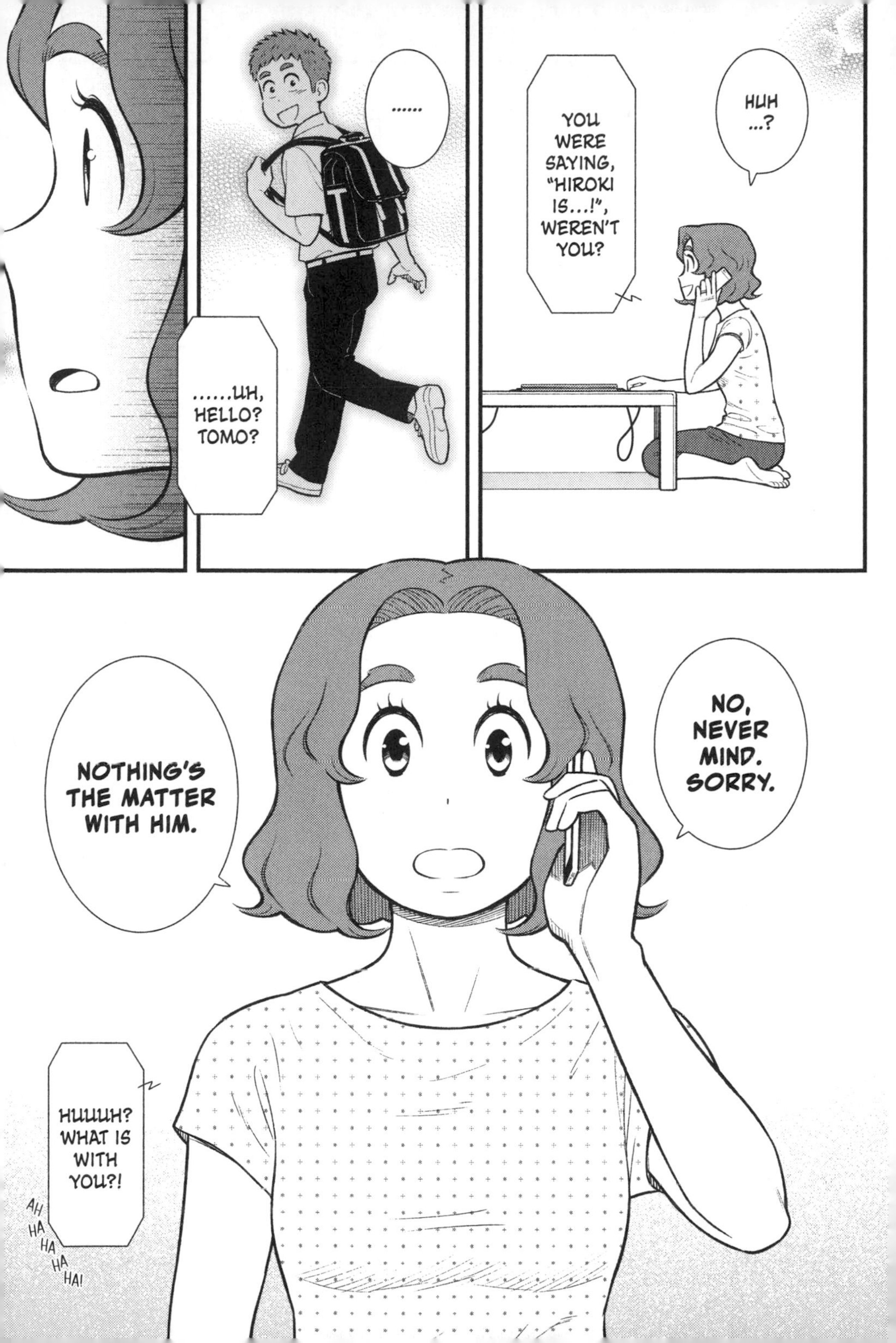
HUH ...?
YOU WERE SAYING, "HIROKI IS...!", WEREN'T YOU?
......
......UH, HELLO? TOMO?
NO, NEVER MIND. SORRY.
NOTHING'S THE MATTER WITH HIM.
HUUUH? WHAT IS WITH YOU?!
AH HA HA HA HA!

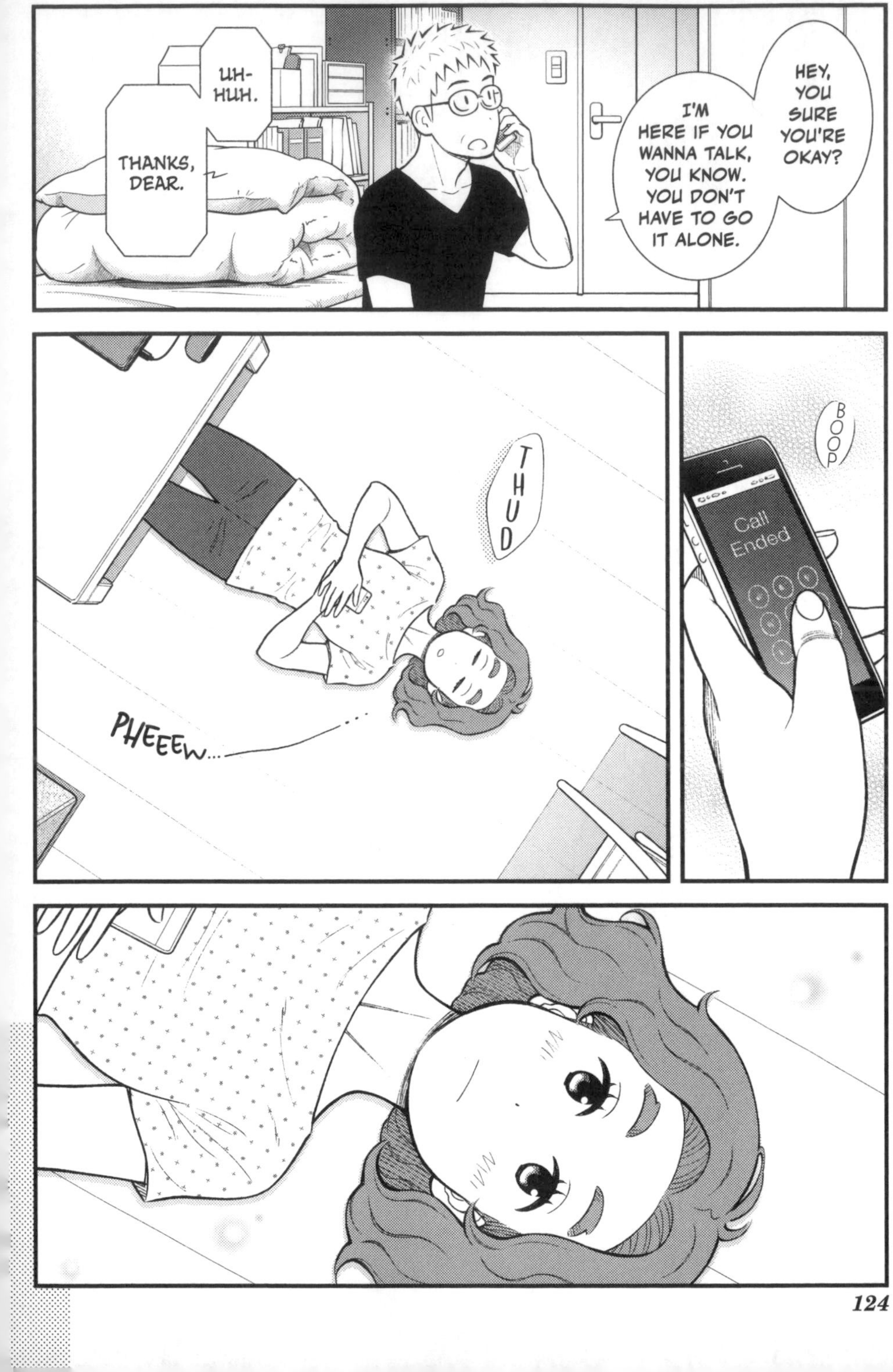
HEY, YOU SURE YOU'RE OKAY?
I'M HERE IF YOU WANNA TALK, YOU KNOW. YOU DON'T HAVE TO GO IT ALONE.
UH-HUH.
THANKS, DEAR.
BOOP
Call Ended
THUD
PHEEEW...

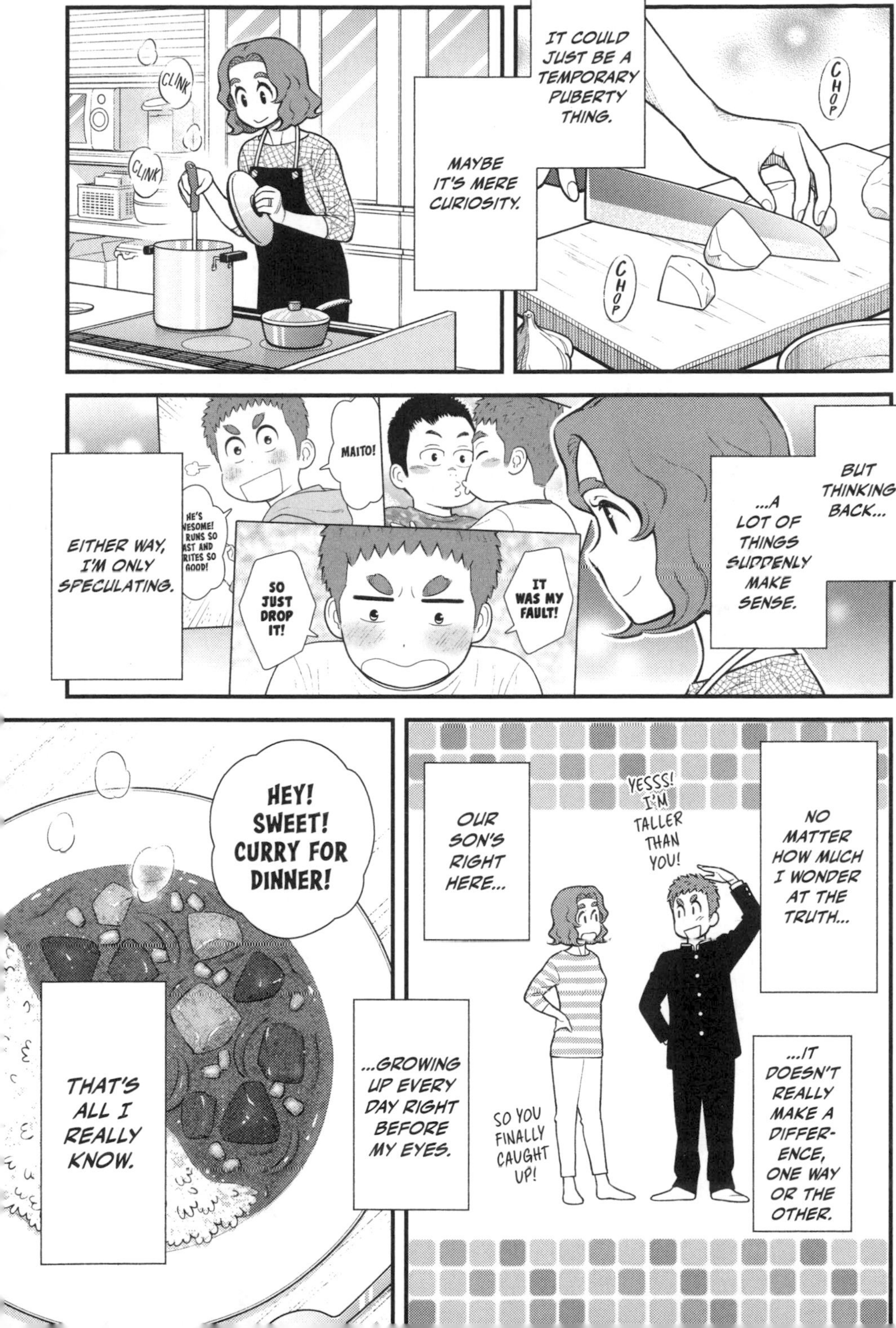
IT COULD JUST BE A TEMPORARY PUBERTY THING.
MAYBE IT'S MERE CURIOSITY.
CHOP
CHOP
CLINK
CLINK
BUT THINKING BACK...
...A LOT OF THINGS SUDDENLY MAKE SENSE.
IT WAS MY FAULT!
SO JUST DROP IT!
MAITO!
HE'S WESOME! RUNS SO AST AND RITES SO GOOD!
EITHER WAY, I'M ONLY SPECULATING.
NO MATTER HOW MUCH I WONDER AT THE TRUTH...
OUR SON'S RIGHT HERE...
YESSS! I'M TALLER THAN YOU!
...IT DOESN'T REALLY MAKE A DIFFER-ENCE, ONE WAY OR THE OTHER.
...GROWING UP EVERY DAY RIGHT BEFORE MY EYES.
SO YOU FINALLY CAUGHT UP!
HEY! SWEET! CURRY FOR DINNER!
THAT'S ALL I REALLY KNOW.

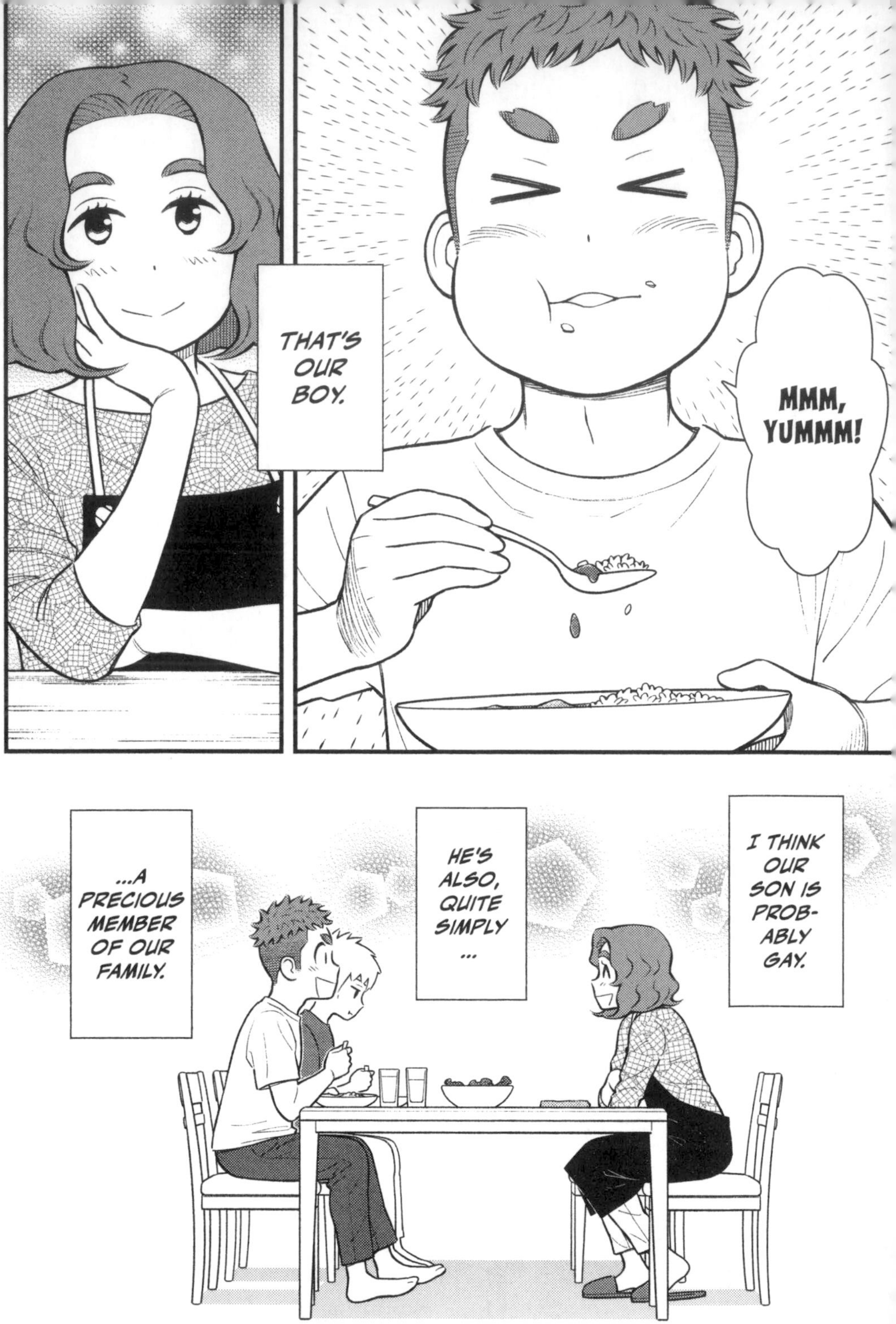
MMM, YUMMM!
THAT'S OUR BOY.
I THINK OUR SON IS PROB-ABLY GAY.
HE'S ALSO, QUITE SIMPLY ...
...A PRECIOUS MEMBER OF OUR FAMILY.

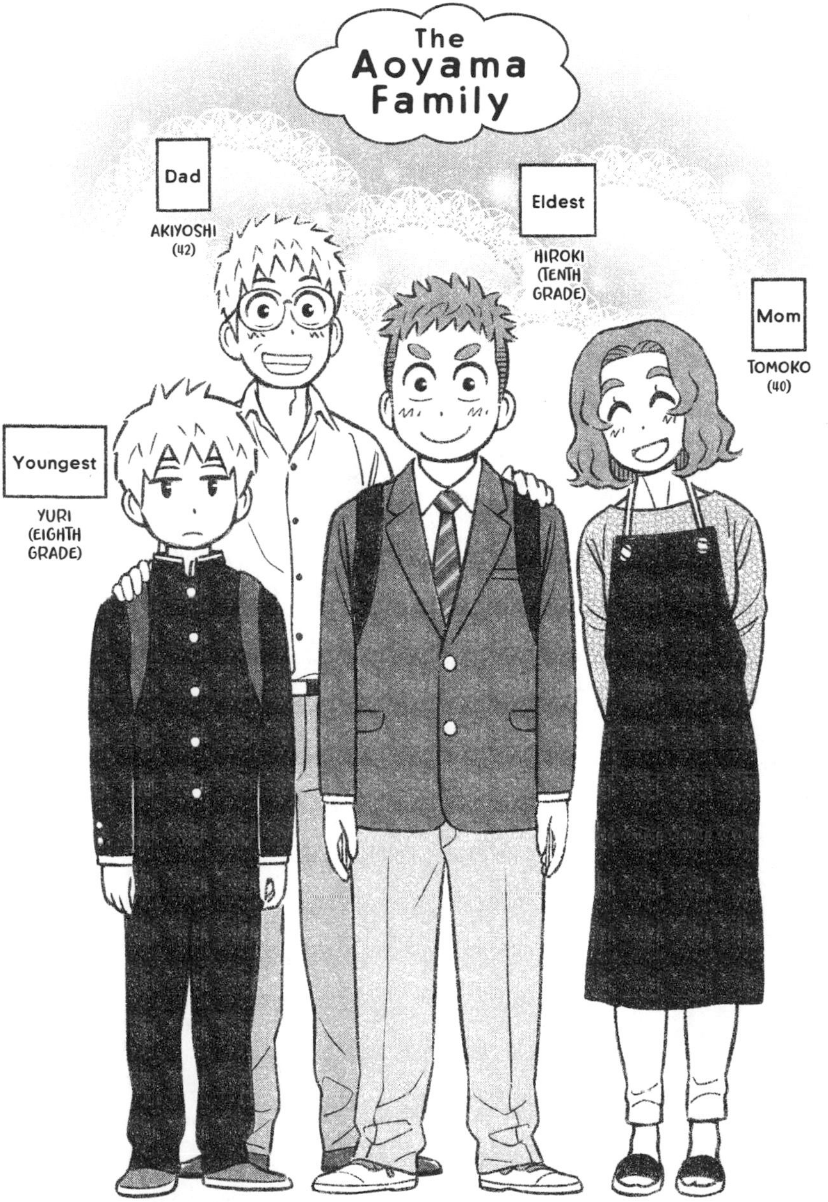
The Aoyama Family
Dad
AKIYOSHI (42)
Eldest
HIROKI (TENTH GRADE)
Mom
TOMOKO (40)
Youngest
YURI (EIGHTH GRADE)

I Think Our Son Is Gay

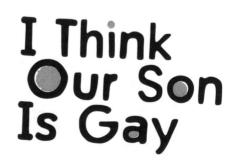

AFTERWORD

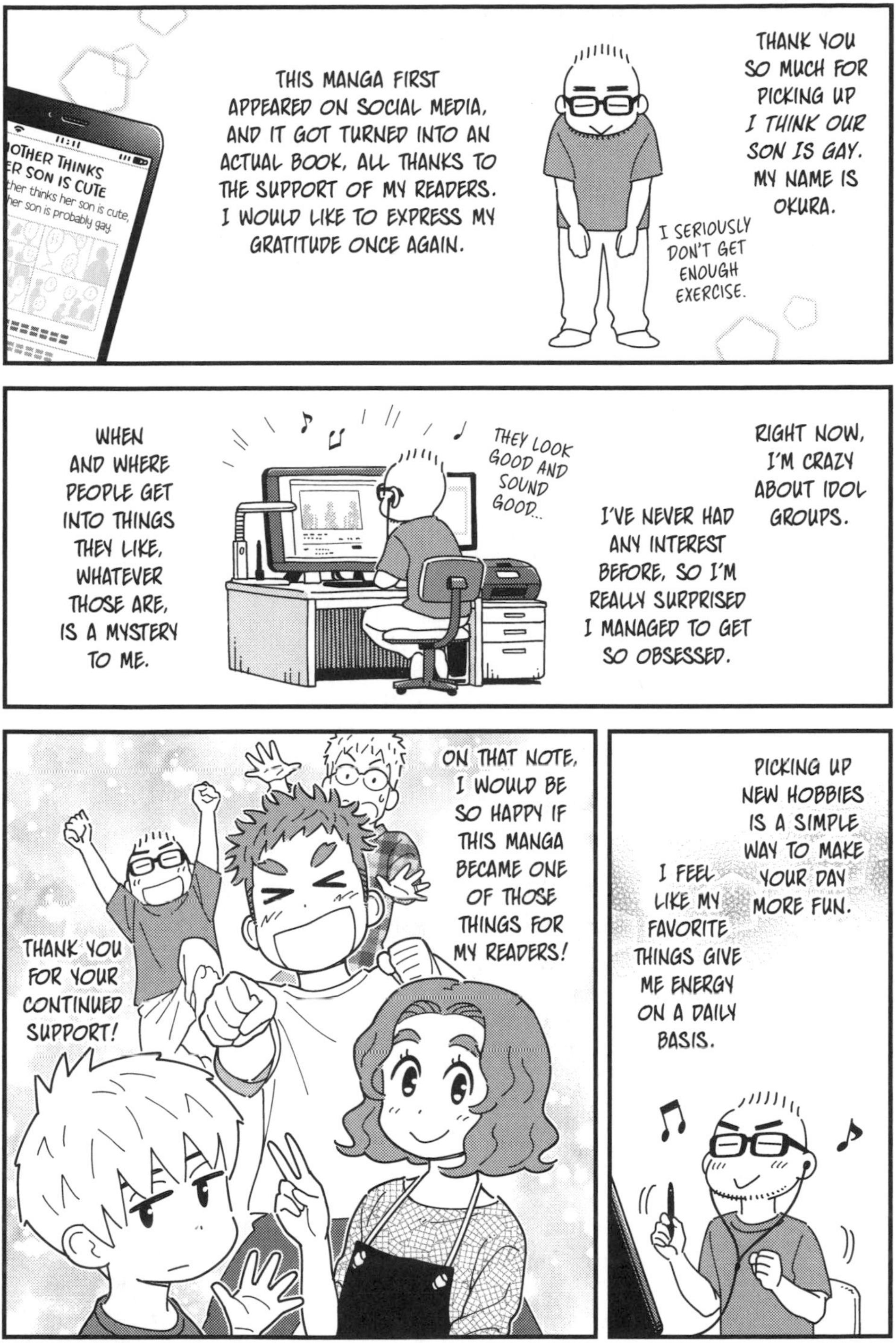
THANK YOU SO MUCH FOR PICKING UP I THINK OUR SON IS GAY. MY NAME IS OKURA.
I SERIOUSLY DON'T GET ENOUGH EXERCISE.
THIS MANGA FIRST APPEARED ON SOCIAL MEDIA, AND IT GOT TURNED INTO AN ACTUAL BOOK, ALL THANKS TO THE SUPPORT OF MY READERS. I WOULD LIKE TO EXPRESS MY GRATITUDE ONCE AGAIN.
RIGHT NOW, I'M CRAZY ABOUT IDOL GROUPS.
I'VE NEVER HAD ANY INTEREST BEFORE, SO I'M REALLY SURPRISED I MANAGED TO GET SO OBSESSED.
THEY LOOK GOOD AND SOUND GOOD...
WHEN AND WHERE PEOPLE GET INTO THINGS THEY LIKE, WHATEVER THOSE ARE, IS A MYSTERY TO ME.
PICKING UP NEW HOBBIES IS A SIMPLE WAY TO MAKE YOUR DAY MORE FUN.
I FEEL LIKE MY FAVORITE THINGS GIVE ME ENERGY ON A DAILY BASIS.
ON THAT NOTE, I WOULD BE SO HAPPY IF THIS MANGA BECAME ONE OF THOSE THINGS FOR MY READERS!
THANK YOU FOR YOUR CONTINUED SUPPORT!

2019/7 OKURA

I Think Our Son Is Gay

1

OKURA

Translation: Leo McDonagh
Lettering: Lor Prescott
Cover Design: Andrea Miller
Editor: Tania Biswas

I THINK OUR SON IS GAY Volume 1
© 2019 Okura/SQUARE ENIX CO., LTD.
First published in Japan in 2019 by SQUARE ENIX CO., LTD.
English translation rights arranged with
SQUARE ENIX CO., LTD. and SQUARE ENIX, INC.
English translation © 2021 by SQUARE ENIX CO., LTD.

ISBN: 978-1-64609-092-1

Library of Congress Cataloging-in-Publication
Data is on file with the publisher.

Printed in the U.S.A.

10 9 8 7 6 5 4 3 2

SQUARE ENIX
MANGA & BOOKS
www.square-enix-books.com